THE LANGUAGE OF CHILDREN
A KEY TO LITERACY

THE LANGUAGE OF CHILDREN
A KEY TO LITERACY

Head of Division of Child Studies
Mount Gravatt College of Advanced Education
Brisbane, Australia

N. W. M. HART

Assistant Director
Mount Gravatt College of Advanced Education
Brisbane, Australia

R. F. WALKER

Psycholinguist
Mount Gravatt Language Research Team
Brisbane, Australia

B. GRAY

▲ **ADDISON-WESLEY PUBLISHING COMPANY**

Reading, Massachusetts · Menlo Park, California · Don Mills, Ontario

Sydney · Melbourne · Brisbane · Amsterdam · London · Manila · Paris · Singapore · Tokyo

45462

Cover photograph and photographs appearing on pages 10–11 and 26–27 courtesy of Mr. Kingsley Neale, Mount Gravatt College of Advanced Education.

ISBN 0-201-05301-2
ABCDEFGHIJ-AL-7987

FOREWORD

The material in this book is the product of fifteen years' research undertaken by Dr. Norman Hart and others into young children's oral use of English. One important practical outcome of this research has been to show that it is necessary to use the language of children as a basis for creating language-reading materials if these are to be most effective in promoting the easy transfer of what children themselves know about oral language to written symbols. But where does one find such source material? What is the nature of this language we are talking about? What changes take place as the child matures?

In order to answer these questions the authors have gone to the children. They have analyzed children's language. They have set down the results of their inquiry in a way which shows those sequences and words which are used over and over again by children in their normal communication with their peers and adults.

Teachers, parents, and writers in addition to those researching the language development of children will see at a glance how valuable this material is as a practical source book. Its universality is confirmed by analysis of children's language which has been collected in areas as far apart as Bristol, England and Toronto, Canada.

The source material available in this book, and the practical application, supported by a clear exposition of the theoretical position taken by the researchers are likely to influence the future planning of language arts curricula.

W. Wood
Chairman, Board of Advanced Education
Queensland, Australia

CONTENTS

45462

LIST OF TABLES

CHAPTER ONE

THE LANGUAGE RESEARCH PROJECT AT MOUNT GRAVATT COLLEGE

As can be judged from the title of this book, the authors share the now fairly general belief that literacy is an extension of oracy—that the ability to communicate effectively in oral language must precede and is inextricably interwoven with the development of ability to create and interpret language in its written form. It follows that insights into child language, including the ways in which children use language at various stages of their development, will greatly assist teachers and parents in fostering both oral language competence and the ability to read and write.

This volume, the product of extensive research directed specifically toward the obtaining of such insights, is intended as a resource book for teachers, parents, writers, and others concerned with young children. A description is given in Chapter 4 of a language and reading program compiled on the basis of this research; but the authors believe that the outcomes of their analyses have application well beyond the construction of such programs. For this reason, this book contains word and word sequence lists, a brief account of the theoretical basis and methodology of the research, and guidelines for the use of these lists.

BASIC CONCEPTS BEHIND THE MOUNT GRAVATT PROGRAM

A basic principle which teachers apply over and over is to move from what is known to what is unknown. They realize that the child must relate new knowledge to old through a process called assimilation. The very act of relating will change a child's original concepts; and his or her cognitive framework will change or broaden to accommodate the new. To quote Piaget (1964), "learning is possible only when there is active assimilation."

It seems logical to apply this principle when children are learning language, or learning to read and write, as well as to other learning. The problem is that little has been discovered about what language children know at any particular stage of their development.

This, then, was the problem that the Mount Gravatt Research Project was designed to attack. Large samples of the language of normal children of various ages were collected and analyzed to discover what words and sequences of words were used at each age level, and how and with what meaning intention they were combined to form utterance. The researchers believed that such a procedure would supply a solid foundation for fostering child language competence and for relating teaching strategies and reading materials to the oral language system of the children to be taught.

The assumption on which the project was based is that development of language and cognitive development of a child are intimately related to one another and that both depend on the way the child organizes his or her world. At any relevant stage of language development, children possess an oral language system which is complete and consistent in itself and not merely an incomplete or deformed version of an adult model. It is adequate for satisfactory communication at that stage and is completely functional.

THE RESEARCH PROJECT

Dr. Norman Hart began the research task in 1967 (Hart, 1968, 1970) by collecting and analyzing random samples of the natural language of 2½, 3½, and 4½ year old children. (This research was funded by a Van Leer Foundation grant to the Queensland, Australia, Department of Education.) The lists of words and word sequences used by children of that age, and provided in this volume, are based on that research. Information on the language of 5½ and 6½ year old children was obtained in research funded by the Committee for Educational Research and Development and undertaken by a research team at Mount Gravatt College of Advanced Education (Queensland, Australia) during 1972–75.

Each age-group sample was confined to children of approximately the same language ability, and the language collected was that used in ongoing, normal activity. It was assumed that there would be sufficient commonality in the language used at one age level and sufficient differences between that used at different age levels to reveal both the essential features of the respective language systems and the important developments in language system associated with growth.

Since the objective was to make generalizations regarding all children of each particular stage of language development, care was taken to obtain a random selection of children from the entire population of the city of Brisbane, Australia. For the preschool ages, this involved seeking out the children of a particular age who lived nearest to randomly selected points on a map of that city. At school ages, it involved obtaining lists from all school principals of all children born in a particular month (August) of the relevant year and then randomly selecting children from these lists. Before any language samples were collected, all the children selected were tested with the Illinois Test of Psycholinguistic Abilities to exclude those with a language age more than one standard deviation from the I.T.P.A. norm for mean scaled scores (mean = 36, standard deviation = 6). To ensure that language was sampled across a very wide and normally distributed variety of situations, it was decided to record all the language spoken by each child (on a randomly chosen day) from the time the child got up in the morning until he or she went to bed at night. In the case of school children, the day was chosen to be a school day.

The Collection of Language

During the day, each child wore a specially designed vest in which was fitted a radio-microphone and small transmitter. Considerable care was taken before the day of actual recording to familiarize the child and his or her playmates or classmates with the wearing of the vest. In the school situation, for example, spare vests were worn for some days by various children in the class, and the language was collected only after the sight of the vest had become unremarkable. At the start of a language-collection day, two research assistants arrived at the child's home with a portable receiver-recorder and, operating from prearranged positions, recorded the speech of the child and those speaking to the child. One of the assistants monitored the input to the recorder, jotting down as much of the speech as possible (with timings), while the other noted the situations and what the child was doing (again with timings). In this way, it was possible to bring together later the utterances and the circumstances of the utterances. This procedure continued throughout the day. The range of the receiver varied according to circumstances; but usually it was over one hundred meters, so that researchers did not have to intrude on the in-school or play activities of the children.

The language collected during the day was then transcribed by the two researchers who collected it. Consultation between the researchers and the notings of situations greatly aided interpretation of the recordings.

It was thought that commonalities extracted from samples of utterance collected in this way would be representative of the language of all normal children of a particular level of language development, at least in the city of Brisbane. Comparison with language collected in other places would reveal the extent to which these commonalities extended across English-speaking communities.

Table 1 gives the average mean scaled scores and standard deviation for language functioning of children included in the sample at each age level. Table 2 gives the mean chronological age and standard deviation for each sample group.

Age label	Mean scale score	Standard deviation
2½ years	37.6	2.5
3½ years	38.6	3.2
4½ years	38.4	2.8
5½ years	37.8	2.4
6½ years	37.9	2.6

**TABLE 1
AVERAGE MEAN
SCALE SCORES ON
THE I.T.P.A. FOR EACH
AGE LEVEL**

Age label	Mean age	Standard deviation
2½ years	2 years, 8 months	1.84 months
3½ years	3 years, 8 months	1.85 months
4½ years	4 years, 9 months	2.44 months
5½ years	5 years, 8 months	1.41 months
6½ years	6 years, 8 months	1.68 months

**TABLE 2
CHRONOLOGICAL
AGE OF EACH SAMPLE
GROUP**

TABLE 3
**NUMBER OF
CHILDREN AND
NUMBER OF WORDS
PROCESSED AT EACH
AGE LEVEL**

Age label	Number of children	Number of words
2½ years	13	8,953
3½ years	18	10,932
4½ years	22	10,386
5½ years	18	65,665
6½ years	22	78,829

The amount of language collected from each age group varied and so did the number of children studied, but the samples were found to be adequate as bases for the purposes of the investigation. Table 3 gives the number of children and the number of words processed at each age level.

The Compilation of Word and Sequence Lists

The language data collected was computer-processed by means of a concordance program which brought identical words and strings of words together in alphabetical order within the immediate verbal context. A sample page of the printout is reproduced in Figure 1. As the sample shows, the printout provides a count of the use of each word and two-word sequence, together with a listing of the children (by code number) who used that language unit and the number of times each used it. A four- or five-figure number at the end of each line indexes that line back into the printout of full verbal context, thus allowing easy access to wider verbal context and the notations of nonverbal context. It was from these resources that judgments were made regarding the meaning which children intended for words and sequences of words and the way in which they systematically strung together their utterances in various situational contexts.

The word and word sequence lists included in this volume were compiled according to an index of frequency of use. With both single words and word sequences, raw frequency of use was multiplied by the percentage of the total sample of children who used the word or sequence. This gave an adjusted index of use, which was called the *communication index*. The purpose of the adjustment was to reflect the generality of the usage rather than reflect that degree of repetition that might be peculiar to one or two children. Alphabetical lists of words used, with their index of use, and listings in the order of frequency of use were both compiled for each age level. These are presented in Chapters 6 and 7.

The procedure just described was sufficient for producing an index which reflected the usefulness of single words as communication units, but a further refinement was necessary in calculating the communication index for the word sequences.

Traditional grammatical descriptions as well as recent semantic studies have recognized that there are meaningful units in the construction of language. Classification of English syntax in terms of prepositional phrases, noun phrases, clauses, etc., represents one attempt to impose a formal classification system on these meaningful units, e.g. "*on* the roof," "*the* tall red building," "*when* he

SAMPLE PAGE OF COMPUTER PRINTOUT FROM THE LANGUAGE OF 6½ YEAR OLD CHILDREN

MT. GRAVATT TEACHERS' COLLEGE – LANGUAGE RESEARCH PROJECT   DATE 18107X PAGE   443

```
L . HEY GRANT LOOK AT MY LONG TAIL . ? WHAT . ? WHY .        I-M GOING HOME IN THAT WHITE CAR . +GOIN . WITH TWO TEAC    11314   51
DIANE . THE ONE THAT CAME UP IS DIANE . GUESS WHAT .         I-M GOING HOME WITH THEM TONIGHT BECAUSE THEY-RE AH STAY    9191   22
                                                                609            1
                                                                611            1
                                                             4 MORPHEMES    2 SPEAKERS
E . OOH . OKAY NOW YOU-RE IN YOUR OWN SEAT . +YA . NO        I-M GOING IN MY OWN DESK . +GOIN . NO . +NUH . MATTHEW-S    11221   51
T HANKY OVER THERE . OVER THERE ON THE TABLE . /RES .        I-M GOING LIKE THAT . GOODY I-M FINISHED . ? CAN I GO DO    58105   47
NOW . ELEPHANT . NO . THAT-S MR BROWN . I WILL . AND         I-M GOING TO ASK PETER TOO . +GOIN . ? WHAT BEGINS WITH     52023   14
UT I DID IN THAT ONE . I UP TO THE NEXT SIDE . /RES .        I-M GOING TO BACK TO NUMBER FOUR . /RES . +GONNA +TA . H    11112   46
P . BOX OF MARKER-SS . /RES . YUK . /RES . BE EARLY .        I-M GOING TO BE EARLY TODAY . MUM . XMUM X3 . ? DO I HAV    58066   51
DONT BLAME IT ON ME . I NEVER EVER STEAL . XEVER X4 .        I-M GOING TO BRING A TWO CENT . AND PUT IT THERE AND SEE    7358   33
NK MICE ARE RATHER NICE . MUMMY . PULL MY ZIPPER UP .        I-M GOING TO BURP SOON . TAKE THIS BELT OFF ME . ? WHAT    59297   16
NT YOU GET DOWN THERE . DUMBELL . NO JUDO LESSON-SP .        I-M GOING TO CHUCK IT AT YOU . BEEP . XBEEP X4 . I CAN T    7513   13
+YEAH . YES DONT . QUERY STOP IT . IF YOU DO IT AGAIN        I-M GOING TO CLEAR YOU OUT QUERY . +GONNA . YES YOU DID    60173    7
THE LAST FIRST ONE . LOOK ROY . YOU-VE GOT :BOX :CO         I-M GOING TO COLOUR IN SANTA . +GONNA . SISTER . THERE .    11096   34
LL MY EGG . O GUESS WHERE I-M GOING TO CRACK MY EGG .        I-M GOING TO CRACK IT ON THE RUBBISH BIN . FOR BIG LUNCH    9124   45
. MUM DIDNT HAVE TIME TO SHELL MY EGG . O GUESS WHERE        I-M GOING TO CRACK MY EGG . I-M GOING TO CRACK IT ON THE    9124   17
ASS-SP ARE CUT ALREADY . ALRIGHT . OO . YES . +YEAH         I-M GOING TO CRACK THAT ON THE BIN . +GONNA . QUERY . I     9166   30
                                                                609            3
                                                             5 MORPHEMES    1 SPEAKERS
SAYS HERE . FINGER PAINTING . I DONT WANT THAT ONE .         I-M GOING TO DO A FINGER PAINTING . +GONNA . YES . I THI    52053   49
. NOT NOW . ? BUT WE USED TO DIDNT WE . NO . XNO X?         I-M GOING TO DO A SPOTTED DOG . +GOIN . OH BOY . MY HAND    52080   68
                                                                652            2
                                                             6 MORPHEMES    1 SPEAKERS
E LEE SOME . ? WHAT ARENT YOU TEACH TOGETHER . /RES .        I-M GOING TO DO ALL THE DAY-SP OF THE WEEK IN RUNNING WR    59294    8
FINGER PAINTING . +GONNA . /RES . THIS ONE . I MEAN         I-M GOING TO DO FIREWORK-SP . +GONNA . SHE-S HELPING AS    52061   16
WHAT BEGINS WITH :E INSTEAD OF ELEPHANT . I KNOW WHAT        I-M GOING TO DO FOR :M . +GONNA . NO . MARGARET . WELL I    52024   35
LLO MARIE . SHE HEARD ME . YES . +YEAH . THIS IS WHAT       I-M GOING TO DO LISA . WHEN YOU GO HOME LEE AND MAUREEN    59056    6
SOM . XI XTHOUGHT XTHAT . ONE BOSOM . O YOU KNOW WHAT        I-M GOING TO DO ON ME SISTER . +GONNA /RES . O YOU KNOW    7380    6
NG TO DO ON ME SISTER . +GONNA /RES . O YOU KNOW WHAT       I-M GOING TO DO ON ME MOTHER . +GONNA /RES . TWO BOSOM-S    7380   67
                                                                607            2
                                                             6 MORPHEMES    1 SPEAKERS
-SP . AW . I-M BEATING YOU . +BEATIN . LOOK AT THAT .        I-M GOING TO DO SEVEN THIS AFTERNOON . +GONNA . O HAVE I    7555   32
CE . ? HELLO . HOW ARE YOU . YUMMEE . O YOU KNOW WHAT       I-M GOING TO DO . +Y . I-M GOING TO PUT PAINT ALL OVER Y    52073   36
                                                                659            2
                                                                607            3
                                                                652            5
                                                             5 MORPHEMES    3 SPEAKERS
R FINGER-SP . O COMING ANM . A SCOTLAND LADY . /RES .        I-M GOING TO DRAW A TRIANGLE AND A . LOOK WHAT I DID . O    52118   26
PLAY WITH YOU AND YOUR CAR-SP . OKAY . AND MICHELLE .        I-M GOING TO DRIVE THIS CAR . +GONNA . I-LL KEEP IT IN M    7265   12
. I-VE DROP MY MARBLE . /RES . LAND IN THAT PUDDLE .        I-M GOING TO DROP IT IN THE PUDDLE . +GONNA . OH I DROPP    10242   10
EEP . XBEEP X3 . OKAY . WAIT A MINUTE . GO TO SLEEP .        I-M GOING TO FALL OVER WHEN YOU WAKE UP . +GONNA . WHEN    10203    9
WELL I-M GOING TO TRY AND DO IT A GOOD WAY . +GONNA .        I-M GOING TO FIGGER IT OUT MYSELF . +GONNA . ? CAN YOU D    8169   12
E . ? WHAT DO YOU CALL THIS STUFF MUM . +MA . CORAL         I-M GOING TO FIX THIS CORAL DOWN THE SPOKE . THAT-S HOW    58024   37
E SHE-S CAUGHT . SHELLY . SHELLY . XSHELLY . I KNOW .        I-M GOING TO GET A DRINK . ? WHO WANTS DRINK . /RES . CO    60084   38
EQUALS TWELVE . ONE TIMES ONE TWELVE EQUALS TWELVE .        I-M GOING TO GET A WHOLE ROW RIGHT . +GONNA . YOU HAVENT    11165   54
                                                                660            1
                                                                611            1
                                                             6 MORPHEMES    2 SPEAKERS
ES . DAVID . YOU GO DOWN AND GET THE CLEANING ONOUN .        I-M GOING TO GET ANOTHER DRINK . +GONNA . YES . SURE CAN    60050    9
LITTLE FINGER . 660 ? WILL WE GO NOW . FINISHED . NOW       I-M GOING TO GET SOMETHING . ? MUM . CAN WE DO THIS NOW    60001   39
E . YOU WAIT HERE AND I-LL GO UPSTAIRS AND GET SOME .       I-M GOING TO GET SOMETHING . ALRIGHT YOU CAN WAIT THERE    59078    1
                                                                659            1
                                                                660            3
                                                                611            1
                                                             5 MORPHEMES    3 SPEAKERS
:R . LEFT RIGHT :R . XLEFT X4 . :E . GIVE IT TO ME .         I-M GOING TO GIVE IT TO HIM . +IM . LEFT RIGHT :R . XLEF    7349    9
WASHING MACHINE . +YA . +A . ? WHERE IS IT NOW . OH .       I-M GOING TO GO AND GET IT . +GONNA . +AN . OH BOY . WHA    8011    1
. KEEP THAT LIKE THAT TO SHOW DAD . OH YES . +YEAH .        I-M GOING TO GO AND LOOK THROUGH YOUR BOOK . +GONNA . ?    8029   52
                                                                608            2
```

arrives," "*I'm* a girl." Regardless of the classification system, it seems to be the nature of the English language that these meaningful units ("building blocks," "developmental units," "meaningful sequences") have one characteristic in common—the unit begins with a signalling word such as those italicized above.

Further, as an inspection of the lists of single words in this book will show, the words most frequently used are signalling words. It was decided that this feature of the language could help in identifying meaningful sequences of words. The communication index for sequences was accordingly weighted so that those beginning with signalling words would generally be high on the lists. This preserves the pattern set in the single-word lists and throws up those strings of words which, since they begin with widely and frequently used words, are likely to be functionally the most useful.

In calculating the communication index of sequences, the index of the first word was multiplied by an index for each subsequent word. The frequency of the *first* word was always taken as that in the *single*-word index (i.e. over the total body of language). The index for the second or third word used in the calculation was the actual frequency of occurrence in the particular sequence. The sequence index was again adjusted for generality of use across the whole sample, as with that of single words.[1]

THE WORD AND WORD SEQUENCE LISTS

In Chapter 6, a combined alphabetical listing is given for all the frequently used single words in the language of the $2\frac{1}{2}$, $3\frac{1}{2}$, $4\frac{1}{2}$, $5\frac{1}{2}$, and $6\frac{1}{2}$ year old children in our samples. The communication index at each age level is given for each word, and, as an indication of developmental trend, the mean of the communication indices is set down separately for the age ranges $3\frac{1}{2}$–$4\frac{1}{2}$ and $5\frac{1}{2}$–$6\frac{1}{2}$. This is followed by alphabetical lists for two-word sequences and three-word sequences, given separately for ages $2\frac{1}{2}$, $3\frac{1}{2}$, $4\frac{1}{2}$, $5\frac{1}{2}$, and $6\frac{1}{2}$. In Chapter 7, single words, two-word sequences, and three-word sequences are ordered according to communication index.

The most useful lists for those concerned with language and reading programs for young children are those of two-word and three-word sequences. They are much less ambiguous and more informative than single-word lists. For example, to know that "I" is very frequently used at $6\frac{1}{2}$ years is not as useful as to know that "I'm going," "I'm not," and "I've got" are very frequently used. The single word "what" is ambiguous, but the phrase "what's that" is not, and the fact that this is the most frequent three-word sequence beginning with "what" is fairly specific information.

Comparative Use of the Communication Index

Because the communication index is adjusted for the differing amounts of language collected at the various age levels, it is possible to compare usages

---

1. A fuller explanation of the calculation of communication indices is provided in Appendix A.

TABLE 4
**INDEX RANGES
WITHIN WHICH THE
FIRST 100 SINGLE
WORDS OCCUR AT
EACH AGE LEVEL**

Frequency range (groups of ten)	Index range				
	2½ years	3½ years	4½ years	5½ years	6½ years
1–10	389–229	450–144	445–132	499–140	523–132
11–20	161–137	142–113	126–85	133–86	129–90
21–30	128–77	112–69	84–58	83–64	90–75
31–40	74–44	66–48	53–36	63–48	73–54
41–50	43–33	48–31	36–26	47–36	53–43
51–60	31–22	31–20	26–20	33–29	41–30
61–70	22–16	20–15	19–15	29–22	30–25
71–80	16–11	14–12	14–12	22–18	25–20
81–90	11–9	11–9	11–9	18–15	20–16
91–100	9–7	8–6	9–7	15–12	15–14

across those age levels. The listings in Chapter 7, which include the 100 most frequent words and sequences at each age level, allow just such a direct comparison of the usage of the most frequent words and sequences.

There is a need, however, for the reader to have some concept of the relative importance of a word or sequence once it has been located in the alphabetical listings. In Table 4, the 100 most frequently used single words are classified into groups of ten by frequency of occurrence. For each group of ten the range of index values is given for each age level. Thus, the ten words most frequently used at age 6½ have index values between 132 and 523, while the ten words most frequently used at age 5½ have index values between 140 and 499. Tables 5 and 6 give similar information for two-word and three-word sequences at each age level.

Given the communication index for a word or sequence, we can find out where that language unit fits within the 100 most frequently used words or sequences at each age level simply by using Tables 4, 5, and 6. For example, the

TABLE 5
**INDEX RANGES
WITHIN WHICH THE
FIRST 100 TWO-WORD
SEQUENCES OCCUR
AT EACH AGE LEVEL**

Frequency range (groups of ten)	Index range				
	2½ years	3½ years	4½ years	5½ years	6½ years
1–10	143–39	243–33	273–35	350–72	415–83
11–20	31–13	32–14	27–15	65–29	83–35
21–30	12–9	14–10	13–10	26–17	33–26
31–40	9–6	10–8	10–7	17–15	26–20
41–50	6–5	8–6	7–5	15–11	19–18
51–60	5–4	6–5	5–4	11–10	17–15
61–70	4–3	5–3	4–3	10–9	14–12
71–80	3–2	3–3	3–2	8–8	12–10
81–90	2–2	3–2	2–2	8–7	10–9
91–100	2–2	2–2	2–2	7–6	9–8

TABLE 6
**INDEX RANGES
WITHIN WHICH THE
FIRST 100
THREE-WORD
SEQUENCES OCCUR
AT EACH AGE LEVEL**

Frequency range (groups of ten)	Index range				
	2½ years	3½ years	4½ years	5½ years	6½ years
1–10	1986–49	4999–114	3707–114	6126–366	9531–578
11–20	25–0.01	111–27	107–32	333–154	496–370
21–30	—	25–12	30–11	153–99	348–241
31–40	—	11–3	11–4	86–58	224–124
41–50	—	3–0.2	4–1	57–43	120–91
51–60	—	0.1–0.01	1–0.02	41–33	81–67
61–70	—	—	—	33–27	66–57
71–80	—	—	—	27–25	56–40
81–90	—	—	—	23–18	40–36
91–100	—	—	—	17–16	36–30

alphabetical listing in Chapter 6 tells us that the word "like" has the following indices at each age level:

Age	2½	3½	4½	5½	6½
Index	22	37	26	28.6	37

From Table 4 we can see that these indices correspond to the following frequency ranges:

Age	2½	3½	4½	5½	6½
Frequency range	51–60	41–50	41–50	71–80	51–60

**COMPARATIVE
ANALYSIS OF
LANGUAGE SAMPLED
IN ENGLAND,
CANADA, AND U.S.A.**

To test the universality of the language sequences collected in the Mount Gravatt program, words and sequences collected there were compared with those from the language of children in Bristol, England. The Education Research Unit at Bristol University, under the direction of Mr. Gordon Wells, is recording the natural speech of children as part of a long-term project on language development. The actual language collected by the Education Research Unit at Bristol was subjected to the same analysis as the Brisbane samples.

A sample of child language collected by Prof. Richard Handscombe of York University and Glendon College, Toronto, Canada, and another from the language of kindergarten black children provided by the South-West Regional Laboratory (SWRL) at Los Alamitos, California, are presently being analyzed to test further the universality across English-speaking countries and cultures of the words and word sequences listed in this volume. It appears likely that, despite superficial differences, the core of frequently used words and sequences is remarkably similar at comparable stages of language development.

The samples of language from Bristol, England and Toronto, Canada were both taken using chronological ages as a means of separating one age from the other. On the other hand, the Australian sampling technique used a language test to select children of "average" language ability for each chronological age sampled. Table 7 shows the single words and two-word sequences which are common over the 100 most frequent in the language of 2½, 3½, 4½, 5½, and 6½ year old Brisbane children and the 100 most frequent in the language of 3¼ year old Bristol children and 5 year old Toronto children. From this comparison it would seem that some children from Bristol (age 3¼) were in fact operating at a higher level. The tables generally increase as one moves up the age scales. This is apparent, too, on the Canadian sample. We await with interest our results for language taken from 8½ year old children as the trend is now marked, with the Canadian sample rising sharply from a 60% commonality for single words at 2½ years and 85% commonality at 6½ years (see Table 7).

There is one further difference in sampling of the Canadian language sample. The children were not using "naturalistic language" in the sense that it is used for Australian and Bristol samples. In the Australian and Bristol samples language was collected randomly from the ongoing daily speech of children. Three specific situations were set up for the Canadian sampling: (1) children were placed in a monologue situation, (2) children were placed in a dialogue situation, (3) children were placed with their peers in a group situation. This had

TABLE 7
BRISTOL (ENGLAND) AND TORONTO (CANADA) SAMPLES COMPARED WITH BRISBANE SAMPLE

Age levels (Brisbane children)	Single words			
	% common		Concurrence correlation	
	Bristol	Toronto	Bristol	Toronto
2½ years	75	60	0.64	0.49
3½ years	77	67	0.70	0.56
4½ years	78	75	0.70	0.63
5½ years	79	78	0.71	0.66
6½ years	80	85	0.71	0.72

Age levels (Brisbane children)	Two-word sequences			
	% common		Concurrence correlation	
	Bristol	Toronto	Bristol	Toronto
2½ years	44	0.20	0.36	0.14
3½ years	53	0.32	0.41	0.23
4½ years	47	0.44	0.40	0.33
5½ years	67	0.43	0.52	0.35
6½ years	59	0.42	0.48	0.32

RECORDING LANGUAGE

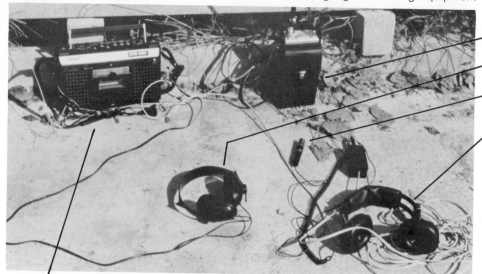

Language Recording Equipment

FM receiver

headphones for
equipment monitoring

microphone
for observer

headphones
for observer

stereo recorder

Child wearing
transmitter and
microphone in
playground during
recording.

Child wearing transmitter and microphone during lunch break with friends.

Monitoring and recording the language.

Operating the equipment. Female observer is describing the interaction situations that are occurring.

Observing and describing the interaction situations in which the recorded language occurs.

	Single words		Two-word sequences	
Age levels (Brisbane children)	% common	Concurrence correlation	% common	Concurrence correlation
$2\frac{1}{2}$ years	71	0.62	46	0.37
$4\frac{1}{2}$ years	80	0.71	51	0.42
$5\frac{1}{2}$ years	81	0.71	47	0.37
$6\frac{1}{2}$ years	80	0.70	42	0.31

TABLE 8
$2\frac{1}{2}$, $4\frac{1}{2}$, $5\frac{1}{2}$, AND $6\frac{1}{2}$
YEAR-OLD BRISBANE
CHILDREN
COMPARED WITH $3\frac{1}{2}$
YEAR-OLD BRISBANE
CHILDREN

a very different influence on the way these children put words together. For instance, they used "and" in numerous combination situations to extend their sentences. Thus, although "and" as a single word is in the top 10 most frequently used single words for $4\frac{1}{2}$, $5\frac{1}{2}$, and $6\frac{1}{2}$ year old Australian children, it is not used in combination with specific words such as "the," "I," "then," "we," "a," "they," "he," "my" with high frequency, as is the case with the Canadian sample. If these two-word sequences are omitted the percentage of language in common rises to 49% and the concurrence correlation to 0.39.

The only way we have of producing some comparative data is to compare the Australian $3\frac{1}{2}$ year old language with each of the other Brisbane age group collections as in Table 8. When this is done we get a top percentage in common of 81% and a concurrence correlation of 0.71. Thus the Canadian sample, with its 85% common and 0.72 concurrence correlation, stands up well, as does the Bristol sample, with 80% common and 0.71 concurrence.

When the two-word sequences are compared in this way the best Australian percentage in common is 51% and the best concurrence correlation is 0.42. Once again, the Canadian sample comparative figures are 44% and 0.33 (if the atypical usage of "and" combinations are taken out, this becomes 49% and 0.39). The comparative figures for Bristol two-word sequences are 67% and 0.52. Considering sample collection, this is a satisfactory result.

Conclusions

When the different sampling techniques are taken into consideration, we conclude that the language used by Canadian children is so similar to that used by children from Australia and Great Britain that it is possible to extract common "signalling sequences" and that these sequences are likely to be used with a high degree of semantic and pragmatic concurrence. Further cross-cultural checking of these concurrences is currently in progress.

CHAPTER TWO

CHILD LANGUAGE AND LEARNING TO READ AND WRITE

It is widely recognized that a disturbing percentage of children find it very difficult to learn to read. Estimates of the proportion of normal children who encounter reading difficulties vary from as low as 5 percent to as high as 25 percent. The disagreement in estimates within a given society appears to arise from differences in the criteria used; but the overall picture seems fairly constant across English-speaking cultures.[1]

Much recent research in psycholinguistics has emphasized the role of the child's oral language as an important factor operating in the reading situation. The Bullock enquiry into the problem of reading in Great Britain, reviewing research in this area, made the following statement:

A printed text is easier to read the more closely its structures are related to those used by the reader in normal speech . . . Reading material which presents children with . . . unreal language therefore lacks predictability and prevents them from making use of the sequential probability in linguistic structure. (Bullock Report, p. 92)

By the time a child is of school age he or she has internalized a highly developed system of oral language which is consistent with that particular child's level of cognitive development and which is functionally adequate for communication in the world in which that child lives. Children therefore come to school with a conception of language as a useful means of communication and with a store of language through which they can communicate their knowledge and experiences.

What is most important about the oral language system of young children is that it is established at an automatic[2] as well as a cognitive level of functioning.

---

1. The Ministry of Education, Britain (1957) estimated at least 21 to 25 percent of children at grade 4 level had reading quotients of 80 or below. In the United States, Austin, Bush, and Huebner (1961) found that approximately 16 percent of children in grades 3 to 9 needed special help in reading. The Victoria Education Department, Australia (1965), found that 20 percent of grade 2 children had serious difficulties in learning to read.

2. Kirk, McCarthy, and Kirk (1969) define this level as that in which "the individual's habits of functioning are less voluntary but highly organized and integrated. The automatic chain of responses of the latter level is involved in such activities as visual and auditory closure, speed of perception, ability to reproduce a sequence seen or heard, rote learning, synthesizing isolated sounds into a word, and utilizing the redundancies of experience." It seems likely, however, that automatic language functioning is similar, in the final analysis, to other automatic motor sequencing such as learning to walk. It certainly involves memory of all the fine motor movements which are required for producing speech. It may well be that the memory involved in oral language sequencing is essentially one of motor sequences monitored by what the ear hears resulting from this sequencing. Because integration of sequencing behavior appears basic to virtually all human activity, it is likely

Five-year-olds cannot express their language rules formally, yet they have a language system that is governed by complex grammatical rules. This internalized language system is the basis from which they must necessarily operate to interpret sequences of language in the visual modality.

Research using the Illinois Test of Psycholinguistic Abilities (I.T.P.A.) suggests that reading is dependent on underlying automatic-sequential (integrative) language functions (Bateman, 1963; Bateman and Weatherell, 1965; Ferrier, 1963; Foster, 1963; Hart, 1963, 1964, 1968, 1970; Kass, 1962, 1966; McLeod, 1967).[3] It seems logical, then, to make use of this internalized language system in helping children learn to read.

THE PROCESS OF READING AND LEARNING TO READ

How does the internalized language system of children relate to the actual process of reading?

In dealing with auditory language, children tend to group sequences of sounds into meaningful units (Werner and Kaplan, 1950; Huttenlocher, 1964). This takes place in a time dimension; the beginning and the end of each meaningful unit are separated in time and it is necessary to remember the first elements (whatever their nature) until meaning is complete. Short-term memory and long-term memory must be involved in this process.

In the written form, language sequences take on a spatial dimension. Visual sequences are interpreted from left to right. It is the order of interpretation which gives rise to a time sequencing across a visual array. The meaningful unit is again an important concept, for now children must be able to take meaningful units from the array of symbols that are presented in left-to-right sequence. Assuming the development of an automatic integrated conceptual system for units that are orally meaningful, it seems desirable to give beginning readers material in which the meaningful units correspond with those predominant in their oral language. If this is done they are freer to concentrate on the decoding problems associated with reading. Language structures to which the internalized system does not apply would seem to represent stumbling blocks in the transition from a knowledge of spoken language to the interpretation of written language.[4]

Learning to read, then, involves extension of language competence from the auditory to the visual mode. The process of reading may be regarded as the

---

that language sequencing may best be understood if the integration involved is defined in terms applicable to all automatic motor sequencing rather than as development from cognitive or representational levels as suggested by Kirk and McCarthy.

3. In a series of studies with cerebral-palsied, visually handicapped, deaf, mentally retarded, and normal children, Hart (1970) found that these groups of children made significant progress in reading after working through a short language program based on the I.T.P.A. and the automatic use of language structures without special reading tuition. He concluded that "inability to use language at an integration (automatic-sequential) level appeared to be an important key to understanding deficits in children's language development."

4. As indicated above, this sequencing would not normally take place at a level of conscious cognitive rules. Interference which directs conscious attention to discrete elements of an integrated automatic sequence may cause at least temporary retrogression in sequencing competence.

extraction of meaning from an array of graphic symbols arranged in a spatial dimension. Such an array could be composed of pictorial units (such as in a wordless comic strip) from which meaning can be extracted without knowledge of any particular language; or it could consist of a more sophisticated graphic code, the units of which are representative of auditory units of a particular oral language.

Faced with the written code, the reader basically has two processing options. One is to take meaning directly from the written code; the other is to first recode the written code into an oral code and then take meaning from that. (We operate in the latter way when we recode Morse signals into the alphabetic code before we can interpret the meaning of the message.)

The first option, that of proceeding directly to meaning from the written code, is generally assumed to be the process employed by very fluent readers. The achievement of this level of proficiency should be the ultimate goal of any reading program. The second option, that of recoding first into the oral code through either overt vocalizing or subvocalizing, is generally assumed to be the pathway through which the great majority of beginning readers pass. Indeed, a large number of readers never achieve more than this level of proficiency.

With regard to this second approach, Smith, Goodman, and Meredith (1974) differentiate between the terms "decoding" and "recoding." Decoding is the process of taking meaning from what the writer has encoded. Recoding, however, is a process of transferring from one code to another with no understanding of meaning. For the beginning reader, the recode-decode process may be diagramed as follows.

| graphic code | —— recoding ⟶ | oral code | —— decoding ⟶ | meaning |

That is, the reader first recodes from the graphic code to an oral code before attempting to decode for meaning. This is necessary because phonemes or words, decoded as separate entities, are not enough to allow the child to go straight to total meaning. Once they are recoded to the oral form, however, the child has a unit of language from which he or she can extract the meaning intended by the author.

Reading involves identifying, through distinctive features,[5] graphic units which are meaningful because they represent semantic "chunks" of the reader's organized interpretation of his or her world. This is true whether the reader decodes directly from written language or must first recode. In the latter case, however, the process of extracting meaning is more difficult. The beginning reader must learn that certain distinctive features of graphic sequences consistently represent distinctive features from known oral sequences, so that both sets of distinctive features refer to the same semantic "chunk." If this learning does not occur, the child may indeed learn to recode an array of graphic symbols, in the sense of producing the sound sequences to which that array corresponds, but

---

5. For a discussion of distinctive features and the process of learning to read, see Frank Smith (1971).

may do so with little verbal understanding. The result is not reading in the usual sense of the word.[6]

If reading is to be a form of communication, beginning readers must be able to identify "chunks" of graphic symbols and relate them to corresponding semantic "chunks" which originate in the organized interpretation of their life-space. Since children have built up an organized system of meaningful oral language before they begin school, sound sequences have already been associated with meaningful "chunks" from within their life-space. When graphic "chunks" translate into familiar "chunks" of auditory sequencing, these graphic units are immediately meaningful. If not, the child faces a virtually impossible task in extracting meaning.

In summary, when we examine the children in the average school who are failing to learn to read, we see that the great majority have an excellent oral command of the automatic use of language structure. They are successful language users. If we capitalize on the automatic use of language structure which already exists in the oral mode when we present reading material to these children, the material must become easier to decode in a meaningful way.

It is likely also that we will provide an easy transition to creative writing as children master the reading process. The capacity to read, using latent structure,[7] is but a short step from a desire to express oneself graphically in the same way.

CONTROLLING LANGUAGE FOR USE IN TEACHING PROGRAMS

Word Frequency Control

Early attempts to control language in books for children were based on lists of frequently used words taken from material written for and by children. The use of these lists as a basis for reading and language development programs is, however, open to criticism, partly because of the methods employed in their compilation and partly because single-word listings, by themselves, do not provide sufficient information for them to be of much use in language programs.

A well-known word frequency count is the one given by Thorndike and Lorge (1944) in *The Teacher's Word Book of 30000 Words*. This count was extracted from books likely to be used by children, such as school readers, textbooks, the Bible, and the English Classics. Two other American lists, Gates (1935) and

---

6. This does not imply that teaching reading should not include training in the recognition of elements of the visual code which are not meaningful in themselves. This book does not set out to delineate a preferred method of teaching reading, but merely to present language units, the use of which is likely to facilitate reading, as defined above, irrespective of the teaching strategies used. Certainly children need to be taught what words are and, later, what elements may be clues to verbal meaning.

7. The term "latent structure" refers to the child's capacity to create novel sentences. In the Mount Gravatt Program the term at first refers to the capacity to recombine signalling sequences with content sequences (see pages 18–19).

Dolch (1950), were built mainly from Thorndike's vocabulary. It is evident that these studies, based on words that adults think that children ought to know, may not correlate well with children's usage.

Rinsland (1945) produced a list based mainly on the writing of grade 1 children, to which was added some conversational material. This study, as well as those of Thorndike, of Gates, and of Dolch, counted only the number of times the word occurred. *Words Your Children Use,* by Edwards and Gibbon (1964), was also compiled from material written by children, and contained lists of single words ordered according to an index that was calculated by multiplying frequency of occurrence by the percentage of children using the word. This was an improvement over the frequency count alone.

The most comprehensive and authentic list of single words based on reading materials is contained in *The American Heritage Word Frequency Book,* by Carroll, Davies, and Richman (1971). The source of the words and their frequencies is the material read by children from grades 3 to 9. Lists are both alphabetical and according to frequency of usage. Word frequency is given both by grade and by subject.

Although the lists just described have their usefulness, a reliance on written language as the source of material to use with beginning readers is suspect. The production of written language is a skill which is learned *after* the child comes to school, very often in conjunction with the type of language presented in reading books. For example, the 250 words most frequently used in writing by children aged 5 and up, in *Words Your Children Use,* include no question markers ("why," "which," "where," "who," etc.), yet these are very frequent in the oral language of $5\frac{1}{2}$ year old children. Similarly, of the 250 words most frequently used by $5\frac{1}{2}$ year olds in the Mount Gravatt study, only 115 are in the corresponding list in *Words Your Children Use.*

Moreover, single-word listings produce only a partial and sometimes misleading picture to the teacher concerned with language development programs. The meaning signalled by a single word is almost always ambiguous until it is placed in a context, e.g., "like" could be used as a verb, as in "I like it," or as a preposition, as in "I want one like that." The resolution of such ambiguity is important, for although "like" is frequently used at the $2\frac{1}{2}$, $3\frac{1}{2}$, $4\frac{1}{2}$, and $5\frac{1}{2}$ year old level, its use as a verb is far more frequent, and its use as a preposition develops at a much slower rate. With single-word vocabulary lists, we just do not know which meaning is to be inferred from a particular word.

To be sure that a given single word is meaningful to the child, it needs to be in the context in which the child uses it. Studies of young children's conception of word boundaries seem to indicate that it is often sequences of words, rather than single words, that are the important carriers of meaning in a sentence. It is clear, also, that when children enter school they do not perceive a word as a separate unit according to printing conventions. As Holden and MacGinitie (1972) point out, a first grade teacher cannot take for granted that children will understand her when she talks about "words" and their printed representation.

Nor can she assume that the concepts related to their usage can be quickly and easily taught.

Word frequency lists do not give enough information about how children use words. One of the purposes of the Mount Gravatt Lists of Word Sequences is to provide information on how children put words together. This provides additional knowledge of the meaning intention of the children.

Control of Structure through Signalling Units

The language signalling units (single words, and two- and three-word sequences) presented in this volume provide valuable insights into the "combinability" of words used by children. In fact, they provide us with basic elements of language structure which are used over and over to form novel sentences by children. Oller (1972) demonstrated that new sentences are not wholly novel to a speaker, but that their "newness" consists in the fact that they constitute new combinations of "familiar units." It is these "familiar units" that are listed in this book.

Basic to Oller's "familiar units" of language, which are meaningful in the sense discussed above, are structure (or function)[8] words which act as signalling devices in the sequencing of units. Words like "a," "the," "can," "do," "in," and "on" occur again and again because they combine readily with thousands of other words. Such words, in their proper place, make up the communication framework or core upon which the rest of the language is built, and they signal, syntactically and semantically, what is to follow them. Combinability is not limited to what are commonly known as structure words, however. Verbs like "put," "take," "give," and "get" can combine with a large number of nouns, verbs, adverbs, and prepositions. A number of adjectives, e.g., "big" and "little," can combine with a relatively large number of nouns; and pronouns occur with very high frequency.

Structure words have often been regarded as having no definitive meaning. In the sense of not having a direct referent this is true; for example, you can't see or touch an "in" or a "the" or a "but." (This most probably is why it is so hard to teach these simple words to children). However, it is not true that they lack meaning, when you consider their dynamic function in language. They take on meaning when they become part of a group of words and contribute to the overall meaning of a sentence. They serve to express and signal the structural relationships that exist in a sentence. This is most important when you consider that children enter school with no concept of structure words as separate entities in the adult sense. Their only experience with structure words has been in

---

8. *A note about function words and content words:* Content words are those which designate a particular action or object in a specific situation. In other words, their reference is limited. They include nouns, adjectives, and some verbs. Structure or function words, on the other hand, are used over a great variety of differing situations in combination with a variety of content words, i.e., their reference is much wider than that of content words, They include the prepositions, the conjunctions, the pronouns, the adverbs, and certain verbs, such as "to be" and "to have."

speech. They are familiar with them as parts of meaningful units and find it difficult to separate them out as individual words.[9]

For the reasons outlined in Chapter 1 (page 6), the language sequences isolated at Mount Gravatt are generally introduced by and contain these function words. The word sequences in turn act as signalling units within language, giving cues of what is to follow and relating to what is past. When used in material for beginning readers, such sequences help preserve the natural rhythm and intonational patterns of children's speech and so help them to transfer the rhythm and intonation to reading. It appears also that they serve to mark off meaningful "chunks" of language within the material.

The most frequently used sequences, which begin with one or more of the structure words, are crucial to children's use of latent structure (i.e., the ability to form new sentences). Because the signalling units (sequences) contribute to the structural meaning rather than specifying a direct referent, they are not tied to one particular situation but are used over and over again by all children to communicate in a great variety of situations. For example, in the phrase "in the box," "in the" contributes structural meaning. It adds meaning to what has preceded and also signals an expectation of what is to follow. This expectation is fulfilled when "box" appears. "Box," however, has a direct referential meaning, i.e., a concrete object called a box exists apart from the phrase "in the box."

Language signalling units are remarkably consistent in the way they appear in the language development of children. After the age of $3\frac{1}{2}$, once signalling units appear in the language, they then consolidate their position and increase in usage, becoming well established through the child's continued use of latent structure (i.e., he uses these units as components of novel sentences over a great variety of communication situations). These signalling units provide the teacher with more than a surface investigation of the child's language structure. They tap the child's communicating capacity. They are basic elements in the child's latent structure and form a communication core for his language.

Naturally, to use these signalling units to their greatest potential, we need to understand fully the meaning intention which the child attaches to the usage of a particular signalling unit. It is not practicable to specify the semantic and pragmatic context[10] of these signalling units in this volume. However, the lists presented provide much information that can be applied by the teacher wishing to understand and make use of the language of children in teaching programs.

---

9. Consider, for example, "He puts the bag *in* _____." At this point in the sentence there is an expectation concerning the fulfilment of meaning and this is likely to be different from "He puts the bag *with* _____." So it is not true to say that "in" and "with" have no meaning in isolation. Rather, they provide additive meaning to what has preceded them and also signal expectations of what is to follow. Thus structure words (or function words), which constitute approximately two-thirds of any text, serve to indicate the expectation of several possible meanings. The *definitive* meaning for these words comes from their use in conjunction with other words. This is probably why young children find it difficult to understand these words in isolation.

10. By pragmatic context we mean the situational context in which the signalling unit is appropriate for the child.

A COMPARISON OF
THE STRUCTURE OF
CHILD LANGUAGE
AND THAT OF
CURRENT
INTRODUCTORY
READERS

Sufficient information is available from a count of word sequences to indicate that the sequences most frequently used in reading books are not the ones most frequently used in children's language. It follows that the language in most readers is not child language in the sense of being readily understood by children.

An analysis of the structure of the language used in four introductory reading series commonly used in England and Australia reveals some interesting contrasts when compared with children's oral language and with a series of readers recently prepared at Mount Gravatt College. The Mount Gravatt Readers were developed using the signalling units presented in this report[11] rather than the traditional method of controlled vocabulary.

The reading books analyzed comprised those which would normally be considered appropriate for the first two years of school. The Mount Gravatt Readers were analyzed for only the first level, however, as subsequent levels were still in preparation at the date of analyses. The other reading series are listed as series A, B, C, and D.

None of the readers analyzed were based on a purely phonic approach to the teaching of reading. Series A readers were part of an experientially based program for which it was claimed that the books were written largely from stories dictated by children. Series B, C, and D were written in a more conventional way, using standard word lists and controls.

Table 9 compares the 100 most frequently used single words, two-word signalling units, and three-word signalling units (word sequences) in each of the reading series with the 100 most frequent single words, two-word sequences, and three-word sequences in $5\frac{1}{2}$ year old oral language. Table 10 compares the $5\frac{1}{2}$ year old children's language and that of $2\frac{1}{2}$, $3\frac{1}{2}$, $4\frac{1}{2}$, and $6\frac{1}{2}$ year old children.

As Table 9 shows, there seems to be little difference among the reading series, including the Mount Gravatt Readers, as regards the percentage of single words that are also found in $5\frac{1}{2}$ year old children's language. That is, for single words, the Mount Gravatt Readers provide only marginally better correspondence than the other series. However, from Table 10 it is also evident that

TABLE 9
**PERCENTAGE OF
SINGLE WORDS AND
WORD SEQUENCES
COMMON TO BOTH $5\frac{1}{2}$
YEAR OLD LANGUAGE
AND THAT OF EACH
OF THE READING
SERIES ANALYZED
(using the 100 most
frequent words and
sequences)**

Reading series	Percentage in common with $5\frac{1}{2}$ year old language		
	Single words	Two-word sequences	Three-word sequences
Series A	54%	17%	2%
Series B	53%	12%	2%
Series C	48%	11%	2%
Series D	52%	17%	0%
Mount Gravatt	61%	43%	30%

---

11. Basic concepts behind the Mount Gravatt Reading Program are given in Chapter 1.

Age levels of samples	Percentage in common with 5½ year old language		
	Single words	Two-word sequences	Three-word sequences
2½ years	85%	39%	6%
3½ years	81%	49%	17%
4½ years	82%	59%	21%
6½ years	92%	81%	62%

TABLE 10
PERCENTAGE OF SINGLE WORDS AND WORD SEQUENCES COMMON TO BOTH 5½ YEAR OLD LANGUAGE AND THAT OF CHILDREN OF OTHER AGES (using the 100 most frequent words and sequences)

5½ year old children's language does not differ much from that of 2½, 3½, 4½, and 6½ year old children at the single-word level. The truly striking differences in both comparisons occur with two-word and three-word signalling units. As Tables 9 and 10 show, the Mount Gravatt Readers are using language structure that is much closer to 5½ year old children's language than the other readers. Special note should be taken of the differences in the three-word sequence column of Table 9.

The following statements summarize important points about the analysis of the four reading series.[12]

a) Only a small proportion of the words and an almost negligible proportion of the sequences which occur in 5½ year old children's language occur also in the reading series. Samples of current Mount Gravatt books are relatively much closer to the language children use.

b) In terms of the relative importance assigned to common words and sequences (as judged by frequency of use), 5½ year old children's language differs greatly from that of each of the current readers with the exception of the Mount Gravatt Readers.

c) The 100 words and sequences most frequently used in children's language and in each reading series account for a high proportion of the total volume of language in the sample.

d) At the level of single words, the language in the four reading series differs from that of 5½ year old children largely because an abnormal weight is given to content words. This contrasts with natural language, where individual content words occur infrequently, and the most frequent words and sequences are structure words or sequences of structure words.

e) In terms of two- and three-word sequences, the difference between the current introductory reading books (series A, B, C, and D) and children's language appears to be a direct consequence of the frequent repetition of content words (nouns, verbs, adjectives, etc.). The few sequences which are common to the reading series and children's language are those which are closely associated with noun phrases, and because of the high degree of repetition of noun phrases, such sequences are used at an abnormal level.

12. A full analysis of the differences was made in Chapter 2 of Report 4 to the Australian Advisory Committee on Research and Development in Education.

The predominant use of repetitive noun phrases constricts the language structure, destroying natural language flow, and thus diminishes the likelihood that the child can predict structure on the basis of his intuitive knowledge of language. Clearly, this compounds the task facing the beginning reader.

The principle of repetition as a basis for learning is often followed in the preparation of reading material. However, the repetition of words in natural language operates completely differently from the way it is used in the preparation of many contemporary readers. Obviously, it would be impossible to repeat each word exactly the same number of times and produce recognizable language. This is because of the relative distribution of word types which must occur in natural language. Structure words are few in relation to the total number of different words, but each of them usually occurs very frequently. Conversely, content words are numerous, but each particular word occurs infrequently.

The various combinations of the structure words provide flexibility and variety. If, in a reading book, content words are repeated more frequently than in normal language, the majority of structure words in the text must then be associated directly with these specific content words, and the combinations of structure words (sequences) available for use must also be specifically associated with the particular content words repeated.

If the child has difficulty with sequencing, then it seems inadvisable to force him to construct new rhythmic patterns, especially without relating them to the pragmatic dimension of language. Breaking up the rhythmic pattern of language has the same effect as changing the structural flow—both are interdependent. By breaking up the structural flow, the ability to use language in its automatic function is reduced. Consequently, greater loads are placed on the child's short-term memory.

A factor peculiar to reading series which helps to break the rhythmic flow of language is the omission of certain contracted forms (e.g. "I'm" and "he's") which are common to children's language. Of the series studied, only series A used any type of contracted form. Table 11 presents a comparison of two-word sequences which occur within the first 20 in each reading series, but not within the first 100 in 5½ year old children's language, with those which occur within the first 20 in 5½ year old children's language, but not within the first 100 of each series. As Table 11 shows, those sequences which occur very frequently in reading books, but not at a high frequency level in children's language, are mainly of two types: (1) those associated with nouns (e.g. "the children"), and (2) those which are elaborations of forms normally contracted (e.g. "it is," "it's," etc.).

Usually the contracted form and the elaborated form have different meanings when the child uses oral language. In the child's oral system, if the elaborated form is used it is mainly for emphasis (e.g., "I will" versus "I'll"). This distinction is not commonly made in the written form. In some cases, the elaborated form simply does not occur in children's language (e.g., "I cannot" versus "I can't").

Occur only in 5½ year old language	Occur only in series A	Occur only in 5½ year old language	Occur only in series B
I'm	my mum	I'm	the dog
it's	my teacher	I'll	the water
I don't	the tree	it's	the ball
I got	the cat	I don't	here is
I know	the children	I got	the shop
you're	my friend	I know	like the
that's	the baby	I've	the children
I can't	to my	you're	and Jane
I want	the little	got a	Peter and
I think	the doctor	that's	the tree
I didn't	the street	I can't	is in
's a	the tea	I think	the fish
you know	the kettle	I didn't	like to
I was	a big	's a	is here
I did	is big	you know	the bus
	we have	I was	the boat
		I have	the toy
		I did	is a

Occur only in 5½ year old language	Occur only in series C	Occur only in 5½ year old language	Occur only in series D
I'm	the ball	I'm	the children
I'll	the tree	I'll	the little
it's	I will	it's	the cow
I don't	the little	I don't	the caravan
I got	the dog	I got	the car
I know	I cannot	I know	look at
I've	the children	I've	the track
you're	the kite	you're	the calf
got a	the five	got a	the farm
that's	the monkey	that's	Andrew said
I can't	the mud	I can't	the truck
I want	and said	I want	the snake
I think	the kitten	I think	the paddock
I didn't	the mother	I didn't	
's a	the seat	's a	
you know	will get	you know	
I was		I was	
I have		I have	
I did		I did	

TABLE 11
TWO-WORD SEQUENCES VERY FREQUENT IN 5½ YEAR OLD LANGUAGE, BUT MISSING FROM FIRST 100 IN EACH READING SERIES, AND VICE VERSA

Goodman and Smith (1971) point out that when children begin learning to read, the material they are presented with should not be stereotyped.

Rather, a child appears to need to be exposed to a wide range of choices so that he can detect the significant elements of written language. Experiments [Goodman and Burke (1968) (1969)] have shown that even beginning readers look for, and use, orthographic, syntactic and semantic redundancy in written language—but, whoever thinks of trying to "teach" a child about that? The child learning to speak, seems to need the opportunity to examine a large sample of language, to generate hypotheses on the basis of feedback that is appropriate to the unspoken rules he happens to be testing.

The point hardly needs to be made that for children just learning to read, the only "unspoken" rules that are available for testing exist within their oral language system. The language in early reading material must be such that those rules can be applied to it and used as a stepping stone for the generation of hypotheses about regularities underlying written language.

CHAPTER THREE

TOWARD A DESCRIPTION OF CHILD LANGUAGE DEVELOPMENT

We have made it clear that the lists of words and sequences of words in this book are not based on raw word counts from surface structure. The sampling procedures and the method used to calculate the communication index of each item were aimed at producing more useful outcomes than would a raw count. Nevertheless, it may not be evident that to develop the language/reading program, the analysis had to be carried beyond the production of these lists. In this chapter we shall show how these lists fit within a longer-term project aimed at producing a developmental description of child language, one which rests on a theory of the way in which children function in their use of language.

As will be pointed out in Chapter 5, the lists in this book have a wide variety of applications. The communication index serves to identify those words and short sequences of words which seem to be functionally the most useful to normal children at each age level, since they are used again and again over a wide spectrum of situations by a large proportion of the children of that particular stage of language development. The lists also reveal the age at which particular units of language come into what we are calling the *core language* of normal children, and they indicate the relative usefulness of each of the units at the various ages. They provide, therefore, a means of comparing the surface structure of the various corpora of language in respect to the frequency of use of the words and strings of words which are contained within them—whether these units of language be signalling, connecting, subordinating, "content," or whatever in function. The fact that the comparison can be made over sequences of two or three words as well as over individual words renders the lists particularly useful and informative.

In respect to language functioning, we believe that this type of surface structure indexing also identifies the most common of those segments of utterance which children, from long practice, use in an automatic or semiautomatic way to link words which have a more specific reference to particular situational contexts. It seems evident that human utterance does *not* normally involve a conscious decision before each word is added to another in the stream of discourse. It seems more likely that the cognitive activity associated with connected utterance is normally concerned with processing larger units than a word, and operates perhaps by matching the meaning obtained from monitoring the utterance against the intended function of the utterance. The degree of automatism and the length of the segments of utterance being processed as single units will vary with language competence, as will the extent of cognitive activity

LANGUAGE ACTIVITIES LEAD TO READING

The language activities depicted in these photographs were used in preparation for the reader, "The Magician".

Talking about "magic" things.

Playing at being a magician.

"I'm going to make a . . . ."

Selecting sequences
to make some stories.

Making sentences
on a felt board.

Making imaginary magic
with a hat.
Guessing what has been
taken out from clues
given by the "magician".

involved in stringing together these segments; but it seems evident that ability to sequence words and sequences of words automatically is fundamental to human language activity at all stages of development.

If this is so, we cannot describe language or the development of language competence in terms which will reflect at all truly the way in which language is used until we have identified segments of utterance which are used in automatic or semiautomatic fashion and have examined the way in which these are manipulated within the stream of utterance. This is why we regard communication index lists as a key to an understanding of language and language functioning; but they are only a key. For example, arising from a surface structure count as they do, communication index lists are not sufficiently descriptive of a corpus to serve as the sole basis for a language or reading program. There remains too much ambiguity, and too little information is available from the lists alone to match the structure of larger segments of language with what the children have been found to process in their oral language.

To take an example, the sequence "I'm going" occurs frequently in the language of children from $3\frac{1}{2}$ to $6\frac{1}{2}$ years. It is a highly practiced and useful sequence and one which, in whatever situation and with whatever meaning intention it is used, is likely to be processed in an automatic fashion. One cannot tell from the lists, however, what the distribution of usage is across such possibilities as "I'm going to (a place)," "I'm going to (do something)," "I'm going (home)," or "I'm going (swimming)" at each stage of language development. Nor do the lists supply enough knowledge of the verbal or situational contexts which give rise to the use of the sequence or the ways in which it is combined with other sequences or "content" words within those contexts. In the Mount Gravatt project, however, the concordance produced for each language sample was such that all the occurrences for "I'm going" (and other sequences which were alike in surface structure) were brought together and the verbal context of each was shown. Each occurrence was tagged in such a way that there was easy access to it within the full corpus and to the notings of the situational context of the occurrence. The language/reading program was developed from this kind of knowledge of the language units around which it was written.

The use of the pragmatic approach in the language program ensured that the units of language on which each segment was based would have psychological reality for the children in the particular situation in which they were to be used—the situation around which the readers had been written. In this approach, the utterances had to arise naturally from the pragmatic situation and there was a very good chance that children would use the units in conjunction with content words without the intrusion of the teacher. If there was any doubt as to the meaning or range of meanings which children expressed by recourse to these units in their oral language, then this doubt could be, and in fact was, resolved by observation during trial of the program. The ways in which the units were incorporated into connected utterance were similarly tested in practice. Although the units come from an extensive survey and are used very frequently by all children of the various age groups, for psychological reality to occur, sentences must be originated by the children and must relate to the pragmatic situation.

There are at least two available methods, then, by which a communication index analysis of the surface structure of a language corpus can be extended through to the pragmatic and semantic dimensions. The first is to investigate the verbal and situational contexts in which the various language units have occurred. The second is to observe the use of particular language units by children of that stage of language development. One of the present objectives of the research is to develop these methods to further stages of sophistication.

An outcome of this kind of analysis is a means of comparing individual corpora. For the reasons outlined, language corpora which are found to differ widely on the communication index count are very likely to differ also on their semantic and pragmatic dimensions, provided that the sample is sufficiently large and the language sampled arises from or has reference to a sufficiently wide variety of situations and corresponding meaning intentions. After all, some 60% of an entire corpus of more than 80,000 morphemes of naturalistic utterance is accounted for by the 100 most frequently used words, and a considerably higher percentage is included when the most frequently occurring two-morpheme sequences are also taken into account. Thus it seems clear that if a communication index reveals a wide discrepancy in the "core" words and word sequences in two corpora, there are fundamental differences in the nature of the two corpora. It is interesting to note, however, that the reverse is not necessarily true. The language of $5\frac{1}{2}$ and $6\frac{1}{2}$ year old children was found to be closely matched in the core words and sequences identified. Further analysis associated with the writing of the language/reading materials for those ages revealed considerable differences on the semantic dimension. The sequences remain the same but semantic elaboration and consequent sentence lengthening is evident.

In summary, we believe that the analysis of language carried out in the developing of the language/reading program points to a very promising way of describing and comparing language corpora, and in particular, of detecting and describing growth in language competence. We consider that the corpora already available to us at Mount Gravatt, together with those to be collected in the next stage of the research, will be a sufficient data base for such a description of child language development. We hope to publish an attempt at this kind of description, together with the outcomes of analyses of language at higher age levels, when the research is completed.

CHAPTER FOUR

THE MOUNT GRAVATT DEVELOPMENTAL LANGUAGE READING PROGRAM

BASIC PRINCIPLES

The Mount Gravatt Developmental Language Reading Program was developed as an outcome of the Language Research Program. The basic principles behind the program are as follows.

1. In the program the *teacher* controls the "signalling units" which are to be used in a pragmatic language experience lesson. Examples of such units might be "I'm," "that's," "I'm going to." These are units used by most children in the English-speaking world.[1]

2. In the program the *children* control the oral words which they expect to follow these signalling units. The completion of sentences by the children, of course, arises out of their observations of events in a lesson, based upon, for example, the life cycle of the frog. Content units, such as "the tadpole," "a frog," would be expected to follow the signalling units "that's," "I'm," "it's," etc. Thus the oral sentences completed will be the children's, and these must therefore be meaningful to them, e.g. "I'm *a tadpole*," "It's *a tadpole*."

3. The teacher thus is "in control" of the sentences which whole groups of children will make naturally. The teacher extracts the particular signalling units that he or she wishes the children to practice, from their talk about the objects in the lesson, and can make this a remedial lesson for some children if need be. The remediation comes at the right time if children who have not experienced "normal" language sequences are taught these during their oral language lessons.

4. It is possible for children to combine and recombine signalling units with different content units. They might, for example, combine the signalling units "I'm," "that's," "it's," "I'm going to," "look at," "I've got," in a variety of ways with such content units as "the tadpole," "a frog," "the tadpoles," "a creek," "two legs," "a tail."

5. Once sufficient practice is attained in combining oral signalling units with oral content units it is time to present the equivalent written units on cards. These can be used in the same way but should always be related back to the well-rehearsed

---

1. This has been confirmed in England (Bristol) and in Canada (Toronto) and confirmation is now being sought in the U.S.A.

and meaningful oral language units and to the pragmatic language situation (in this case, a natural science lesson dealing with the life cycle of a frog).

6. The children need not know which of the various combinations of signalling units and content units will appear in their reader when it is presented. Indeed, there could be some quite novel combinations. If the previous stages have been well rehearsed, however, the children can be expected to have immediate success in reading the book.

7. Once the children have "caught on" to the decoding game, that is, extracting meaning from written sentences, activities aimed at analyzing and synthesizing the sound elements of words could begin.

FURTHER DETAILS OF THE PROGRAM

The reading books of the program were written around themes which employ central concepts which children normally develop during their early years. The children learn to use the language units in the language lessons within the scope of these themes. The language lessons and the experiences given to the children may occupy up to two weeks for each reader. Once a given child is readily decoding written material in the language lessons, he or she is presented with the relevant reader. In most cases the child will succeed in reading it on the first attempt.

The Mount Gravatt reading program does not differ greatly from other experiential programs. However, it is unique in that it provides teachers with the *core language* used by children to communicate. This, at last, enables the teacher to control the language lesson and yet maintain the child's natural language without the immense task of constructing a reader for each individual child.

These readers are designed to help teachers be more efficient in using whatever approach to reading they are convinced is the "right" approach. Increased efficiency results because the children's use of written language matches their phonological, morphological, syntactical, and semantic use of oral language much more closely than is possible with other contemporary readers.

For example, the teacher who thinks that phonic analysis and synthesis of language are the key to teaching reading can still insist that the children practice those skills to whatever level of efficiency is required. (Sound-blending techniques should, however, be postponed until the children have shown they understand how to decode written language.) In the Mount Gravatt program children apply their intuitive knowledge of the rules which govern their oral language to the matching written form *first*. Once they have succeeded in decoding the written form, they are strongly motivated to learn any extra skills which will help them attack new words.

Similarly, those who use the *"look-say"* approach will find useful material here. Not many of these teachers should object to changing the direction to that of a "say-look" approach. This means that when the children "say," the teacher makes sure that *what* they "say" is meaningful to them first in oral language and then in written language. Moreover, it ensures that the teacher still controls the language.

The Mount Gravatt system also simplifies the task of those teachers who favor an "experiential approach." Such teachers experience difficulty in progressing from the individual "story written down" stage to a more generalized class approach. The Mount Gravatt program, through "common core language," controls the experiential approach from the child's first introduction to reading.

These comments have by no means exhausted the numerous "methods" of teaching reading. It seems clear, however, that any current approach to reading, any special skills a teacher may have, or any particular method he or she may use can only be enhanced, if the children are first given a chance to maximize the transfer of their own knowledge of oral language to the written form.

One further point is that motivation is of paramount importance in reading. Success breeds success. By using the readers after children have experienced their language orally, the teacher can maximize the children's chance of success when *first* they approach each reader. This is particularly true because the readers, by their design, allow the teacher to make the language-reading lesson part of the total curriculum. Language development becomes an integral part of cognitive development. Children learn through experience that reading can be fun and that reading is part of learning, just as oral language has been in their past experience.

CONTROL OF LANGUAGE IN THE READERS

It will be evident to the teacher that the concept of language control in the Mount Gravatt reading books differs greatly from that employed in most traditional readers, because control is of the language "signalling units" only. Signalling units have a generality of use in child language: They are *core elements* of language that are used over and over in many different situations. The "content units" in the program are controlled by the pragmatic situation about which the book is written.

In the Mount Gravatt program repetition does not take the form of using the same words over and over in the reader. Orally, the children do practice repetition of the signalling units and their use in conjunction with content units in the experiential language-concept development lesson. Only then are they presented with the relevant reading book, and there, repetition of signalling units does not occur in an artificial way. Instead, repetition occurs in a natural way over a number of books and over a variety of language development lessons. This serves to demonstrate the generality of the use of the signalling units. The readers are looked upon as a reward, since they are presented only when success is assured. Thus "reading" becomes associated with success and is also a form of evaluation, for success usually is marked by proof of the accomplishment of a task—the task in this case being the mastery of the written form of language units in various combinations.

A. *Oral language work*

1. *Providing the pragmatic situation and encouraging discussion and interaction, using the children's own signalling units and content words*

The teacher, with the help of a "real-life" situation, draws from the children the language sequences they regard as appropriate to the situation. For example, in preparation for the reader about a frog, the teacher may

a) introduce such things as an aquarium, frogs, and tadpoles to the classroom,
b) encourage children to express their observation and ideas in their own words,
c) elicit the use of those language units which are being controlled for that reader,
d) provoke activities aimed at blending language activity and experience within this situation.

2. *Extracting or incorporating the desired controlled language units and accepting or suggesting content words and sequences*

This step will not prove difficult. The signalling units in the reading books are taken from the actual communication language of children. They are used frequently by a high proportion of children in their everyday experiencing of the world. The content units in the books relate directly to the pragmatic situations.

In such a language interaction situation the teacher will hear the language units being used over and over. The teacher should be able to capitalize on the children's use of both signalling and content units. When children are interacting the teacher should *not* discourage the children from using sequences other than the controlled sequences, but when the children do use the desired sequences the teacher should emphasize them in some way. Such emphasis can come from

a) reinforcing by repeating the phrase with affirmation (Yes, *it's* jumping"),
b) expanding the statement ("Yes, *that's* a frog and *that's* a tadpole and *that's* an egg"),
c) picking up and using the sequence again at every later opportunity.

The teacher can suggest signalling units and content units if necessary. However, they must be introduced in a natural way and be appropriate to the situation. They must also be units previously elicited from the children.

3. *Continued practice in oral language, where latent structure is encouraged by combining and recombining signalling units and content units*

In addition to endeavoring to elicit the required signalling units and content units over and over again, the teacher must actively demonstrate, in each pragmatic situation, the various combinations of sequences and content units that can be achieved. One way of doing this is to combine a sequence with whatever content words are available within the confines of the pragmatic situation.

For example, if a child says "That's a frog," the teacher can answer "Yes, that's a frog and that's a tadpole and that's an egg." He or she should encourage children to expand on their own statements in the same way. As the children move from one activity to another, this sort of substitution of language units will occur across situations, over a period of time. The teacher can also reverse the principle and illustrate the combination of a number of sequences with a particular content unit whenever an opportunity arises, for example, "That's a frog," "I'm a frog," "It's a frog." Note, however, that activities must be kept meaningful and appropriate to the ongoing situation. For example, as children are acting out being frogs it is appropriate to encourage them to refer back to the real frog—"That's a frog and I'm a frog." Again, a variety of such combinations will occur as activities progress over time.

At this stage the teacher should not move out of the realm of direct reference to a meaningful situation. For example, it would not be advisable to enlarge a statement of "That's a frog" by suggesting that the child could also say "I've got a frog," unless the child actually has a frog.

B. *Linking of oral units with their written form*

1. *Introduction to written forms*

When it is seen that the children are using the oral units freely, the teacher can then move to the introduction of the written form. This must be accomplished within the pragmatic situation—with the actual frogs and tadpoles, etc. The required unit is drawn from the children in the form of a sentence, for example, "That's a tadpole." The sentence is then made up for the children using a card containing the signalling unit "that's" and another containing the content unit "a tadpole":

$$\boxed{\text{that's}} \quad \boxed{\text{a tadpole}}$$

The children should then make up the sentence using their own unit cards.

2. *Practice in the use of written and oral forms (interchange) with reference to the pragmatic situation*

The children should be given practice, within the pragmatic situation, in using the written units to form sentences. The teacher should emphasize with the written form, as with the oral, that the same signalling units and content units can be combined in various ways to form new sentences. As sentences are drawn from children in the pragmatic situation the children can be given practice at recreating these using the language units.

Another way of achieving this might be to structure the pragmatic situation so that some form of open-ended sentence results. For example, during an observation lesson about a frog the teacher could get any of these sentences—

I've got / a head
/ green skin
/ legs
/ eyes

or

I'm / a tadpole
/ an egg

or

I'm going to be / a frog
/ a tadpole

Once children are able to make up sentences from the pragmatic situation the procedure should be reversed. Practice should then be given in reconstructing the pragmatic situation from sentences. For example, the children or teacher could make up sentences using unit cards. The children should then read each sentence and interpret it either by referring it directly to the situation it specifies or by acting it out.

C. *Word attack skills*

1. *Phonics*

The development of the ability to make use of cues as an aid to word recognition is an important aspect of learning to read. There need be no conflict between the need to introduce children to reading through their natural oral language and the need for phonic analysis and synthesis. That is, the Mount Gravatt program does not require the adoption of any particular method for the development of word attack skills. For convenience of teachers, however, the words used in level 1 and level 2 readers have been examined and a phonics program has been designed which will allow the teacher to anticipate children's difficulties in attacking new words. This phonics program is included in the Teachers' Edition.

2. *Reinforcement of language sequences*

One of the methods used in the program to make children very familiar with the integration of signalling units into sentences is through Musical Games (also found in the Teachers' Edition). A musical game has been written for each reader. The amount of repetition of words and word sequences which can be written into a reader without destroying the natural rhythm, juncture, and stress of language is limited. However, children can be given this practice, without monotony for them and without upsetting the natural language within the reader, simply by using these specially written musical games.

D. *Presentation of reading book*

When the children are manipulating signalling sequences and content units successfully with the pragmatic language situation (both oral and written), novel combinations of these sequences which form new sentences are presented to the children. Because of their previous experience they are assured of success. The actual reading lesson takes a relatively small amount of time—the time a child takes to read a short story. Thus reading of a book is always associated with success and novelty.

TABLE 12
FLOW DIAGRAM FOR PRODUCTION OF LANGUAGE PROGRAM LEADING TO READING (READERS) AND CREATIVE WRITING

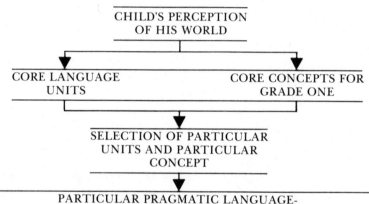

CHILD'S PERCEPTION OF HIS WORLD

CORE LANGUAGE UNITS

CORE CONCEPTS FOR GRADE ONE

SELECTION OF PARTICULAR UNITS AND PARTICULAR CONCEPT

PARTICULAR PRAGMATIC LANGUAGE-CONCEPT DEVELOPMENT LESSON

A. *Oral Language Work*
   1. Child's own sequences and content words (oral).
   2. Teacher extracts or includes desired controlled language units—accepts or suggests content words.
   3. Continued practice in oral language where *latent structure* is encouraged—ringing the changes on combinations of our units and content words.

B. *Linking of Oral Language Units with Their Written Form*
   1. Introduction to written forms.
   2. Practice of use of written and oral forms (interchange) with reference to pragmatic language situation.
   3. Practice at tracing language units.

READING BOOK (READING)

Presentation of reader away from pragmatic language situation.

Use of illustrations as a substitute.

Sentences contain new combinations of signalling units and content units.

CREATIVE WRITING

Sentences containing recombinations of signalling units and content units.

E. *Children's literature program*

Each reader and its associated language program is developed around a theme. Concepts are carefully selected from the curricula which suit children of this age level. In the Teachers' Edition a section called "Children's Literature" contains a bibliography, ordered in such a way that teachers may have readily available some supplementary material suited to whatever theme they are developing.

Table 12 is a flow chart illustrating the steps for teaching the pragmatic lesson *prior* to the presentation of the reader.

CHAPTER FIVE

ADDITIONAL APPLICATIONS FOR THE WORD AND WORD SEQUENCE LISTS

The unique characteristics of the word and word sequence lists have been described and illustrated in the preceding chapters. These characteristics, together with the theoretical viewpoint of the reader, will determine what applications are found for the lists in addition to those already described or implied. Here we merely indicate a possible range of likely applications.

A. Use of Language Units by Teachers

1. *Preschool—as norms of language development program*

The word sequences could be used systematically in relation to pragmatic situations. Because the sequences range over ages $2\frac{1}{2}$ to $6\frac{1}{2}$ years, there is sufficient material to plan for differential progress in language function.

Content words and sequences would normally be taken directly from the pragmatic situation which the child is experiencing. They can usually be obtained easily from the child because children learn to label very early in language development.

2. *Primary*

a) Again, these language units provide very useful information on language usage at the different age levels, suggesting the minimum oral proficiency which children should have attained before attempting to read.

b) The units provide a way of applying some scheme of grading to the language of the children in a given class. The use of the communication index, in conjunction with data on the proportion of the children who used that sequence in the population sampled, should be an aid in the grading of the sequences.

c) It is suggested, also, that once sequences are ordered according to frequency of usage, concepts which children in early grades could be expected to acquire in the various subject areas be used as topics for experiential lessons in which children practice their use of the particular language sequences selected for that stage. Content words should not be controlled as in the usual vocabulary-controlled language and reading programs. Nouns, adjectives, etc., used with the language units can easily be obtained from the children in the experiential situation. If these content words are not already known by children, the teaching of such "labelling" words is not difficult in such a situation.

Whatever sequences have been selected as core should be carefully introduced by the teacher so that children are led to use these in a normal language lesson around the selected topic. Children will use the sequences controlled by the teacher and those they suggest themselves, in combination with content words arising from the practical experience, to make their own oral sentences.

Once children are adept at relating oral language to the particular pragmatic situation (e.g., study of the life cycle of a frog), the teacher can relate the oral language directly to its written form. After this is done, a "reader" can be prepared which uses language sequences and content words that have been previously practiced, but now arranged in sentences which contain *different* combinations of these units. Suitable pictorial illustrations of the topic help.

B. Use by Authors of Books for Children

One reason that some authors of books for children are successful may be that they express themselves in words which the children are familiar with in their oral language. These lists should make it possible for authors of children's books to check their word usage against that of young children.

It was found at Mount Gravatt, for example, that Hungarian folk songs which had been used successfully with Hungarian children lost much, particularly in rhythm, intonation, stress, etc., when translated. When the most common English sequences were used in writing lyrics, a much more satisfactory situation was obtained. Use of these sequences ensures that signalling devices, which are so important to young children and which are integral to the rhythm of language, match those of the language which children know.

C. Use in the Education of Migrants

The learning of English as a second language by migrant adults need not follow the same pattern as the language learning of children. Nevertheless, these lists can provide information which is invaluable to the teachers of migrant parents who are attempting to communicate with their young children in English. By consulting the lists such teachers can order the introduction of English language units so that, for example, those units which apparently form core language for children are introduced early.

D. Use in Language Testing

From these units, it should be possible to develop normative tests. In the Van Leer and other projects, tests were used which were based on the ability of the child to repeat sentences successfully. Such tests were based on intuitive understanding of words children used or on words extracted from intelligence and other normative tests. The lists in this book could provide a more reliable basis for selection of items for tests of the oral language development of children.

E. Use for Communication with Children

Professionals who work with young children have an urgent need to communicate efficiently with them. Some experience great difficulty. There could be a number of reasons for this difficulty, but one important reason may be an insensitivity to the surface structure used by children. By examining these lists and noting sequences with high communication indices, this sensitivity may be increased. Our writers found that there is a definite carry-over when they turn to the writing of a children's story after working in other areas with these units: they find themselves using children's sequences in a natural fashion.

F. The Production of Additional Information from Single-Word Frequency Lists

Although we have pointed out reasons for using language sequences rather than words, teachers can obtain much background information about the develop-

TABLE 13
DEVELOPMENTAL
FREQUENCIES OF USE
OF PERSONAL
PRONOUNS
CLASSIFIED
ACCORDING TO TYPE

Pronoun type	Pronoun	Word usage indices				
		2½ years	3½ years	4½ years	5½ years	6½ years
Subject	I	290	450	445	499	523
	he	288	138	66	57	52
	she	4	2	14	48	35
	we	14	125	86	62	78
	they	36	32	33	52	63
	you*	172	257	291	293	344*
	it*	195	249	225	310	307*
Object	me	169	73	63	81	75
	him	97	31	6	15	11
	her	1	0.8	2	11	13*
	us	2	8	2	18	10
	them	8	17	25	32	43
Possessive (A)	mine	35	13	17	12	14
(mine)	his	—	0.8	—	—	8*
	hers	—	0.1	0.1	0.4	—
	ours	—	0.4	—	0.7	10*
	theirs	—	—	0.2	—	—
	yours	2	0.3	0.1	3	—
Possessive (B)	my	104	63	53	86	73
(my)	his	7	18	0.7	9	8*
	her	—	1	0.2	4	13*
	our	0.4	3	0.2	9	10*
	their	—	0.8	0.2	1	3
	your	4	30	4	26	48
	its	—	0.2	—	—	—
Reflexive	myself	—	—	—	—	0.7
	himself	—	—	—	—	—
	herself	—	—	—	—	—
	ourselves	—	—	—	—	—
	themselves	—	—	—	—	—
	yourself	—	—	—	—	0.4
	yourselves	—	—	—	—	—
	itself	—	—	—	—	—

* "You" and "it" belong to both the subject and the object groups.

ment of a child's communication competence by reference to the frequency listing of single words from the Mount Gravatt list. The stress here should be on the developmental aspect of function words and others as they are used in larger units within sentences. For example, comparison of the developmental frequencies of the different types of personal pronouns[1] can produce valuable information about their usage, as shown in Table 13. From this table it appears that some personal pronoun types are not well integrated into the child's oral language even at the age of 5½. Subject and object type pronouns do appear to be well integrated. But both types of possessive pronouns occur less frequently than subject and object type pronouns in children's speech. (Exceptions are "mine/my" and "yours/your," which have a high frequency.) And reflexive type pronouns occur very infrequently. These findings are summarized in Table 14.

Another aspect of the integration of personal pronouns into the language system of children is the substitution of object or possessive type pronouns into the positions usually reserved for nominal types. For example, 2½ year old children used "me" for "I" in about 30 percent of subject positions and "my" for "I" in about 3 percent of the subject positions. ("I" was never used incorrectly for "me," "my," or "mine" by any age group.) By contrast, 3½ year old children used "me" for "I" and "my" for "I" in only 3 percent of cases. All older children used the pronouns correctly with an insignificantly small number of exceptions. Thus, in the data for 2½ year olds, about 50 percent of the occurrences of "me" and 7 percent of the occurrences of "my" were for subject. Among 3½ year olds about 7 percent of the occurrences of "me" and 3 percent of the occurrences of "my" were used for subject. These figures are reflected in Table 13, where the index for "I" rises steeply between the 2½ year old level and the 3½ year old level, and where the index for "me" is reduced by half in the same period. Similarly, the index for the occurrence of "my" drops sharply between the 2½ and 3½ year old levels.

The age at which various prepositions are first introduced is set out in Table 15. The 3½, 4½, and 6½ year old levels see the introduction of few new prepositions in comparison with the 2½ and 5½ year old levels. Comparison of the frequencies of use over these five age levels gives part of the explanation for this. Such a

Pronoun type	Pronoun	Frequency
Subject	I	Most frequent
Object	me	↑
Possessive (A)	mine	↓
Possessive (B)	my	
Reflexive	myself	Least frequent

TABLE 14
ORDER OF FREQUENCY OF USAGE OF FIRST-PERSON PRONOUN TYPES

1. Dennis M. Muchisky (Teaching Assistant at University College, University of New Mexico, Albuquerque) has completed an in-depth study of frequencies of different types of personal pronouns in the Mount Gravatt sampling of the language of 2½ year old children.

	2½ years	3½ years	4½ years	5½ years	6½ years
TABLE 15 **PREPOSITIONS INTRODUCED INTO CHILD LANGUAGE AT DIFFERENT AGE LEVELS**	in	after	about	from	without
	on	into	by	away	until
	up	inside	through	around	till
	out			as	
	down			before	
	to			near	
	for			round	
	with			into	
	over			behind	
	at			along	
	like			across	
	off			underneath	
	under			except	

comparison is set out in Table 16. As this table shows, the use of most of the prepositions that are introduced at the 2½ year old level actually decreases as the child grows older, reaching a low point at the 4½ year old level. There seems to be a slight recovery at the 5½ year old level, and usage increases substantially at 6½ years.

At the 2½ year old level these prepositions are used in a restricted way. They are used always in close association with a verb, e.g., "Put it on," "Take it in there." The number of verbs these prepositions are used with is restricted also. "At" is used almost universally in the form "look at." However, the child gradually learns to use these with a greater variety of verbs, and by the 4½ year old level he or she has started to use prepositional phrases to qualify nouns, e.g., "Do you know the lady in the brown dress?" (although these are still infrequent at this age level). It appears that the child, during the 3½ and 4½ year old levels, is still resolving and generalizing the usage of those prepositions introduced at the 2½ year old level, and it is not until the 5½ year old level that they are integrated into the child's communication competence.

It is possible to extend this analysis widely to cover classifications of other parts of speech in child language. For example, the teacher could examine the use of conjunctions, and although it is helpful to be able to look up the computer listings for more information about their use, much information can be obtained merely by extracting the relevant conjunctions from the single-word frequency lists and comparing their usage at different age levels. Thus, from Table 17 it is possible to see that conjoined sentences do not appear with any great strength until the 3½ year old level. Also, the dominant function of "and" as a conjunction through all age levels is clearly shown. However, the table also shows the gradual introduction of other conjunctions, which express more than the "additive" functions of "and," for example, "because" (causal), "then" (temporal), "if" (conditional), "or" (disjunctive), "but" (adversative).

Age at which introduced	Preposition	Word usage indices				
		2½ years	3½ years	4½ years	5½ years	6½ years
2½ years	in	204	153	126	95	101
	on	138	142	92	101	120
	up	119	111	47	64	78
	out	67	34	20	46	53
	down	43	43	15	37	40
	at	44	33	15	32	30
	to	137	113	141	189	228
	of	22	24	44	39	61
	for	10	48	25	37	41
	with	3	15	38	33	28
	over	8	14	8	20	27
	like	3	14	6	16	37
	off	16	14	19	17	25
	under	5	7	—	4	3
	away	2	6	3	5	6
3½ years	after	—	1	7	2	3
	around	—	7	1	5	6
	into	—	3	1	3	8
	inside	—	2	0.7	2	0.8
4½ years	about	—	—	5	5	12
	by	—	—	2	3	1
	through	—	—	2	0.2	5
5½ years	from	—	—	—	5	11
	as	—	—	—	3	5
	before	—	—	—	2	1
	outside	—	—	—	1	1
	near	—	—	—	1	0.6
	round	—	—	—	0.9	2
	onto	—	—	—	0.8	0.2
	behind	—	—	—	0.4	0.4
	along	—	—	—	0.3	0.6
	across	—	—	—	0.2	0.4
	underneath	—	—	—	0.2	0.2
	except	—	—	—	0.2	0.2
6½ years	without	—	—	—	—	0.2
	until	—	—	—	—	0.5
	till	—	—	—	—	2

TABLE 16
FREQUENCIES OF OCCURRENCE OF PREPOSITIONS IN 2½, 3½, 4½, 5½, AND 6½ YEAR OLD CHILDREN'S LANGUAGE, GROUPED ACCORDING TO YEAR OF INTRODUCTION

Word	Word usage indices				
	2½ years	3½ years	4½ years	5½ years	6½ years
and	39	125	180	170	157
when	1	18	13	19	30
but	0.8	7	20	28	27
because	—	13	14	41	28
then	—	4	13	16	20
if	—	4	9	22	26
or	—	0.7	2	6	10
till	—	1	—	0.4	2
than	—	0.4	—	4	2
where*	30	20	21	33	56
why*	2	8	2	10	19

* "Where" and "why" appear only as question markers.

CHAPTER SIX

ALPHABETICAL LISTS

The alphabetical lists in this chapter make it possible to find quickly the communication index at each age level for those words and sequences most frequently used by children in the Mount Gravatt study.

For single words (pages 46–60), the indices at all five age levels are given together for ease of comparison. In some cases a word used by Australian children is not found in the language of other English-speaking children, or has a different meaning in Australia than elsewhere. In these cases a North American equivalent is supplied in parentheses beside the entry.

The lists for two-word and three-word sequences contain information about the frequency of use and number of speakers as well as the communication index. They are accordingly grouped separately by age level as follows.

SINGLE WORDS FREQUENTLY USED BY AUSTRALIAN CHILDREN, AGES 2½, 3½, 4½, 5½, AND 6½—ALPHABETICAL LISTING

Word	2½ Index	3½ Index	4½ Index	5½ Index	6½ Index	3½ & 4½ Mean Index	5½ & 6½ Mean Index
a	272	296	275	183.7	179.7	285.5	181.7
able					1		0.5
about			4.5	4.8	11.6	2.25	8.2
ache				0.1			0.05
across				0.3	0.4		0.35
aeroplane (s)					0.1		0.05
after		1.1	7	2.3	2.7	4.05	2.5
afternoon				0.4	2		1.2
again	6.1	9.4	2	7.9	7.5	5.7	7.7
ago				0.3			0.15
air					0.3		0.15
all	17	38	43	27.7	33.4	40.5	30.55
alligator		0.4				0.2	
allowed			0.7			0.35	
alone				5.3	5.8		5.55
along				0.6	0.6		0.6
already				0.3	0.6		0.45
alright	1.2			1.1	0.8		0.95
always				5.1	5.1		5.7
am ('m)	11	52	64	1.5	1.9	58	1.7
an	1.8			73.7	90.3		82
and	39	125	180	170.4	157	152.5	163.7
Andrew	9.2				1.8		0.9
another		9.5	2.5	6.4	7.5	6	6.95
answer (s)				0.6	0.3		0.45
any	4.1	4.1		6.3	7.2	2.05	6.75
anybody							0.4
anyone							0.35
anything						2.2	2.5
anyway				2.2	2.5	0.6	2.35
anywhere							0.15
apple (s)				0.2	0.2	0.1	0.2
are ('re)	67	107	58	82.9	90	82.5	86.45
area		6		0.1	0.1		0.1
aren't	6		2	2.1	3.8	4	2.95
arm (s)				0.1	0.1		0.1
around	7.6		1.1	5.1	6.4	4.35	5.75
as				3	4.7		3.85
ask	44	33	17	2.3	2.2	25	2.25
asleep				0.2			0.1
at	0.8			31.9	29.8		30.85
ate				0.3			0.15
awake					6.1		3.05
away	2.1	6	2.5	4.5	6.1	4.25	5.3
baby (s)	9.2	4.4		2.3	1.5	2.2	1.9
back	27	20	5	14.1	21.5	12.5	17.8
backwards				0.1	0.2		0.15
bad				0.8	0.4		0.6
badge				0.1			0.05
bag (s)	4.2			0.2	0.2		0.2
ball (s)	5			2.9	0.6		1.75
balloon	1.2						
band (s)				0.3			0.15
bang	1.4	2.5	0.6	1	0.7	1.55	0.85
bar				0.5			0.25
basket	0.8						
bat							
bath				0.4			0.2
battery (s)			0.5	0.5	0.6	0.25	0.55
be	19	13.3	15	24.1	35.5	14.15	29.8
beach				0.2	0.1		0.1
bead (s)			0.8			0.4	
beak (s)					0.1		0.05
bean (s)					0.1		0.05
bear (s)	2.8	1.6		0.3	0.1	0.8	0.2
beat		1.1		2.8	0.6	0.55	1.7
beaut							
(beautiful)				0.3			0.15
beautiful				0.5	0.4		0.45
because	10	13	14	40.5	27.7	13.5	34.1
bed (s)		4.2	0.7	0.5	5.5	2.45	3
bee (s)		0.4		0.1		0.2	0.05
been				3.8	4.2		4
beep					0.3		0.15
before		0.6	0.6	2.2	1.1	0.6	1.65
beg				0.2			0.1

SINGLE WORDS FREQUENTLY USED BY AUSTRALIAN CHILDREN, AGES 2½, 3½, 4½, 5½, AND 6½—ALPHABETICAL LISTING (cont.)

Word	2½ Index	3½ Index	4½ Index	5½ Index	6½ Index	3½ & 4½ Mean Index	5½ & 6½ Mean Index
behind				0.4	0.4		0.4
being					0.2		0.1
bell				0.3	0.4		0.35
best				0.5	1.3		0.9
bet				0.9	0.5		0.7
better	1.1	2.6	2.5	12	9.3	2.55	10.65
bickie (cookie)		0.2				0.1	
big	38	27.1	18	18	13.7	22.55	15.85
bigger				0.9	0.3		0.6
biggest				0.2	0.4		0.3
bike (s)		0.3		0.3	0.3	0.15	0.3
bin					0.6		0.3
bird (s)	22	1.5		0.9	0.3	0.75	0.6
biro (ball point pen)				0.1			0.05
birthday (s)	1.8	0.4	0.5	0.5	0.2	0.45	0.35
biscuit				0.5	0.2		0.35
bit (s)	2	6.9	2.4	6.2	5.6	4.65	5.9
bite (s)	10.6	4.4		0.3	0.5	2.2	0.4
black		1.3		5.8	2.8	0.65	4.3
blow (s)				0.6	1		0.8
blue (s) (blue crayon)				0.1			0.05
board (s)		1.3		0.2	0.2	0.65	0.2
boat (s)	11	4.2		0.4	0.6	2.1	0.5
body (s)					0.3		0.15
bomb (s)				0.2	0.2		0.2
bone (s)				0.2	0.2		0.2
boo (s)					0.7		0.35
book (s)	6	3.5		6.7	10.4	1.75	8.55
boom				0.4			0.2
boot					0.1		0.05
born					0.1		0.05
boss				0.2			0.1
both				0.6	1.1		0.85
bottle (s)				0.4	0.1		0.25
bottom				0.9	0.5		0.7
bought	1.4				0.1		0.05
bowling					0.1		0.05
bow wow		0.2				0.1	0.35
box	9.7		2.5	2	0.6	1.25	1.3
boy (s)	12.9	15.3	9.5	10	11.8	12.4	10.9
Brad					0.5		0.25
bread				0.1			0.05
break			1.5	1.2	1.1	0.75	1.15
Brett					0.2		0.1
brick (s)	7.1				0.4		0.2
bridge (s)	1.2	0.7			0.8	0.35	0.4
bring				2.8	2.7		2.75
broke				0.6	1.4		1
broken	9			0.6	0.3		0.45
brother (s)				3.8	0.4		2.1
brought	1.4				0.8		0.4
brown			0.4	0.8	1.9	0.2	1.35
brush (s)				0.2			0.1
bub (boy)				0.1			0.05
bubba (s) (baby)							
bubble gum							0.8
build	1.1			0.4			0.2
building	1.4		0.5	0.1		0.25	0.05
bump (s)							0.05
bunny		0.4		0.1		0.2	0.05
burn		0.7	0.8			0.75	
burning	0.4				0.1		0.05
burnt				0.2			0.1
bus (s)				0.3	2.3		1.3
but	0.8	7.1	20	28.4	26.7	13.55	27.55
butter					0.2		0.1
button (s)		0.4		0.4	0.6	0.2	0.5
buy		1		0.8	1	0.5	0.9
by	0.8		1.6	2.8	1.4	0.8	2.1
bye				0.7	0.3		0.5
cakes	3.5			1	0.5		0.75
call		1.6	1.8	1	1.5	1.7	1.25

SINGLE WORDS FREQUENTLY USED BY AUSTRALIAN CHILDREN, AGES 2½, 3½, 4½, 5½, AND 6½ — ALPHABETICAL LISTING (cont.)

Word	2½ Index	3½ Index	4½ Index	5½ Index	6½ Index	3½ & 4½ Mean Index	5½ & 6½ Mean Index
called				1.6	0.1		0.85
came				2.6	5.5		4.05
camera		0.2				0.1	
can	46	95	85	60.3	79.8	90	70.05
can't	20	20	16	30	24	18	27
captain					0.3		0.15
car (s)	24	15	5	5.7	7.7	10	6.7
card (s)					1		0.5
care				0.4	0.3		0.35
careful					0.2		0.1
carrot (s)					0.2		0.1
carry				0.1	0.5		0.3
case					0.2		0.1
cat	7.5	13.7		1.7	1.3	6.85	1.5
catch		0.6		3.9	1.4	0.3	2.65
caught				1.3	0.7		1
cement					0.2		0.1
cent (s)				0.8	1.5		1.15
chair (s)				1.3	1.3		1.3
chalk				0.2			0.1
chance					0.3		0.15
change				0.1	0.5		0.3
chase	0.8						
channel					0.4		0.2
check					0.1		0.05
chicken	0.4				0.3		0.15
children					0.1		0.05
chimney (s)				0.1			0.05
chip					0.1		0.05
chocolate (s)				0.8	0.2		0.5
Christmas				0.1	0.2		0.15
chuck					0.2		0.1
circle				0.7	0.2		0.45
class (es)				2	0.4		1.2
classroom				0.3			0.15
clean	0.8			0.9	0.3		0.6
climb		0.7				0.35	
climbing		3.9			0.1	1.95	0.05
clock					0.3		0.15
close (adv)				1	0.2		0.6
close (verb)	0.9			0.2	0.2		0.2
clothes				0.3	0.3		0.3
coat (s)					0.3		0.15
coffee	3.8			0.1			0.05
cold				1.3	0.8		1.05
colour (s)	0.8	1		1.3	1.3	0.5	1.3
(color)							
coloured				0.1			0.05
(colored)							
colouring				0.2			0.1
(coloring)							
come	74	78	31	47.1	48.2	54.5	47.65
comes				4.6	4.3		4.45
coming				3.6	7		5.3
copy				0.4			0.2
cord					0.1		0.05
cordial			0.3			0.15	
corner			1.6			0.8	
could		0.7	13.6	10.9	8.9	7.15	9.9
couldn't				2.7	2.2		2.45
count				0.3	0.7		0.5
couple					0.1		0.05
course					0.3		0.15
cow (s)	1.4	2.8	1.6			2.2	
crash					0.1		0.05
crazy				0.1	0.1		0.05
cream				0.3	0.2		0.25
cross (s)				0.2	0.2		0.2
cry							
crying					0.1		0.05
cubby (tree-house)	2.1						
cup (s)	3.1	2.8		0.6	1.7	1.4	1.15
cupboard				0.1	0.1		0.1
cut		1.2	0.6	1.2	3.3	0.9	2.25
Dad				5.8	3.2		4.5

SINGLE WORDS FREQUENTLY USED BY AUSTRALIAN CHILDREN, AGES 2½, 3½, 4½, 5½, AND 6½ —ALPHABETICAL LISTING (cont.)

Word	2½ Index	3½ Index	4½ Index	5½ Index	6½ Index	3½ & 4½ Mean Index	5½ & 6½ Mean Index
Daddy	19	4	1.8	5.6	10.2	2.9	7.9
dare					0.1		0.05
dark				0.3	0.7		0.5
darling					0.8		0.4
Darrea					0.1		0.05
David					2.8		1.4
day (s)		2.8	2.5	7.6	6.4	2.65	7
dead				0.3	0.2		0.25
dear					0.3		0.15
deep					0.1		0.05
desk				0.4	0.7		0.55
Diane					1.3		0.65
did	9	4.7	11	35.6	32.3	7.85	33.95
didn't	1.4	2.8		25	14.5	1.4	19.75
die					0.1		0.05
different			0.6	1.8	0.5	0.3	1.15
dig					0.2		0.1
dinner		1.7			0.3	0.85	0.15
dip					0.1		0.05
dirt	1.2	1.2			0.5	0.6	0.25
dirty			2	0.9	0.7	1	0.8
do	23	190	73	76.5	82.6	131.5	79.55
does			1.1	2.5	6.6	0.55	4.55
doesn't	1.1	2.7	0.6	6.6	6.9	1.65	6.75
dog (s)	29.6	4.2		1.5	1.7	2.1	1.6
doing	6			8.1	7.8		7.95
doll (s)				0.5	0.1		0.3
dollar (s)			0.7	0.2	0.3	0.35	0.25
dolly	1.6	1.8				0.9	
done				4.4	5.2		4.8
don't	56	69	43	77.9	72.7	56	75.3
door (s)	6.5	0.2		3	3.6	0.1	3.3
dot (s)				0.2			0.1
double					0.2		0.1
down	43	43	15	40.3	36.8	29	38.55
downstairs			1.4	0.1	1	0.7	0.55
draw				1.8	1.6		1.7
drawed (n)				0.2			0.1
drawing (s)				0.5	0.2		0.35
dress		0.5	0.5	0.2	0.1	0.5	0.15
dressed					0.3		0.15
drink (s)	3.8	0.7		4.8	1.1	0.35	2.95
drive		1		0.6	0.8	0.5	0.7
driving					0.2		0.1
drop				0.2	0.5		0.35
dropped				0.1	0.1		0.1
dry				0.2	0.1		0.15
duck (s)	1.1			0.9	0.6		0.75
dug					0.2		0.1
dumb				0.2			0.1
each				0.4	0.5		0.45
ear (s)				0.4	1		0.7
early				0.3	0.3		0.3
easy			0.2	0.6	1.2	0.1	0.9
eat	5.4	4		5.4	2	2	3.7
eating				0.5	0.1		0.3
egg (s)				1.2	0.8		1
eh					0.3		0.15
eight				3.1	4		3.55
either				0.6	0.4		0.5
elephant	2.1				0.2		0.1
eleven				0.2	0.6		0.4
else			0.6	4	2.3	0.3	3.15
end				0.9	1.2		1.05
engine		0.8			0.1	0.4	0.05
enough			0.7	0.4	0.6	0.35	0.5
equals					2.2		1.1
erk (awk)					0.1		0.05
even		0.3	1.4	3.2	5.1	0.85	4.15
ever			1.1	0.3	0.1	0.55	0.2
every		1.9		0.3	3	0.95	1.65
everybody				0.9			0.45
everyone				0.2	0.3		0.25
everything			1.5	0.2	0.8	0.75	0.5
except				0.2	0.2		0.2
excuse					0.9		0.45

SINGLE WORDS FREQUENTLY USED BY AUSTRALIAN CHILDREN, AGES 2½, 3½, 4½, 5½, AND 6½—ALPHABETICAL LISTING (cont.)

Word	2½ Index	3½ Index	4½ Index	5½ Index	6½ Index	3½ & 4½ Mean Index	5½ & 6½ Mean Index
eye (s)	1.6			2.6	1.3		1.95
face				1.6	0.8		1.2
fall	4	1.3		0.8	0.9	0.65	0.85
falling					0.1		0.05
falls					0.1		0.05
far				0.7			0.35
fast				0.3	1.9		1.1
faster				0.2			0.1
fat				1.3	0.6		0.95
father (s)				1.1	2.1		1.6
favourite (favorite)					0.1		0.05
feel			0.7	0.9	1	0.35	0.95
feet				1.2	0.3		0.75
fell		1.5		1.3	0.5	0.75	0.9
fellow	0.4						
felt (s) (felt pens)							0.1
fence					0.1		0.05
fifteen					0.3		0.15
fifty					0.5		0.25
fight					0.2		0.1
fill					0.1		0.05
find			2.4	2.8	4.5	1.2	3.65
finger(s)		0.55	1.6	1	1.6	1.07	1.3
finish	2.1	0.24	2.2	0.6	0.3	1.22	0.45
finished				1.8	3.8		2.8
fine			1.1	0.4		0.55	0.55
fire (s)	2.0	1.1	·	0.4	0.7	0.55	0.55
first			0.7	3.9	6.1	0.35	5
fish (s)	2.7	1.8		1	0.2	0.9	0.6
fishing				0.1			0.05
fit				0.2	0.4		0.3
five (s)		0.6	1.1	8.8	14.7	0.85	11.75
fix				0.9	0.6		0.75
fixed				0.3	0.1		0.2
flat					0.2		0.1
floor		0.7		0.4	0.2	0.35	0.3

Word	2½ Index	3½ Index	4½ Index	5½ Index	6½ Index	3½ & 4½ Mean Index	5½ & 6½ Mean Index
flower (s)		0.8	1.8	1.1	0.7	1.3	0.9
flying		0.4			0.2	0.2	0.1
follow					0.5		0.25
foot				0.4	1.4		0.9
football				0.8	0.2		0.5
for	10	48	25	36.6	40.6	36.5	38.6
forget				0.5	0.5		0.5
forgot				1.6	2.6		2.1
forgotten					0.2		0.1
fork (s)				0.2	0.3		0.25
forty				0.1	0.1		0.1
found			3.8	2.6	2.1	1.9	2.35
four (s)		0.8	1.3	12.3	17.6	1.05	14.95
fourteen					0.3		0.15
fourth					0.1		0.05
fox					0.3		0.15
free					0.1		0.05
friend (s)			1.6	4.3	1.4	0.8	2.85
frog (s)	10						
from				4.6	11.3		7.95
front				0.7	1		0.85
full				0.3	1.1		0.7
fun				0.2	0.5		0.35
funny	0.9	2.5	0.9	1	2	1.7	1.5
game (s)			0.5	0.5	3.3	0.25	1.9
garden (s)					0.2		0.1
gate (s)	1.4			0.2	0.5		0.35
gave				4.3	1.3		2.8
gee				0.6			0.3
get	70	58	36	62.7	78.7	47	70.7
gets				0.8	1.8		1.3
getting				3	6.3		4.65
giant					0.1		0.05
girl (s)	3.7	0.4	3.5	12.6	8.6	1.95	10.6
give				12.9	10.5		11.7
giving				0.2			0.1
glass				0.3			0.15
glue					0.1		0.05

SINGLE WORDS FREQUENTLY USED BY AUSTRALIAN CHILDREN, AGES 2½, 3½, 4½, 5½, AND 6½—ALPHABETICAL LISTING (cont.)

Word	2½ Index	3½ Index	4½ Index	5½ Index	6½ Index	3½ & 4½ Mean Index	5½ & 6½ Mean Index
go (s)	121	82	67	59.3	75.2	74.5	67.25
goal				0.2			0.1
God	1.1	12	6	1.4	0.3	9	0.85
goes				4.6	6.5		5.55
going	60	71	61	69	64.5	66	66.75
gold					0.1		0.05
gone	14.8			1.3	1.6		1.45
good	8.1	6.7		18.1	20.8	3.35	19.45
goody				0.2	0.8		0.5
got	161	144	96	93.3	96	120	94.65
grade (s)				3.3	1.3		2.3
Graham					0.2		0.1
Grandma				0.4			0.2
grass		3.9		0.2		1.95	0.1
great				0.3	0.4		0.35
green (s)				3.8	2.2		3
Greg					0.7		0.35
grey (gray)		1		0.2		0.5	0.1
ground				0.7	0.4		0.55
grow		1.3		3	1.6	0.65	2.3
guess				0.3			0.15
gum					0.3		0.15
gun (s)	1.1	0.8	0.5		0.7	0.65	0.35
ha	1.1						
had ('d)		2.7	10	22.5	19.1	6.35	20.8
hair		0.7		4	1.1	0.35	2.55
half (s)			0.6	1.8	1.8	0.3	1.8
hand (s)	2.7	1	1.3	5.7	4.9	1.15	5.3
handle				0.1	0.1		0.05
hang				0.5	0.2		0.3
hanging					0.2		0.1
hanky				0.3	0.1		0.25
happen					0.1		0.05
happened				0.6	0.9		0.75
happens					0.1		0.05
hard			1.8	4.8	3.4	0.9	4.1
has	34	8.3	16	19.7	21.9	12.15	20.8
hasn't				1	0.7		0.85

Word	2½ Index	3½ Index	4½ Index	5½ Index	6½ Index	3½ & 4½ Mean Index	5½ & 6½ Mean Index
hat (s)	0.8	1.6	1.4	0.2	0.5	1.5	0.35
hate				0.4	0.3		0.35
have ('ve)	95	66	104	94.2	113.5	85	103.85
haven't		8.3	2.5	6	10.8	5.4	8.4
having	1.1		0.7	3.4	2	0.35	2.7
he	288	138	66	57.3	51.8	102	54.55
head (s)	1.1	9.3	0.8	3.2	4.2	5.05	3.7
hear			3.2	6.7	12.9	1.6	9.8
heard				0.6	1.6		1.1
heavy				1.4	1		1.2
hello	16	3.3	6	6.4	6.2	4.65	6.3
help	1.2		1.4	3.6	3.1	0.7	3.35
her	2.1	3.7	4.4	19.9	13.3	4.05	16.6
here	245	117	50	60.1	63.4	83.5	61.75
herself					0.1		0.05
hey		17	34	32.7	54.3	25.5	43.5
hi				0.3	1.8		1.05
high				1.7	0.7		1.2
hill				0.4	0.2		0.3
him	97	31	6	15.4	10.8	18.5	13.1
his	6.5	21	0.7	8.9	7.6	10.85	8.25
hit	0.8			2.7	1.7		2.2
hm					0.7		0.35
hold		2.7	0.9	8.5	2	1.8	5.25
Holden (make of car)							
hole (s)			0.2	2.1	0.8	0.1	1.45
holiday		1.1		0.1		0.55	0.05
home	2.7	8.8	2.5	8.9	9.3	5.65	9.1
homework					0.1		0.05
hooray							0.05
hop				0.1	0.1		0.1
hope				0.2			0.1
horse (s)	9.2	1.3	0.4	0.5	0.7	0.85	0.6
hot				2.9	1.1		2
hour (s)					0.3		0.15
house (s)	24	3.7	7	9.4	5.6	5.35	7.5
how	1.6	3.7	7	20.4	27.2	5.35	23.8

SINGLE WORDS FREQUENTLY USED BY AUSTRALIAN CHILDREN, AGES 2½, 3½, 4½, 5½, AND 6½—ALPHABETICAL LISTING (cont.)

Word	2½ Index	3½ Index	4½ Index	5½ Index	6½ Index	3½ & 4½ Mean Index	5½ & 6½ Mean Index
huh					2.2		1.1
hundred (s)				1	1.6		1.3
hurry		1.5		0.8	0.7	0.75	0.75
hurt	0.6	0.8		3.2	0.8	0.4	2
hurts					0.4		0.2
I	290	450	445	499.2	523	447.5	511.1
ice					0.4		0.2
iceblock (s) (ices)						0.15	
icecream				0.2	0.3		0.25
idea					0.2		0.1
if		3.7	9	22	26.4	6.35	24.2
in	204	153	126	94.5	100.8	139.5	97.65
ink				0.2			0.1
inside		1.5	0.7	1.8	0.8	1.1	1.3
instead				0.2	0.1		0.15
into		2.7	1.1	3	8.1	1.9	5.55
is ('s)	357	319	247	243	283.5	283	263.25
isn't	2.3	4.4	3.8	4.6	8	4.1	6.3
it	195	252	225	310.1	306.8	238.5	308.45
jacket				0.5	0.1		0.3
James					0.4		0.2
Jan					0.7		0.35
Jeffrey					0.6		0.3
John					0.2		0.1
joke (s)					0.2		0.1
Julie					0.7		0.35
jump (s)		3.7		0.6	1.7	1.85	1.15
jumped				0.6			0.3
jumper (s)				0.3	0.5		0.4
just		7	14	29.4	39.1	10.5	34.25
kangaroo		0.7				0.35	
Karen	1.1				0.2		0.1
keep			1.6	2.8	5.8	0.8	4.3
keeps				0.2	0.3		0.25
key (s)			0.3		0.3	0.15	0.15
kick (s)				1.7	0.3		1
kicked				0.2			0.1
kid (s)			1.6	0.4	1.7	0.8	1.05
kill			3.1	0.3	0.3	1.55	0.3
killed				0.1	0.2		0.15
kind			0.4	0.3	0.2	0.2	0.25
kindy (kindergarten)		3.7	2.5			3.1	
king					0.2		0.1
kitchen					0.1		0.05
knew				0.2	0.4		0.3
knife					0.2		0.1
knock (s)				0.3			0.15
knot (s)					0.1		0.05
know	6	27	65	64.5	63	46	63.75
knows				0.2	0.4		0.3
lady (s)	54		1.5	8.8	4.6	0.75	6.7
last				2.7	4.6		3.65
late				0.2	0.4		0.3
lead					0.1		0.05
leader				0.3	0.3		0.3
leave	2.2	1.3	8	10.2	5.2	4.65	7.7
leaves					0.1		0.05
left				1	2.8		1.9
leg (s)	1.8	2		1	1.5	1	1.25
lend					0.2		0.1
let (s)	7.5	16	2.7	14.4	14.1	9.35	14.25
letter (s)		1		0.2	0.1	0.5	0.15
library					0.3		0.15
lift					0.2		0.1
light (s)	0.8			1.5	1.2		1.35
like	22	37	26	28.6	37	31.5	32.8
likes					0.1	0.05	0.05
line (s)				2	1.1		1.55
lion (s)	1.9	2.2			0.7	1.1	0.35
listen				0.5	1.2		0.85
listening					0.1		0.05
little	19	31	22	17.8	16.8	26.5	17.3
live			1.2		0.8	0.6	0.4
lives				0.2	0.3		0.15

SINGLE WORDS FREQUENTLY USED BY AUSTRALIAN CHILDREN, AGES 2½, 3½, 4½, 5½, AND 6½—ALPHABETICAL LISTING (cont.)

Word	2½ Index	3½ Index	4½ Index	5½ Index	6½ Index	3½ & 4½ Mean Index	5½ & 6½ Mean Index
lock					0.2		0.1
locked				0.2			0.1
lolly (s) (candy)	0.9			0.7	0.7		0.7
long	0.5	2.5	2	3.5	4.2	2.25	3.85
look	363	125	97	50.8	47.5	111	49.15
looked					0.3		0.15
looking				0.4	0.6		0.5
looks				1.4	3.2		2.3
loose				0.2			0.1
lose				0.2	0.3		0.25
lost			1	2.4	0.4	0.5	1.4
lot (s)				1	2.2		1.6
loud				0.2	0.2		0.2
love				2.5	0.4		1.45
lovely				0.3	0.2		0.25
loves				0.2			0.1
lucky				0.3	0.7		0.5
lunch	1.1	0.9		1.9	1	0.45	1.45
mad				0.5	0.6		0.55
made		1.1	3.8	2.9	2.5	2.45	2.7
magic					0.1		0.05
make	35	14	26	14.5	11.6	20	13.05
makes				1.6	0.4		1
making				2.3	0.6		1.45
man (s)	17	2.5	10	2.8	3.6	6.25	3.2
many		0.9		3.2	4.8	0.45	4
marble					0.5		0.25
Marie					0.2		0.1
mark (s)					1.6		0.8
match (s)					0.1		0.05
Mathew					0.1		0.05
matter				1	2.5		1.75
may				0.5	1.6		1.05
me	169	73	63	81.2	74.8	68	78
mean		4.4		2.2	5.2	2.2	3.7
means				0.3	0.4		0.35
meant					0.1		0.05
meat				0.2			0.1
men				0.1	0.2		0.15
mermaid		0.9				0.45	
mess (s)				0.2			0.1
Michael					2.1		1.05
Michelle					0.2		0.1
microphone				2	8.1		5.05
middle				0.4	0.5		0.45
might	1.5	10	15	10.3	7.1	12.5	8.7
mike					1.7		0.85
milk	1.2	1.3		1.9	0.4	0.65	1.15
mind				0.4	0.7		0.55
mine	34.6	13	17	11.8	13.6	15	12.7
minus					0.5		0.25
minute (s)		0.9		3.2	5	0.45	4.1
miss		1.7	7	0.3		4.35	0.15
missed				0.9	0.7		0.8
missing					0.1		0.05
Miss				5.5	10.1		7.8
mm (before morning)					2.7		1.35
Monday				0.6			0.3
money			0.2	1.7	0.5	0.1	1.1
monkey (s)		1.7		0.1	0.2	0.85	0.15
moon		2.2				1.1	
more	11	8.8	2	8.8	10.5	5.4	9.65
morning	1.5		0.4	2.5	2.2	0.2	2.35
most				0.2	0.2		0.2
Mother (s)		1.7		4	3.8	0.85	3.9
motor		0.3		0.1		0.15	0.05
motorbike (s)					0.1		0.05
mouse				0.4			0.2
mouth	3			1.2	0.3		0.75
move (s)	2.1			1.9	0.9		1.4
moved					0.1		0.05
Mr.		0.7		2.2	2.1	0.35	2.15
Mrs.		0.9	2.7	5.3	7.8	1.8	6.55
much		0.9		2.2	4	0.45	3.1

SINGLE WORDS FREQUENTLY USED BY AUSTRALIAN CHILDREN, AGES 2½, 3½, 4½, 5½, AND 6½ — ALPHABETICAL LISTING (cont.)

Word	2½ Index	3½ Index	4½ Index	5½ Index	6½ Index	3½ & 4½ Mean Index	5½ & 6½ Mean Index
mud				0.2	0.2		0.2
Mum (Mom)	143			14.8	11.9		13.35
Mummy		1.3	6	11	20	3.65	15.5
must		1.6	0.9	1.9	2.8	1.25	2.35
my	104	63	53	86.1	73.2	58	79.65
myself				0.9	0.7		0.8
nail (s)			0.3			0.15	
name (person)				203.7			101.85
name (s)		2.8		9.6	4.1	1.4	6.85
Nanna					0.2		0.1
naughty	3			1.5	1.3		1.4
near	0.4			0.9	0.6		0.75
nearly				2.3	1		1.65
neck					0.5		0.25
need		0.9	3.4	4.9	4.5	2.15	4.7
needs				0.2			0.1
neo (s) (felt pens)							
never			0.6	0.4		0.3	0.2
new		1		2.5	1.9	0.5	2.2
next		0.8	2.2	3.1	2.8	1.5	2.95
nice	9.7	1.1	0.6	1.8	0.6	0.85	1.2
night				1	1.6		1.3
nine				2.1	3.3		2.7
nineteen					0.7		0.35
no	232	125	84	122.9	122.9	104.5	122.9
nobody				0.5	0.5		0.25
noise (s)	1.4			0.4	1.2	0.65	0.8
none				0.7	0.5		0.25
nope					0.5		0.35
nose				1			0.75
not	30	64	35	57.8	56.7	49.5	57.25
nothing			1.5	2.1	3.4	0.75	2.75
now	33	34.4	36	39.9	44.1	35.2	42
nuh (no)				0.4	0.4		0.2
number (s)				2.1	3		2.55
nut (s)				0.2	0.4		0.3

Word	2½ Index	3½ Index	4½ Index	5½ Index	6½ Index	3½ & 4½ Mean Index	5½ & 6½ Mean Index
o'clock				0.7	1.2		0.95
of	22	24	44	39.1	61	34	50.05
off	16	14	19	16.8	24.6	16.5	20.7
oh	43	31	34	96.4	85.7	32.5	91.05
ok, okay		2.7		6.5	17.6	1.85	12.05
old			0.8	2.8	1.7	0.4	2.25
on	138	142	92	101.4	119.8	117	110.6
once (s)				1.4	1.3		1.35
one (s)	138	116	132	110.2	132	124	121.1
only	2.1	11	3.5	18.4	20.1	7.25	19.25
onto				0.8	0.2		0.5
open	3.5	2	0.4	3	1.4	1.2	2.2
or		0.7	2.2	6.4	10.1	1.45	8.25
orange (s)				2.4	1.3		1.85
order (s)					0.1		0.05
other (s)	5.7	2.7	6	6.9	11.4	4.35	9.15
ouch				0.4	1.1		0.75
our (s)		3.6	2.5	7	9.7	3.05	8.35
out	67	34	20	46.3	52.6	27	49.45
outside				1.4	1.3		1.35
over	7.5	14	8	20.4	26.5	11	23.45
own				1.3	1.5		1.4
pack					0.1		0.05
packet					0.2		0.1
page (s)				1.5	0.5		1
paint (s)				1	0.6		0.8
painting		10	2.7		0.2	6.35	0.1
pants	1.4			0.7	0.6		0.65
paper (s)				2.9	0.6		1.75
pardon			0.2			0.1	0.25
park		3.5	0.2	1.3	0.5	1.85	0.75
part (s)			0.6	0.9	0.2	0.3	0.55
party				0.2	0.1		0.15
pass				0.3			0.15
past				1.4	1.2		0.8
pattern				0.1			0.5
Paul					2.1		1.05
pay				0.2	0.3		0.15

SINGLE WORDS FREQUENTLY USED BY AUSTRALIAN CHILDREN, AGES 2½, 3½, 4½, 5½, AND 6½—ALPHABETICAL LISTING (cont.)

Word	2½ Index	3½ Index	4½ Index	5½ Index	6½ Index	3½ & 4½ Mean Index	5½ & 6½ Mean Index
pea (s)				0.1			0.05
peanut (s)					0.1		0.05
pen (s)				0.2	0.7		0.45
pencil (s)	0.8	1.3	2.7	1.7	2.8	2	2.25
people (s)	0.8			1.8	3.2	2	2.5
person (s)				0.1			0.05
Peter					2.7		1.35
phone (s)					0.4		0.2
photo		0.3				0.15	
pick		1.3		1	2.1	0.65	1.55
picked			0.6		0.1	0.3	0.05
picnic				0.3			0.15
picture (s)				1.3	2.1		1.7
pie (s)			0.4	0.4		0.2	0.2
piece (s)	1.1	1.7		2.1	1	0.85	1.55
pig (s)	1.1			0.5			0.25
pin (s)				0.5	0.2		0.35
pink				2.8	1		1.9
place (s)			1.2	1.9	4.1	0.6	3
plastic				0.1	0.2		0.15
plate (s)					0.6		0.3
play	4.2	6.2	7	14.7	16.1	6.6	15.4
played				0.2	0.2		0.2
playing				1	3.5		2.25
please	1.1			7.8	5.3		6.55
plus	1.1			1.3	1.9		1.6
pocket (s)	4.6				1.2		0.6
point (s)	4.5	1.1		0.2		0.55	0.1
poke					0.4		0.2
police	2.8				0.1		0.05
policeman					0.1		0.05
poor		2.7		0.2		1.35	0.1
port (s) (school bag)				4.6	0.8		2.7
pour				0.1			0.05
press				0.2			0.1
pretend				0.1	0.2		0.15
pretty				0.2	1.4		0.8

Word	2½ Index	3½ Index	4½ Index	5½ Index	6½ Index	3½ & 4½ Mean Index	5½ & 6½ Mean Index
probably					1.1		0.55
properly					0.1		0.05
pull	1.6			2.3	1		1.65
pulled				0.3	0.1		0.2
pulling				0.3	0.2		0.25
puppy	5.8	1.5		2.3	0.2	0.75	1.25
purple			0.8	0.5	0.9	0.4	0.7
push					0.1		0.05
pushed							
pushing				0.2			0.1
pussy	5.4	2.5	1			1.75	
put	77	55	30	43.6	43.6	42.5	43.6
putting				1.2	0.5		0.85
quick			0.2	2	1	0.1	1.5
quickly				0.4	0.2		0.3
quiet			0.2	0.2	1.4	0.1	0.8
rabbit (s)	2.3	0.6		0.2		0.3	0.1
race (s)				0.3	0.3		0.3
radio (s)				0.3	0.1		0.2
rain		0.6			0.2	0.3	0.1
ran				0.2			0.1
rather	5.4			2.4	2.4		2.4
read				0.2	0.4		0.3
reading			0.4	0.5	2.3	0.2	1.4
ready				2.6	2.8		2.7
real		1	2	1.5	2.7	1.5	2.1
really		0.8	0.4	0.2		0.6	0.1
reckon				0.2			0.1
record				0.5	1.2		0.85
recorder				3.7	2.6		3.15
red (s)	2.8	0.3	0.8	0.4	1.3	0.55	0.85
remember				0.4	0.1		0.25
rest				0.2			0.1
ride				4.6	0.8		2.7
right	8	3.3	10	22.4	17.8	6.65	20.1
righto					0.1		0.05
ring		0.6			0.5	0.3	0.25
river (s)					0.1		0.05

SINGLE WORDS FREQUENTLY USED BY AUSTRALIAN CHILDREN, AGES 2½, 3½, 4½, 5½, AND 6½—ALPHABETICAL LISTING (cont.)

Word	2½ Index	3½ Index	4½ Index	5½ Index	6½ Index	3½ & 4½ Mean Index	5½ & 6½ Mean Index
road	2.8		0.7	0.6	0.9	0.35	0.75
robot			0.6			0.3	
rock (s)				0.3	0.4		0.35
rod (s)		0.8		0.4	0.8	0.4	0.6
roll				0.3			0.15
roof				1.1			0.55
room			0.5	2.3	0.7	0.25	1.5
Ross					0.2		0.1
round		3.9		0.9	1.9	1.95	1.4
row (s)					0.1		0.05
rub				0.1	0.6		0.35
rubber				0.6	0.9		0.75
rubbish					0.6		0.3
rug					0.1		0.05
ruler (s)	2.5				0.1		0.05
run		4.4	2.6	4.1	2.1	3.5	3.1
running		0.9		0.7	0.5		0.6
said		0.9	2	19.8	14.9	1.45	17.35
sale		1.2				0.6	
salt							
same		0.8		1.8	0.5	0.4	1.15
sandwich (s)				0.2	0.2		0.2
Santa							
Santa Claus	0.8				0.1		0.05
Saturday			0.4	0.1	0.1	0.2	0.1
sausage				0.2			0.1
saw	5.5	4.6	7	2.1	4.7	5.8	3.4
say		0.9	2.5	11.9	19.6	1.7	15.75
saying				0.6	0.1		0.35
says				3.8	3		3.4
scared				0.1			0.05
school		1.1	1.8	8	8.8	1.45	8.4
scratch		0.7		0.9		0.35	0.45
screw					0.1		0.05
scribble				0.2			0.1
sea		0.3			0.1	0.15	0.05
seat (s)				0.2	0.1		0.15
second (s)	1.1			0.9	1		0.95
secret					0.1		0.05
see	106	44	37	33.4	35.6	40.5	34.5
seed (s)					0.1		0.05
seeing				0.4			0.2
seen					0.5		0.25
send					0.6		0.3
set (s)				0.7	0.7		0.7
seven (s)		0.4		4.6	4.4	0.2	4.5
seventeen					0.4		0.2
seventy					0.1		0.05
shake		0.4		0.1		0.2	0.05
shall		0.4			0.1	0.2	0.05
shark		0.4			0.3	0.2	0.15
sharp				0.2	0.1		0.15
sharpen					0.2		0.1
sharpener					0.2		0.1
she	4.3	2.1	13.5	47.7	34.8	7.8	41.25
sheep		0.8	0.6			0.3	
shell						0.4	
shift					0.2		0.1
ship				0.6	0.1		0.35
shirt				0.3	0.4		0.35
shoe (s)	4.9			2	0.6		1.3
shoot	1.5						
shop (s)				0.2	0.3		0.25
shopping				0.1			0.05
short				0.2			0.1
shot				0.1			0.05
should			1.4	1.3	3.5	0.7	2.4
shouldn't					0.2		0.1
show	4.6	5.1	2	5.5	5.5	3.55	5.5
shut	2.5	0.9		0.9	2.5	0.45	1.7
shy					0.3		0.15
sick				0.9	0.3		0.6
side (s)	0.5	2	1.9	2.9	2.3	1.95	2.6
sill				0.4			
silly		0.3		0.6	1.2	0.15	0.8
sing	1.1			0.9	0.6		0.6

SINGLE WORDS FREQUENTLY USED BY AUSTRALIAN CHILDREN, AGES 2½, 3½, 4½, 5½, AND 6½—ALPHABETICAL LISTING (cont.)

Word	2½ Index	3½ Index	4½ Index	5½ Index	6½ Index	3½ & 4½ Mean Index	5½ & 6½ Mean Index
singing				0.2	0.3		0.25
sister				2.3	1.2	1.75	1.75
sit	4.6	3.5		4.8	4.6	1.75	4.7
sitting		1.9		1.3	1.8	0.95	1.65
six (s)				9.3	7.7		8.5
sixteen					0.4		0.2
sixty				0.1	0.2		0.15
skating			0.2	0.2		0.1	
skipping					0.2		0.1
skippy (s) (kangaroo)							
sky	5.8			0.2			0.1
sleep					0.6		0.3
slip		0.6				0.3	
slipped					0.1		0.05
slippery				0.4			0.2
slow			1.8	0.4	0.5	0.9	0.45
smack	1.8			0.1			0.05
small				0.3	0.4		0.35
smaller					0.1		0.05
smart				0.2	0.1		0.15
smash					0.1		0.05
smashed					0.1		0.05
smell				0.3			0.15
snail (s)		0.4	0.4	0.1		0.4	0.05
snake		3.7	13	0.2	0.1	8.35	0.1
so				16.8	16.7		16.75
soccer			0.4	0.2	0.1	0.2	0.15
sock (s)			1.6	0.4	0.6	0.8	0.5
some	6.4	48	14	22.9	22.1	31	22.5
somebody				2.7	0.4		1.55
someone				0.4	3.2		1.8
something	1.2		5.5	6.8	14	2.75	10.4
sometimes				1.2	1.7		1.45
somewhere				0.4	1.2		0.8
song (s)	0.5			0.2	0.4		0.3
soon				0.2	0.5		0.35
sore				0.3			0.15
sorry			0.7	0.7	0.7	0.35	0.7
sort (s)			0.5		0.3	0.25	0.15
soup				0.2			0.1
space (s)			0.4	0.1		0.2	0.05
speak				0.7	0.4		0.55
speaker					0.2		0.1
speaking					0.2		0.1
spell (s)				0.3	0.6		0.45
spelling					0.2		0.1
spider	0.3				0.1		0.05
spill					0.1		0.05
spit					0.1		0.05
spoon (s)		0.2			0.1	0.1	0.05
sport (s)				0.3	0.1		0.2
spot (s)					0.1		0.05
square				0.2			0.1
stair (s)	1.1	0.8		0.1	0.2	0.4	0.15
stand		0.7		2.2	1	0.35	1.6
standing				0.3	0.1		0.2
start				0.9	1		0.95
started				0.2	0.7		0.45
stay		0.7		1.9	5.5	0.35	3.7
staying					0.5		0.25
steal					0.1		0.05
steps		1		0.2	0.2	0.5	0.2
Stephen				0.5			0.25
stick (s)		1.3		2	1.4	0.65	1.7
sticky			0.4			0.2	
still			1.6	5.3	3.3	0.8	4.3
stomach				0.2			0.1
stone (s)				0.2	0.3		0.25
stop	1.4	2.6	4.4	5.2	4.2	3.5	4.7
stopped					0.2		0.1
story (s)				1.1	0.2		0.65
straight				0.4	0.7		0.55
straw				0.5			0.25
street				0.2			0.1
strong					0.1		0.05

SINGLE WORDS FREQUENTLY USED BY AUSTRALIAN CHILDREN, AGES 2½, 3½, 4½, 5½, AND 6½—ALPHABETICAL LISTING (cont.)

Word	2½ Index	3½ Index	4½ Index	5½ Index	6½ Index	3½ & 4½ Mean Index	5½ & 6½ Mean Index
stuck				0.2	0.7		0.45
stuff				0.6	2		1.3
stupid			1.1	0.7	0.5	0.55	0.6
such					0.1		0.05
sum (s)					0.4		0.2
sun				0.1			0.05
Sunday (s)		0.6		0.5		0.3	0.25
suppose				0.2			0.1
supposed				0.6	0.6		0.6
sure				0.9	0.9		0.9
Susan					0.4		0.2
swim	0.8						
swimming		0.8			0.2	0.4	0.1
swing (s)				0.2	1.2		0.7
table	5.7	2.5	0.9	2.2	1.1	1.7	1.65
tail (s)	5.7	2.2			1.2	1.1	0.6
take	43	12	29	13.2	21.3	20.5	17.25
takes					0.1		0.05
taking				0.4	0.8		0.6
talk (s)	12	2	9	4	8.3	5.5	6.15
talked				0.2			0.1
talking				1.8	1		1.4
tape (s)				1.4	6		3.7
tea	7	4.8		2.2	1.5	2.4	1.85
teach					0.1		0.05
teacher (s)				1.1	3.5		2.3
tear				0.1			0.05
teddy	0.8						
teeth				0.4	0.2		0.3
tell		1.3	1.6	14.3	8.7	1.45	11.5
telling			5	1	1	2.5	1
ten (s)				2.1	11.2		6.65
tennis				0.2			0.1
test (s)				0.2	0.6		0.4
testing					0.7		0.35
than		0.4		4.4	1.6	0.2	3
thank				4.9	4.4		4.65
thanks				1	2		1.5
that	341	225	253	180	200.6	239	190.3
the	140	172	230	214.7	246	201	230.35
their		0.8	0.4	1.1	2.7	0.6	1.9
them	8	17	25	31.5	42.5	21	37
then		3.7	13	15.7	19.7	8.35	17.7
there	389	117	70	82.9	98.5	93.5	90.7
these	17	13	22	8.9	11.4	17.5	10.15
they	36	32	33	52.4	63	32.5	57.7
thing (s)	17	31	23	15.3	23.3	27	19.3
think		6.7	8	12.2	14.8	7.35	13.5
thinks				0.2			0.1
third (s)				0.1	0.3		0.2
thirteen				0.2	0.4		0.3
thirty					1.1		0.55
this	82	102	110	89.5	86.7	106	88.1
those	0.2	4.7	21	7	7.9	12.85	7.45
though				0.2			0.1
thought				2.3	3.3		2.8
thousand					0.1		0.05
three (s)	1.4	3.9	2	20.5	28.6	2.95	24.55
through	0.8		2	2.5	4.7	1	3.6
throw		1.4		0.9	3	0.7	1.95
throwing				0.1			0.05
Thursday				0.2			0.1
tidy				0.1	0.1		0.1
tie			1	0.2	0.3	0.5	0.25
tied	2.2						
tiger		0.4			0.3	0.2	0.15
till		1.3		0.4	1.6	0.65	1
time (s)	1.1		5	11.5	14.9	2.5	13.2
times					0.5		0.25
tiny		0.2			0.4	0.1	0.2
tip	4.6				0.1		0.05
tired				0.3	0.2		0.25
to	137	113	141	189.4	227.6	127	208.5
toast					0.1		0.05
today		0.7	2	2.3	6	1.35	4.15
toe (s)				0.9	0.2		0.55

SINGLE WORDS FREQUENTLY USED BY AUSTRALIAN CHILDREN, AGES 2½, 3½, 4½, 5½, AND 6½—ALPHABETICAL LISTING (cont.)

Word	2½ Index	3½ Index	4½ Index	5½ Index	6½ Index	3½ & 4½ Mean Index	5½ & 6½ Mean Index
together					0.4		0.2
toilet				0.7	0.6		0.65
told				2.4	3.3		2.85
tomato					0.1		0.05
tomorrow				0.8	2		1.4
tonight				0.3	0.8		0.55
Tony					0.1		0.05
too	46	19	16	22.8	15.2	17.5	19
took		1.1	2	3.2	0.9	1.55	2.05
tooth				0.3			0.15
top (s)	4.3	0.8	0.4	2.3	2.3	0.6	2.3
touch		2.2		3.7	1.3	1.1	2.5
town	0.4			0.2			0.1
toy	0.5				0.3		0.15
track	1.5			0.1			0.05
train	2.1	2.7		1.9	2.7	1.35	2.3
tree (s)		0.9			0.2	0.45	0.1
triangle (s)				0.2			0.1
trick					0.1		0.05
trip (s)				0.4	0.2		0.3
trouble (s)				0.2			0.1
truck	6.5	6.3	0.7	1.8	1.4	3.5	1.6
try		3.1	0.7	0.9	2.6	1.9	1.75
trying					0.7		0.35
tuckshop (school store)				0.5			0.25
Tuesday				0.2	0.1		0.15
tummy	2.1			0.1			0.05
turn (s)		3.3	2	6.9	9.1	2.65	8
turned				5	1.1		3.05
turning				0.1			0.05
TV				0.3	0.7		0.5
twelve				0.3	2.5		1.4
twenty				0.9	1.4		1.15
twenty-five					0.1		0.05
twenty-one				0.1	0.1		0.1
two	31	25	12	38.1	48.9	18.5	43.5
uh				1.3			0.65
under	4.6	7		3.5	3.4	3.5	3.45
underneath				0.2	0.2		0.2
undone					0.2		0.1
until					0.5		0.25
up	119	111	47	64.3	77.6	79	70.95
upside		0.4		0.3	1.6	0.2	0.95
upstairs							
us				5.8	10		7.9
use			0.9	4.1	3.8	0.45	3.95
used				1.3	1.1		1.2
using				0.4	0.2		0.3
veges (vegetables)							0.05
verandah	0.4			0.1			0.05
very			2	7.6	4.2	1	5.9
voice					0.3		0.15
wait		2.2		3.9	7	1.1	5.45
waiting				0.1	0.4		0.25
wake	0.8						
walk	8.7	2	0.5	1.1	1.5	1.25	1.3
walking				0.4	0.2		0.3
wall					0.2		0.1
want	128	63	35	31	51.3	49	41.15
wanted				0.7	1		0.85
wants				2.6	4.6		3.6
was		8.6	9	32.7	29.8	8.8	31.25
wash				1.5	0.6		1.05
washing					0.1		0.05
wasn't			0.3	1	2.4	0.15	1.7
watch	11	5.3	3	8.7	5.1	4.15	6.9
water	11	4	2	4.9	4.4	3	4.65
way	11	3.7	12	11.7	11.1	7.85	11.4
we	14	125	86	62	77.9	105.5	69.95
wear				0.3	1.4		0.85
Wednesday (s)				0.5	0.3		0.4
week (s)					0.4		0.2
well		10	6	21.2	24.5	8	22.85
went		1.6	0.5	11.1	9.3	1.05	10.2

SINGLE WORDS FREQUENTLY USED BY AUSTRALIAN CHILDREN, AGES 2½, 3½, 4½, 5½, AND 6½—ALPHABETICAL LISTING

Word	2½ Index	3½ Index	4½ Index	5½ Index	6½ Index	3½ & 4½ Mean Index	5½ & 6½ Mean Index
were	1.2	0.3	1	5.3	6.7	0.65	6
weren't				0.2			0.1
wet		0.7	0.7	0.6	1.3	0.7	0.95
what	82	66	109	98	116.8	87.5	107.4
whatever					0.3		0.15
wheel (s)	4	0.7		0.2	0.3	0.35	0.25
when	1.2	18	13	19.3	30.3	15.5	24.8
where	30	20	21	32.5	56.3	20.5	44.4
which				3.6	4.5		4.05
while				0.7	1		0.85
whistle					0.1		0.05
white (s)	2.7	3.7	5	5.8	2.2	4.35	4
who				18.4	11.7		15.05
whole				0.7	1.6		1.15
whoops					0.3		0.15
whose				0.7	1.7		1.2
why	2.1	8.3	2	9.6	18.9	5.15	14.25
will ('ll)	11	64	43	69.6	93.7	53.5	81.65
win				0.3	0.1		0.2
window	1.4				0.9		0.45
wipe					0.2		0.1
wire (s)		0.6		0.2	0.8	0.3	0.5
wish				1.2	0.3		0.75
witch				0.2	0.3		0.1
with	3	15	38	32.5	27.7	26.5	30.1
without					0.2		0.1
wolf (s)				0.7			0.35
woman (s)					0.1		0.05
won				0.6	0.4		0.5
wonder				0.4	0.8		0.6
won't	6	0.8	0.7	9.8	11.9	0.75	10.85
wood (s)				0.4	0.2		0.3
word (s)				1.5	5.3		3.4
work	0.8	0.8	0.7	3	3	0.75	3
working				0.1	0.4		0.25
works				0.1	0.2		0.15
worry (s)					0.4		0.2
would ('d)	2.7	2.7	10	8.2	14.6	6.35	11.4
wouldn't				1.5	4.4		2.95
wow				0.3	0.8		0.55
wowee				0.1			0.05
write	1.2	4.5		3.2	1.1	2.25	2.15
writing				1.2	0.8		1
wrong				2.3	3.2		2.75
wrote					0.1		0.05
yard					0.1		0.05
yeah (yeh)					0.7		0.35
year (s)			1		0.3	0.5	0.15
yellow	1.2			3.2	1		2.1
yes	229	112	88	140.3	128.8	100	134.55
yesterday					2.1		1.05
yet			1.1	2.3	3	0.55	2.65
you	172	257	219	292.9	343.6	238	318.25
your	7.1	28	4.4	28.6	48.2	16.2	38.4
yourself				0.5	0.4		0.45
yuk (ck)				1	2.1		1.55
yukky (yucky)					0.2		0.1
yum				0.5	0.3		0.4
yummy					0.2		0.1
zero				0.1	0.2		0.2
zip				0.1	0.3		0.05

TWO-WORD SEQUENCES FREQUENTLY USED BY AUSTRALIAN CHILDREN, AGE 2½—ALPHABETICAL LISTING

Sequence	Freq.	No. of Speakers	Index	Sequence	Freq.	No. of Speakers	Index	Sequence	Freq.	No. of Speakers	Index
a big	7	4	6.8	I like	6	4	6.1	that mine	7	4	8.5
a look	10	4	9.2	I take	5	3	3.8	that my	7	4	1.7
a mouth	5	3	3.5	I want	56	9	130.2	that on	6	3	3.8
at me	6	3	0.7	in bed	9	3	4.9	that one	16	8	38.9
at the	9	4	1.1	in here	28	5	25.5	that way	6	3	5.5
big boat	6	3	0.6	in the	11	7	14.1	that's (is)	47	10	142.9
big one	8	4	1.1	in there	35	12	76.3	the box	4	4	2
big truck	8	3	0.8	is going	5	3	0.9	the door	5	3	1.8
can get	4	4	0.6	is it	5	5	1.5	there he	6	3	6.2
can make	5	4	0.8	is the	8	5	2.4	there you	8	7	19.5
can't get	5	3	0.2	it down	5	3	2.5	there's (is)	26	6	54.1
can't make	8	4	0.3	it is	6	3	3.1	they're	9	5	1.4
come on	8	3	1.6	it on	6	4	4.1	this is	5	3	1.1
do it	9	5	0.9	it out	6	3	3.1	this off	6	3	1.3
don't want	8	5	2	it up	7	4	4.9	this one	11	7	5.6
down there	10	5	1.9	it's (is)	21	9	31.4	to get	14	4	6.9
fall down	6	3	0.06	I'm	19	8	39.2	to put	7	6	3
get him	20	4	4.9	I'll	9	3	7	to you	5	3	1.8
get me	11	3	2	look at	34	10	110	up here	8	4	3.5
get the	6	3	1.1	look see	8	3	7.6	up the	5	3	1.5
get out	11	4	2.7	look that	12	6	23.2	up there	5	4	2.1
go on	8	4	3.5	make a	30	4	3.7	want a	8	5	4.6
going to	22	10	11.8	me got	15	3	6.8	want it	6	4	2.8
got a	25	7	25.1	my car	5	3	1.4	want that	5	3	1.7
got my	7	3	3.1	no he	8	3	4.9	want this	6	3	2
got one	10	7	10	no I	13	5	13.5	want to	29	9	29.8
got this	5	5	3.5	no that	9	3	5.6	we got	6	4	1.3
got to	7	3	3.1	of tea	7	3	0.4	want that	5	3	1.1
have a	12	6	2.9	on a	6	3	2.2	what's (is)	20	9	13.2
he can't	7	3	5.5	on here	10	4	4.9	where's (is)	15	7	2.8
he going	5	3	3.7	on me	7	4	1.8	yes look	5	3	3
he is	8	5	10.4	on the	9	6	6.6	you are	8	6	7.4
here is	8	6	10.5	one (s) in	7	4	3.5	'm going	8	5	0.4
he's (is)	85	6	131	one of	6	3	2.2	's a	28	7	46.9
he's (has)	14	7	25.1	put his	5	3	1	's going	16	3	11.6
him up	6	5	2.1	put it	12	6	4.9	's my	5	4	4.8
I can	5	3	3.8	put that	6	3	1.2	's not	10	3	7.2
I can't	7	6	10.7	put this	8	3	1.6	's that	6	4	5.6
I did	5	3	3.8	see him	6	3	1.7	's (has) got	14	7	1.6
I don't	7	6	10.7	see look	7	3	2				
I got	26	6	40.3	take it	22	4	3.4				
I have	7	5	9	that a	6	6	10.9				

Sequence	Freq.	No. of Speakers	Index
a big	8	5	6.2
a car	14	6	13
a dog	5	3	2.4
a little	19	11	32.6
a truck	6	3	2.9
and a	8	8	4.3
and he	7	5	2.3
and I	9	7	4.1
and that	6	3	1.1
and then	6	3	1.3
and they	6	4	1.5
and you	5	5	1.6
all the	9	4	0.7
are you	10	5	0.5
at that	6	3	0.3
at the	10	3	0.5
back in	7	4	0.3
big one	8	3	0.4
but you	4	4	0.1
can get	6	5	1.5
can have	8	5	2
can see	14	7	4.9
can I	6	4	1.2
can take	5	3	0.8
can't see	6	5	0.3
climb up	8	5	0.1
come here	6	3	0.8
come on	36	7	10.4
cup of	6	3	0.03
do it	7	5	3.4
do know	28	9	25.3
do like	7	5	3.4
do that	9	6	5.5
do this	4	4	1.5
do want	23	8	18.4
do you	18	8	14.4
don't go	4	4	0.6
don't have	5	5	0.9
don't know	26	8	7.6
don't like	5	4	0.7
don't touch	6	5	1.1
don't want	14	5	2.6
down here	5	5	0.6
down there	7	5	0.8
get in	6	4	0.8
get some	6	4	0.8
get up	14	4	3.4
get out	11	7	2.4
go back	6	4	1.1
go in	5	5	1
go on	14	10	6.1
go to	19	9	7.4
go up	8	5	1.6
going to	52	13	25.3
got a	42	10	32
got all	4	4	1.2
got to	21	8	12.8
have a	9	5	1.1
have to	9	5	1.1
haven't got	7	6	0.2
haven't we	5	4	0.1
he can	8	3	1.8
he can't	4	4	1.1
he got	12	4	3.4
he might	9	5	3.3
here is	7	4	1.7
hey look	7	5	0.3
he's (is)	45	10	32.8
he's (has)	7	5	2.5
him up	7	3	0.3
I can	20	11	52.2
I can't	7	6	9.9
I don't	33	9	70.7
I got	44	12	125.1
I have	9	4	8.6
I haven't	5	5	5.9
I know	11	5	13.1
I put	7	5	8.1
I saw	11	6	15.8
I think	18	5	21.6
I want	25	10	59.4
in a	9	6	6.2
in here	18	9	13.2
in it	7	5	2.8
in the	27	10	21.9
in there	17	8	11
in this	4	4	1.2
is going	14	8	5.9
is it	5	4	1.1
is that	10	7	3.7
is the	6	5	1.6
it goes	6	3	2.5
it in	10	7	9.3
it is	11	6	8.8
it isn't	6	3	2.5
it off	8	5	5
it on	8	5	5.3
it up	9	7	8.3
it's (is)	55	4	29.2
I'll	28	10	66.6
I'm	64	16	243
I've	5	4	4.5
know what	9	4	0.5
like that	9	6	1.1
like this	12	5	1.1
look at	28	8	14.8
make a	8	5	0.3
me have	5	4	0.8
me too	7	4	1.6
name is	5	3	0.02
no I	7	7	3.2
no it	5	5	1.6
no that	9	6	3.6
not going	6	5	1
on the	17	8	10.2
on there	6	5	2.3
on this	6	4	1.8
one day	5	4	1.3
one's (is)	8	4	2.1
out of	5	4	0.4
put him	8	4	0.9
put it	12	6	2.1
put that	10	4	1.2
put some	5	3	0.4
some more	8	5	1
take it	6	4	0.2

Sequence	Freq.	No. of Speakers	Index	Sequence	Freq.	No. of Speakers	Index
that one	12	9	12.8	's going	15	8	14.2
that's (is)	67	14	111.4	's my	8	6	5.6
the car	9	5	4.1	's not	16	5	9.5
the table	5	4	1.9	's that	10	7	8.3
the water	6	4	2.2	's the	12	7	9.9
they're	8	4	0.5	's (has) got	8	8	0.2
this is	24	9	11.6	've got	12	7	0.2
this one	12	7	4.5				
there you	6	5	1.9				
there's (is)	17	9	9.5				
to me	4	4	0.9				
up here	13	7	5.3				
up in	5	3	0.9				
up on	6	5	1.8				
up the	11	7	4.6				
up there	10	6	3.3				
up to	8	5	2.2				
want it	9	5	1.5				
want to	25	9	7.5				
we are	4	4	1				
we got	14	9	8.4				
we have	6	4	1.6				
we're	28	7	12.9				
we've	5	3	1				
what's (is)	10	5	1.7				
when I	4	4	0.1				
when we	5	3	0.1				
when you	4	4	0.1				
yes he	7	4	1.7				
yes I	7	6	2.5				
you are	6	3	2.6				
you better	5	4	2.8				
you can	9	6	7.5				
you can't	10	6	8.2				
you do	5	4	2.8				
you don't	7	5	2.6				
you have	6	3	2.6				
you know	6	5	4.1				
you like	4	4	2.1				
'm going	16	9	3.6				
'm not	9	7	1.6				
's a	47	14	78.1				

Sequence	Freq.	No. of Speakers	Index
a big	16	9	17.9
a car	7	4	3.6
a cow	6	3	2.2
a little	10	8	9.9
a man	4	4	1.9
a real	6	4	3
all these	5	3	0.3
allowed to	5	3	0.01
and he	11	7	6.3
and I	15	10	12.2
and see	4	4	1.3
and that	8	4	2.6
and the	5	5	2
and then	12	5	4.9
and they	6	5	2.5
and we	7	7	4
and you	8	8	5.2
another one	4	4	0.01
at the	6	4	0.2
be in	10	7	0.5
big one	8	4	0.3
but he	4	4	0.1
but it	5	3	0.1
can do	6	6	1.4
can have	7	6	1.6
can hear	4	4	0.6
can see	7	5	1.4
can I	7	5	1.3
can take	4	4	0.6
come and	4	4	0.2
come on	8	5	0.6
could have	5	4	0.1
do it	9	7	2.1
do like	4	4	0.5
do that	6	5	1
do this	4	4	0.5
do you	16	6	3.2
don't know	14	7	1.9
don't need	3	3	0.2
don't you	4	4	0.3
don't want	4	4	0.3
down there	6	3	0.1

Sequence	Freq.	No. of Speakers	Index
get a	8	5	0.6
get out	6	4	0.4
go down	5	3	0.5
go on	6	4	0.7
go there	6	4	0.7
going to	46	16	20.4
got a	29	13	16.4
got on	9	7	4.6
got to	6	5	1.2
had a	9	5	0.2
had to	4	4	0.07
have a	21	11	7
have got	6	5	1.4
have it	4	4	0.5
have to	15	10	4.5
haven't got	5	4	0.02
here is	6	5	0.7
hey look	5	4	0.3
he's (is)	25	14	10.5
he's (has)	7	4	0.9
I can	20	9	36.5
I can't	9	5	8.9
I could	6	5	6.7
I did	4	4	3.1
I don't	19	9	34.7
I found	9	5	8.9
I go	6	4	4.5
I got	30	13	78.8
I had	10	8	16
I haven't	5	3	3.1
I know	10	8	16
I like	7	5	7.1
I made	13	4	10.7
I mean	6	4	4.9
I might	6	4	4.9
I need	13	5	13.4
I saw	12	6	14.7
I think	13	7	18.3
I want	25	12	61
I was	4	4	3.1
if you	4	4	0.06
in here	8	7	3.2

Sequence	Freq.	No. of Speakers	Index
in it	8	4	1.9
in my	8	5	2.2
in the	33	14	26.5
in there	8	7	3.1
in this	5	3	0.9
is all	6	6	1.1
is going	5	4	0.6
is not	14	9	3.8
is on	7	4	0.9
is that	7	4	0.9
is the	20	10	6
is this	4	4	0.5
is what	11	6	2
isn't it	6	5	0.01
it has	10	5	5.2
it on	8	8	6.5
it to	5	3	1.6
it up	7	4	2.9
it was	5	4	2
it's (is)	49	16	80.1
I'll	36	12	87.2
I'm	71	9	272.8
I've	9	7	12.9
know what	39	14	16.1
leave it	6	4	0.09
like that	12	5	0.7
like to	5	4	0.2
look after	5	3	0.7
look at	10	6	2.6
look what	13	5	2.9
make a	6	4	0.4
might be	5	4	0.1
my cat	5	3	0.4
no I	10	6	2.3
no we	4	4	0.6
not going	5	5	0.4
now I	5	4	0.3
on me	7	4	1.2
on the	20	12	10
on this	4	4	0.6
on here	4	4	0.9

Sequence	Freq.	No. of Speakers	Index	Sequence	Freq.	No. of Speakers	Index
other one	5	5	0.06	we're	5	4	0.8
out the	4	4	0.1	we've	8	4	1.3
put the	10	7	0.9	what I	23	10	11.5
saw a	10	6	0.2	what you	5	3	0.8
see the	5	4	0.3	what's (is)	18	9	8.1
so I	5	4	0.1	when I	10	5	0.3
stop it	7	4	0.05	where's the (is)	6	4	0.2
take it	6	5	0.4	where you	6	6	0.3
take this	7	4	0.4	why can	6	4	0.02
talking to	5	4	0.3	with my	5	4	0.3
that and	5	4	2.3	with the	6	3	0.3
that boy	5	3	1.7	yes I	9	6	2.2
that one	12	8	11.2	you are	4	4	2
that way	8	3	2.8	you can	4	3	1.5
that's (is)	62	16	114.1	you can't	7	5	4.4
the big	4	4	1.6	you go	7	4	3.8
the little	6	5	3.5	you got	9	6	7.3
the other	11	8	9.2	you have	10	6	7.9
the water	5	3	1.6	you know	26	11	37.8
there's (is)	13	9	3.5	'll be	7	4	0.4
they're	9	6	0.8	'll take	4	4	0.2
think I	6	5	0.1	'm going	24	13	8.5
this is	23	10	11.6	'm not	5	4	0.5
this off	7	4	1.4	's a	31	13	36.1
this one	12	6	3.6	's going	11	5	4.9
to come	5	5	1.6	's not	15	10	13.4
to do	14	8	7.2	's that	9	4	3.2
to have	7	5	2.1	's (has) got	18	10	0.7
to kindy (to kindergarten)	4	4	1	've got	12	8	0.5
to put	4	4	1				
to see	5	5	1.6				
to take	6	5	2.1				
to the	8	8	4.1				
up here	5	4	0.3				
up there	5	4	0.4				
want a	6	4	0.4				
want to	26	12	5				
was a	4	4	0.06				
we got	6	5	1.2				
we have	7	6	1.6				
we saw	7	4	1.1				

TWO-WORD SEQUENCES FREQUENTLY USED BY AUSTRALIAN CHILDREN, AGE 5½—ALPHABETICAL LISTING

Sequence	Freq.	No. of Speakers	Index	Sequence	Freq.	No. of Speakers	Index	Sequence	Freq.	No. of Speakers	Index
a better	5	2	0.1	all my	7	4	0.06	around with	10	3	0.01
a big	35	11	5.8	all of	11	6	0.1	at all	7	4	0.07
a bit	10	8	1.4	all over	10	5	0.1	at home	12	6	0.2
a black	9	4	0.5	all that	10	3	0.07	at my	14	8	0.3
a book	9	5	0.7	all the	53	15	1.8	at our	14	6	0.2
a boy	11	2	0.3	allowed to	54	9	0.2	at school	22	10	0.6
a car	9	4	0.5	am I	17	9	0.1	at that	13	9	0.3
a chocolate	6	2	0.2	and a	44	14	8.6	at the	50	14	1.8
a crazy	5	1	0.08	and all	8	4	0.4	at this	12	9	0.3
a dark	6	1	0.09	and ask	6	3	0.3	back to	10	7	0.08
a different	9	7	0.9	and do	7	4	0.4	be a	14	8	0.2
a drink	20	8	2.4	and don't	11	5	0.8	be good	5	4	0.04
a envelope	5	1	0.08	and down	7	5	0.5	be the	12	7	0.2
a girl	22	11	3.6	and get	27	9	3.4	beat you	20	8	0.04
a go	10	2	0.3	and he	32	12	5.4	because he	15	10	0.5
a goal	7	2	0.2	and I	121	15	25.3	because I	69	15	3.4
a good	27	8	3.2	and it	39	12	6.5	because it	29	9	0.9
a house	9	5	0.7	and look	9	4	0.1	because she	11	5	0.2
a hundred	14	5	1.1	and me	12	6	1	because they	15	5	0.2
a lady	7	6	0.6	and now	9	3	0.4	because we	15	7	0.3
a little	47	13	9.2	and put	10	7	1	because you	15	8	0.4
a long	14	5	1.1	and see	11	7	1.1	better get	7	6	0.04
a look	19	7	2	and she	29	10	4	better not	12	6	0.07
a lot	6	6	0.5	and that	44	11	6.7	better put	6	4	0.02
a microphone	11	4	0.7	and the	32	12	5.4	better than	12	5	0.06
a minute	23	11	3.8	and then	37	13	6.7	big cars	5	1	0.01
a new	12	6	1.1	and there	17	6	1.4	big lunch	7	7	0.07
a picture	7	2	0.2	and they	34	10	4.7	big one	9	7	0.09
a piece	7	4	0.4	and this	13	9	1.6	bit (s) of	21	7	0.07
a race	5	3	0.2	and three	5	3	0.2	black and	8	4	0.02
a real	8	6	0.7	and we	18	8	2	black hair	11	7	0.04
a rubber	6	4	0.4	and when	11	5	0.8	blue one	5	3	0.01
a sky	5	1	0.08	and you	65	16	14.5	brother's	7	4	0.01
a tape	9	3	0.4	another one	19	9	0.09	but don't	8	3	0.06
a toilet	6	3	0.3	any more	26	10	0.13	but he	9	7	0.1
a tree	10	5	0.8	are been	5	1	0.01	but I	58	15	2
a turn	10	3	0.5	are not	11	7	0.2	but it	19	10	0.4
a yellow	8	4	0.5	are the	9	6	0.1	but not	8	6	0.1
about it	7	3	0.01	are you	72	14	2.6	but you	15	8	0.3
about that	6	5	0.01	aren't they	8	5	0.01	can be	8	4	0.2
all day	6	5	0.07	aren't we	7	4	0.01	can beat	6	3	0.09
all I	7	5	0.05	around and	7	3	0.01	can do	28	9	1.2

Sequence	Freq.	No. of Speakers	Index	Sequence	Freq.	No. of Speakers	Index	Sequence	Freq.	No. of Speakers	Index
can go	15	8	0.6	didn't you	9	6	0.1	from the	8	5	0.02
can have	16	9	0.7	do a	14	8	0.7	gave it	12	7	0.03
can hear	14	8	0.6	do I	12	8	0.6	gave me	21	6	0.08
can I	30	11	1.6	do it	77	12	5.8	get a	20	8	0.04
can make	7	5	0.2	do that	36	12	2.7	get down	13	5	0.13
can play	8	6	0.2	do the	8	6	0.3	get in	19	10	1
can run	9	4	0.2	do this	22	8	1.1	get it	46	10	2.4
can talk	5	2	0.05	do we	11	7	0.5	get my	8	8	0.3
can tell	5	2	0.05	do you	112	15	10.5	get off	11	7	0.4
can you	25	10	1.2	does it	7	5	0.01	get on	10	5	0.3
can't come	6	2	0.03	doesn't matter	13	5	0.04	get out	43	10	2.2
can't do	18	7	0.3	doing it	6	5	0.02	get that	13	7	0.5
can't find	10	5	0.1	done it	9	3	0.01	get the	23	8	0.9
can't get	13	8	0.3	don't care	8	4	0.2	get this	12	7	0.4
can't see	7	5	0.09	don't come	8	6	0.3	get up	25	10	1.3
can't use	5	2	0.03	don't do	14	8	0.7	get you	11	5	0.2
catch me	11	6	0.02	don't have	14	9	0.8	give it	13	7	0.1
come and	16	7	0.4	don't know	150	18	17.2	give me	43	10	0.5
come back	9	4	0.1	don't like	8	5	0.3	give us	16	7	0.1
come down	10	5	0.2	don't pull	8	4	0.2	give you	11	4	0.05
come here	26	7	0.7	don't tell	15	5	0.5	go and	46	12	2.7
come in	8	6	0.2	don't touch	11	8	0.6	go around	6	2	0.06
come on	153	18	10.6	don't want	33	10	2.1	go down	14	7	0.5
come out	9	5	0.2	don't we	8	3	0.2	go in	19	10	0.9
come up	6	3	0.07	don't you	24	11	1.7	go on	38	10	1.8
come with	19	5	0.4	down and	16	8	0.4	go out	13	6	0.4
coming out	7	4	0.03	down here	15	8	0.4	go over	15	7	0.5
could do	7	3	0.02	down the	13	9	0.4	go to	34	15	2.5
could I	11	4	0.04	down there	39	13	1.5	go up	23	11	1.2
could make	6	2	0.01	down to	12	8	0.3	going home	14	6	0.5
could you	12	4	0.04	drink of	8	3	0.01	going in	9	7	0.4
days for	9	1	0.01	every time	6	5	0.01	going to	275	17	26.4
did it	12	8	0.3	find it	13	6	0.02	good morning	9	5	0.07
did so	12	5	0.2	five six	10	8	0.06	good one	13	4	0.03
did that	15	8	0.3	for a	23	9	0.6	got a	556	17	72.2
did you	68	13	2.6	for me	34	11	1.1	got another	8	5	0.3
didn't do	6	4	0.05	for my	8	6	0.1	got any	13	8	0.8
didn't get	7	4	0.06	for the	13	5	0.2	got four	10	7	0.5
didn't have	11	7	0.2	for you	38	9	1	got her	12	2	0.2
didn't I	5	4	0.04	found it	12	5	0.01	got it	54	15	6.2
didn't know	10	6	0.1	four five	28	9	0.3	got no	12	8	0.7
didn't want	8	4	0.07	from here	8	4	0.01	got one	48	15	5.5

Sequence	Freq.	No. of Speakers	Index
got some	15	8	0.9
got that	11	7	0.6
got the	26	11	2.2
got three	10	6	0.5
got to	75	14	8.1
got two	15	8	0.9
grade three	10	3	0.01
guess what	25	8	0.05
had a	27	11	0.5
had it	8	5	0.07
had to	20	11	0.4
half past	12	5	0.01
hand's (is)	6	2	0.01
has to	15	9	0.06
have a	79	16	6.9
have it	11	6	0.4
have one	9	7	0.3
have some	12	6	0.4
have tea	10	2	0.1
have that	11	7	0.4
have the	9	3	0.1
have to	161	18	16
have you	14	8	0.6
haven't got	28	12	0.2
having a	13	8	0.03
he didn't	7	5	0.2
he fell	6	2	0.06
he got	10	3	0.1
he had	8	5	0.2
he is	8	4	0.2
he might	9	7	0.3
he said	16	4	0.3
he was	16	9	0.7
he went	8	5	0.2
hear it	12	6	0.04
hear me	15	4	0.03
help me	12	6	0.02
here and	5	3	0.07
here comes	14	5	0.3
here dad	11	3	0.2
here I	7	4	0.1
here name			

Sequence	Freq.	No. of Speakers	Index
(person)	24	5	0.6
here you	14	9	0.6
here's (is)	33	15	2.4
hey it	7	3	0.06
hey look	13	6	0.2
hey name			
(person)	15	4	5.2
hey what	7	3	0.06
hey where	6	5	0.08
he's (is)	66	16	4.9
he's (has)	31	13	1.9
him in	11	4	0.06
hold it	24	10	0.2
hold on	27	3	0.06
how come	9	4	0.06
how many	32	9	0.5
how much	9	6	0.09
how to	20	8	0.3
how you	9	5	0.08
hurt my	7	5	0.01
I am	36	11	16.2
I aren't	12	6	2.9
I bet	10	6	2.4
I better	11	7	3.1
I can	147	15	90
I can't	88	17	61
I caught	6	4	1
I could	25	8	8.2
I couldn't	7	4	1.1
I did	50	14	28.6
I didn't	66	14	37.7
I do	26	10	10.6
I don't	220	16	143.7
I forgot	13	7	3.7
I found	17	8	5.6
I gave	11	5	2.2
I get	16	11	7.2
I go	28	13	14.9
I going	16	5	3.3
I got	182	17	126.3
I had	42	12	20.6
I hate	8	5	1.6

Sequence	Freq.	No. of Speakers	Index
I have	44	16	28.7
I haven't	27	11	12.1
I heard	8	4	1.3
I hope	5	4	0.8
I just	25	11	11.2
I know	154	16	100.6
I like	32	13	17
I love	19	10	7.8
I made	10	5	2
I mean	14	8	4.6
I might	20	10	8.2
I need	22	9	8.1
I never	16	8	5.2
I not	9	3	1.1
I only	22	10	8.9
I put	18	10	7.3
I said	35	11	15.7
I saw	13	10	5.3
I see	11	8	3.6
I think	77	13	40.9
I thought	18	9	6.6
I told	15	8	4.9
I took	8	6	2
I want	78	17	54.1
I was	57	13	30.2
I wasn't	7	7	2
I went	9	6	2.2
I were	7	4	1.1
I will	13	7	3.7
I wish	10	5	2
I won	7	2	0.6
I wonder	6	3	0.7
I won't	21	11	9.4
I would	8	5	1.6
if I	44	13	1
if it	18	8	0.3
if you	67	15	1.8
in a	33	10	2.6
in grade	25	7	1.4
in here	26	14	2.8
in it	33	10	2.6
in my	61	16	7.5

TWO-WORD SEQUENCES FREQUENTLY USED BY AUSTRALIAN CHILDREN, AGE 5½—ALPHABETICAL LISTING (cont.)

Sequence	Freq.	No. of Speakers	Index	Sequence	Freq.	No. of Speakers	Index	Sequence	Freq.	No. of Speakers	Index
in our	13	7	0.7	it only	6	4	0.6	like this	28	11	0.7
in that	15	8	0.9	it out	30	11	8.4	like to	6	4	0.06
in the	147	18	20.4	it over	13	7	2.3	little baby	10	4	0.06
in there	58	14	6.3	it that	8	6	1.2	little bit	17	8	0.2
in this	9	5	0.3	it there	9	6	1.4	little one (s)	6	4	0.04
in your	24	11	2	it to	36	12	10.9	little piggy (s)	6	1	0.01
is a	18	10	0.5	it up	50	13	16.5	look at	74	15	4.6
is in	6	2	0.2	it was	50	13	16.5	look how	10	6	0.2
is it	52	12	1.8	it went	23	6	3.5	look I	15	10	0.6
is my	13	8	0.3	it when	5	2	0.3	look what	18	10	0.7
is not	6	5	0.08	it with	11	8	2.2	look you	7	4	0.1
is that	34	11	1.1	it won't	11	8	2.2	made a	11	8	0.02
is the	21	11	0.7	it'll	15	4	1.5	make a	32	9	0.3
is this	9	4	0.1	it's (is)	363	17	156.5	make it	19	9	0.2
is too	5	5	0.07	it's (has)	17	10	4.3	makes a	7	5	0.01
isn't it	16	8	0.01	I'd (would)	11	6	2.7	me a	12	8	0.6
it a	8	5	1	I'll	302	17	209.6	me and	17	10	1.1
it again	10	5	1.3	I'm	476	18	349.8	me home	11	2	0.1
it all	9	7	1.6	I've	116	16	75.8	me some	8	4	0.2
it and	21	7	3.7	just a	12	6	0.2	me that	8	5	0.3
it but	7	5	0.9	just because	5	2	0.02	me the	16	5	0.5
it didn't	11	6	1.7	just want	7	4	0.07	me this	10	2	0.1
it doesn't	11	5	1.4	keep on	13	5	0.02	me to	17	8	0.9
it down	12	5	1.5	kick it	21	2	0.01	might be	18	9	0.1
it for	20	9	4.6	know how	23	9	1.1	might break	7	2	0.01
it from	6	3	0.5	know that	21	10	1.1	might get	7	5	0.03
it go	7	4	0.7	know the	8	4	0.2	might have	7	5	0.03
it goes	14	6	2.1	know what	54	13	3.7	mine's (is)	11	8	0.09
it got	11	6	1.7	know where	19	11	1.1	more than	10	6	0.04
it has	7	6	1.1	know who	7	4	0.1	must be	9	5	0.01
it here	9	6	1.4	know why	16	5	0.4	my brother	17	7	0.8
it in	26	11	7.3	lady (s) who	8	1	0.01	my class	18	5	0.6
it is	49	16	19.9	leave it	46	12	0.5	my face	6	2	0.08
it isn't	15	6	2.3	leave me	8	4	0.03	my finger	5	3	0.1
it like	21	8	4.1	leave that	7	4	0.02	my fork	5	1	0.04
it makes	7	3	0.5	let me	29	10	0.2	my friend (s)	35	4	1
it might	12	6	1.8	let you	7	4	0.02	my hand (s)	10	8	0.6
it name (person)	17	7	3	let's get	5	3	0.01	my head	6	4	0.2
it now	8	6	1.2	let's go	25	8	0.09	my house	5	3	0.1
it off	12	9	2.7	let's see	13	7	0.04	my name	13	6	0.5
it on	49	12	15	like a	15	8	0.3	my neo (s) (pen)	12	2	0.2
				like that	53	14	1.7				

TWO-WORD SEQUENCES FREQUENTLY USED BY AUSTRALIAN CHILDREN, AGE 5½—ALPHABETICAL LISTING (cont.)

Sequence	Freq.	No. of Speakers	Index	Sequence	Freq.	No. of Speakers	Index	Sequence	Freq.	No. of Speakers	Index
my port (s) (school bag)	20	9	0.5	oh I	67	15	7.9	our school	5	4	0.01
my set	5	1	0.04	oh look	7	6	0.3	out and	7	3	0.08
my shoe (s)	8	4	0.2	oh no	27	8	1.7	out here	8	6	0.2
my sock (s)	5	3	0.1	oh oh	18	6	0.9	out of	51	13	2.6
name (person) 's	61	15	15.2	oh she	5	4	0.2	out the	15	7	0.4
new one	8	4	0.01	oh sorry	6	2	0.09	out there	7	3	0.08
next to	7	5	0.01	oh that	19	9	1.3	over her	5	2	0.02
no he	13	7	0.9	oh there	6	6	0.3	over here	12	7	0.1
no I	89	13	12.1	oh we	8	6	0.4	over it	9	5	0.08
no it	33	12	4.1	oh well	7	7	0.4	over the	20	8	0.3
no not	12	7	0.9	oh what	10	6	0.5	over there	31	11	0.6
no that	14	8	1.2	oh where	8	3	0.2	over to	9	6	0.09
no they	9	6	0.6	oh yeah	31	11	2.7	part of	10	6	0.01
no yeah	8	4	0.3	oh you	26	9	1.8	piece (s) of	10	7	0.01
no you	45	13	6.1	old one	6	4	0.01	play with	18	10	0.2
not allowed	18	6	0.5	on a	9	7	0.5	put a	9	6	0.2
not going	8	6	0.2	on it	31	14	3.6	put him	13	4	0.2
not playing	7	3	0.1	on me	20	8	1.3	put it	63	14	3.1
not that	8	5	0.2	on my	26	9	1.9	put my	10	7	0.2
not the	8	5	0.2	on name (person)	39	12	3.9	put some	13	5	0.2
not very	8	5	0.2	on that	18	8	1.2	put that	16	7	0.4
now I	46	14	2.1	on the	103	15	12.8	put the	20	9	0.6
now it	12	6	0.2	on there	12	6	0.6	put them	19	10	0.7
now we	11	7	0.3	on this	10	6	0.5	put this	25	12	1.1
now what	8	6	0.2	on you	32	9	2.4	put your	19	10	0.7
now you	19	8	0.5	one and	13	7	0.8	read it	6	5	0.01
of a	6	3	0.06	one day	17	7	1.1	said I	13	8	0.2
of it	23	8	0.6	one hand	5	2	0.09	said no	5	3	0.02
of paper	6	5	0.1	one more	10	7	0.6	said that	6	5	0.05
of that	6	6	0.1	one of	36	11	3.6	said to	11	7	0.1
of the	34	14	1.5	one on	7	5	0.3	said you	11	5	0.09
of them	33	12	1.3	one thing	7	6	0.4	say it	12	6	0.1
of these	8	5	0.1	one two	83	12	8.9	say that	10	5	0.05
of this	9	5	0.1	one (s) in	7	3	0.2	see how	6	3	0.05
of those	11	5	0.2	one's (has)	6	2	0.1	see if	16	9	0.4
of water	8	5	0.1	one's (is)	26	12	2.8	see it	20	10	0.5
off me	6	5	0.04	only got	19	9	0.2	see that	13	7	0.2
oh don't	8	6	0.4	only one	10	8	0.1	see the	7	4	0.08
oh get	7	5	0.3	other one	9	5	0.03	see what	8	6	0.1
oh God	11	2	0.2	other side	7	3	0.01	see you	18	9	0.4
oh he	8	5	0.3	our house	13	5	0.04	seven eight	8	7	0.02
								she can	9	5	0.2

TWO-WORD SEQUENCES FREQUENTLY USED BY AUSTRALIAN CHILDREN, AGE 5½—ALPHABETICAL LISTING (cont.)

Sequence	Freq.	No. of Speakers	Index
she did	7	6	0.2
she didn't	5	4	0.08
she doesn't	7	6	0.2
she got	8	5	0.2
she had	5	5	0.1
she is	7	6	0.2
she said	14	8	0.4
she was	14	8	0.4
she won't	7	4	0.1
she's (has)	7	5	0.1
she's (is)	61	13	3.1
show you	19	10	0.09
sit down	12	6	0.03
six seven	12	7	0.06
so I	16	5	0.1
some more	11	6	0.1
some of	9	8	0.1
somebody else (s)	9	4	0.01
something else	6	4	0.01
stand up	12	5	0.01
stop it	17	11	0.08
take a	7	4	0.03
take it	13	9	0.1
take me	8	1	0.01
take the	9	6	0.06
talk in	10	6	0.02
talk through	7	3	0.01
talking about	12	3	0.01
tape recorder	19	3	0.01
tell him	7	4	0.03
tell me	9	7	0.07
tell on	9	2	0.02
tell you	22	9	0.2
than you	13	7	0.03
thank you	46	12	0.2
that a	11	5	0.8
that again	7	22	0.2
that and	16	9	2.1
that big	14	6	1.2
that I	14	5	1
that is	9	4	0.5

Sequence	Freq.	No. of Speakers	Index
that lady	8	3	0.4
that little	6	5	0.4
that one	81	14	16.7
that part	7	2	0.2
that say	6	5	0.4
that the	7	4	0.4
that thing	10	4	0.6
that time	9	6	0.8
that to	9	4	0.5
that was	24	11	3.9
that wasn't	6	5	0.4
that way	22	6	1.9
that word	9	4	0.5
that you	9	3	0.4
that'll	10	5	0.7
that's (is)	261	17	65.3
the answer (s)	7	4	0.2
the back	22	11	4.3
the ball (s)	22	5	1.9
the big	32	10	3.9
the black	11	4	0.8
the boss	9	2	0.3
the bottom	8	7	1
the car	16	8	2.2
the creature	6	1	0.1
the door	21	8	2.9
the end	9	6	0.9
the front	10	7	1.2
the girl	10	6	1.1
the ground	11	7	1.4
the handle	5	3	0.3
the hill	6	5	0.5
the house	17	8	2.4
the lady (s)	36	8	5
the leader	13	3	0.7
the line	8	4	0.6
the little	15	8	2.1
the lost	5	4	0.4
the microphone	8	4	0.6
the middle	6	4	0.4
the money	5	1	0.09
the next	9	6	0.9

Sequence	Freq.	No. of Speakers	Index
the one	20	8	2.8
the orange	7	1	0.1
the other	34	11	6.6
the paper	15	7	1.8
the pin	7	1	0.1
the puppet	6	1	0.1
the road	7	4	0.5
the roof	16	6	1.7
the saints	5	1	0.09
the same	21	9	3.3
the sport (s)	6	3	0.3
the table (s)	11	8	1.5
the thing (s)	28	11	5.4
the time	14	9	2.2
the toilet	11	9	1.7
the top	16	9	2.6
the track	7	4	0.2
the water	14	6	1.5
the way	12	6	1.3
the witch	7	4	0.2
the wolf	8	3	0.4
them in	13	8	0.3
them on	7	3	0.05
then the	8	5	0.05
then we	7	5	0.05
then you	8	6	0.06
there and	24	10	1.6
there was	20	8	1.1
there's (is)	96	17	11.1
these are	9	5	0.03
they are	21	11	1
they can	12	7	0.4
they have	10	8	0.3
they put	7	4	0.1
they went	9	5	0.2
they were	23	6	0.6
they're	107	16	7.3
think he	6	3	0.02
think I	37	11	0.4
think it	12	6	0.08
this and	12	6	0.5
this in	10	7	0.5

TWO-WORD SEQUENCES FREQUENTLY USED BY AUSTRALIAN CHILDREN, AGE 5½—ALPHABETICAL LISTING (cont.)

Sequence	Freq.	No. of Speakers	Index	Sequence	Freq.	No. of Speakers	Index	Sequence	Freq.	No. of Speakers	Index
this is	67	15	7.4	to wait	5	3	0.2	we could	12	5	0.3
this on	12	7	0.6	to you	16	11	2.7	we did	11	6	0.3
this one	59	16	6.9	told you	10	4	0.01	we do	5	3	0.08
this thing	12	8	0.7	too close	6	4	0.05	we don't	7	6	0.2
this time	9	8	0.5	too late	5	4	0.04	we go	8	7	0.3
this way	16	7	0.8	took it	8	7	0.02	we got	17	8	0.7
those lady (s)	10	2	0.01	touch it	12	4	0.01	we had	12	7	0.4
three four	54	11	1	touch your	9	3	0.01	we have	23	10	1.2
through it	12	4	0.01	try and	12	4	0.01	we know	6	4	0.1
through the	13	5	0.01	trying to	14	8	0.01	we want	6	4	0.1
throw it	8	3	0.01	turn it	10	7	0.04	we went	9	6	0.3
time is	7	4	0.03	two days	9	1	0.03	we were	14	7	0.5
to a	13	8	1.6	two three	73	10	2.3	well I	29	6	0.3
to be	43	16	10.7	under the	12	7	0.02	well it	7	6	0.07
to beat	7	4	0.4	up and	17	10	0.9	well she	7	4	0.05
to catch	10	5	0.8	up here	21	9	1	well they	12	5	0.1
to come	9	8	1.1	up in	13	8	0.5	well we	8	5	0.07
to do	54	14	11.7	up on	18	8	0.8	well you	16	6	0.2
to get	83	15	19.3	up that	8	5	0.2	went to	13	9	0.1
to give	14	6	1.3	up the	24	11	1.4	went up	6	4	0.02
to go	56	17	14.7	up there	48	13	3.3	we'll	27	10	1.4
to have	52	13	10.4	up to	20	10	1.5	we're	66	17	5.7
to keep	6	4	0.4	us it	8	4	0.02	we've	30	13	2
to kick	7	2	0.2	use it	10	7	0.02	what a	15	5	0.6
to make	28	9	3.9	used to	12	5	0.01	what are	38	10	3
to me	31	10	4.8	very quickly	5	2	0.01	what did	16	6	0.8
to move	6	3	0.3	wait for	8	6	0.02	what do	13	4	0.4
to my	14	8	1.7	want a	13	6	0.2	what else	7	3	0.2
to play	42	11	7.2	want it	10	7	0.2	what happened	8	4	0.3
to put	38	14	8.2	want me	11	3	0.08	what I	36	13	3.8
to school	22	12	4.1	want one	8	3	0.06	what is	14	7	0.8
to see	25	13	5	want to	125	16	5.1	what it	17	8	1.1
to show	8	6	0.7	wants to	9	8	0.02	what this	5	1	0.04
to sit	13	6	1.2	was a	28	9	0.7	what time	8	4	0.3
to take	27	11	4.6	was going	11	7	0.2	what was	13	2	0.2
to talk	7	3	0.3	was in	11	6	0.2	what we	7	5	0.2
to tell	28	7	3	was it	10	5	0.1	what you	18	7	1
to that	10	6	0.9	was that	8	2	0.04	what's (is)	86	15	10.3
to the	41	15	9.5	was the	12	6	0.2	when he	7	6	0.07
to this	8	7	0.9	watch out	13	5	0.05	when I	28	12	0.5
to touch	13	4	0.8	watch this	27	7	0.1	when it	19	8	0.2
to use	11	7	1.2	we can	17	10	0.9	when she	6	5	0.05

TWO-WORD SEQUENCES FREQUENTLY USED BY AUSTRALIAN CHILDREN, AGE 5½—ALPHABETICAL LISTING (cont.)

Sequence	Freq.	No. of Speakers	Index	Sequence	Freq.	No. of Speakers	Index	Sequence	Freq.	No. of Speakers	Index
when we	15	6	0.1	you can	71	14	23.8	'll go	24	10	1.1
when you	21	9	0.3	you can't	43	11	11.3	'll have	40	11	2.1
where are	8	5	0.1	you come	9	7	1.5	'll let	5	2	0.05
where did	17	7	0.3	you could	16	9	3.4	'll make	7	3	0.1
where I	8	4	0.09	you couldn't	7	4	0.7	'll put	21	9	0.9
where is	21	8	0.4	you did	17	8	3.3	'll read	12	3	0.2
where it	13	8	0.3	you didn't	17	7	2.9	'll show	14	7	0.5
where the	13	7	0.2	you do	25	9	5.4	'll take	6	4	0.1
where's (is)	54	14	2	you done	9	3	0.6	'll tell	10	9	0.4
which one	10	6	0.02	you don't	41	11	10.8	'll try	6	4	0.1
who did	7	5	0.05	you get	35	11	9.2	'm a	13	7	0.3
who gave	9	2	0.03	you go	30	11	7.9	'm doing	16	9	0.4
who said	12	4	0.07	you going	11	6	1.6	'm going	126	17	2.7
who wants	8	5	0.06	you got	41	12	11.8	'm having	6	3	0.06
who's (is)	25	7	0.3	you have	49	14	16.4	'm hot	8	3	0.07
why do	8	5	0.03	you haven't	9	6	1.3	'm in	7	6	0.1
why don't	8	3	0.02	you just	6	5	0.7	'm not	69	15	3.1
why I	8	4	0.03	you know	87	15	31.3	'm telling	10	4	0.1
will I	13	6	0.06	you miss	5	3	0.4	'm the	11	8	0.3
will you	16	9	0.1	you one	5	1	0.1	're a	15	7	0.4
with a	9	5	0.1	you paint	5	2	0.2	're going	53	12	2.6
with it	17	7	0.3	you put	15	10	3.6	're having	10	5	0.2
with me	33	11	1	you said	14	5	1.7	're in	13	3	0.2
with my	7	6	0.1	you say	11	6	1.6	're just	8	4	0.1
with the	21	7	0.4	you see	10	4	1	're not	74	16	4.8
with this	20	9	0.5	you something	6	4	0.6	're the	10	5	0.2
with you	19	8	0.4	you want	32	10	7.7	's a	146	16	35.6
would be	5	3	0.01	you watch	13	3	0.9	's alright	7	4	1
would you	9	7	0.03	you were	9	5	1.1	's all	25	12	4.6
yes and	24	11	3	your hand	11	6	0.2	's been (has)	6	2	0.01
yes because	8	5	0.5	your mouth	6	4	0.06	's better	7	4	0.4
yes but	24	8	2.2	you name	9	4	0.08	's coming	5	2	0.2
yes I	60	14	9.6	your nose	5	1	0.01	's down	7	3	0.3
yes it	29	11	3.7	your pardon	6	2	0.03	's for	18	10	2.7
yes please	16	5	0.9	your toes	5	1	0.01	's going	48	13	9.5
yes sister	6	2	0.1	yours is	8	6	0.1	's gone	8	5	0.05
yes that	16	6	1.1	you'll	20	10	4.8	's good	9	5	0.7
yes we	12	8	1.1	you're	182	17	74	's got (has)	66	17	1.3
yes you	21	11	2.7	you've	26	11	6.8	's hot	5	4	0.3
you and	18	8	3.4	'll be	30	10	1.4	's show	9	8	1
you are	32	14	10.7	'll do	17	7	0.6	's in	39	11	6.6
you better	10	8	1.9	'll get	36	12	2.1	's loose	8	2	0.2

TWO-WORD SEQUENCES FREQUENTLY USED BY AUSTRALIAN CHILDREN, AGE 5½—ALPHABETICAL LISTING (cont.)

Sequence	Freq.	No. of Speakers	Index
's mine	15	8	1.8
's my	47	13	9.3
's no	8	6	0.7
's not	65	17	16.9
's on	13	9	1.8
's one	13	8	1.6
's only	9	5	0.7
's over	7	4	0.4
's seven	5	2	0.2
's supposed	5	2	0.2
's talking	7	3	0.3
's that	48	13	9.5
's the	68	16	16.6
's there	3	4	0.3
's this	17	6	1.6
's too	11	7	1.2
's up	12	8	1.5
's what	18	6	1.6
's why	6	3	0.3
's wrong	8	5	0.6
's your	20	8	0.6
've been	14	10	0.3
've got	104	15	3.4

TWO-WORD SEQUENCES FREQUENTLY USED BY AUSTRALIAN CHILDREN, AGE 6½—ALPHABETICAL LISTING

Sequence	Freq.	No. of Speakers	Index
a baby	5	3	0.2
a bath	6	3	0.2
a big	35	15	5.7
a bit	30	13	4.2
a book	10	8	0.9
a boy	6	5	0.3
a bridge	8	6	0.5
a car	5	5	0.3
a couple	5	4	0.2
a cup	5	5	0.3
a different	5	4	0.2
a dog	6	4	0.3
a drink	10	8	0.9
a funny	7	5	0.4
a game	9	6	0.6
a girl	12	8	1
a go	16	8	1.4
a good	43	15	7
a hole	8	5	0.4
a hundred	5	3	0.2
a little	45	17	8.3
a long	14	10	1.5
a look	18	8	1.6
a lot	15	11	1.8
a man	11	5	0.6
a marble	16	3	0.5
a microphone	45	10	4.9
a minute	36	14	5.4
a monkey	5	3	0.2
a new	3	4	0.3
a one	6	6	0.4
a pencil	12	5	0.7
a picture	13	8	1.1
a piece	6	4	0.3
a real	10	6	0.7
a tape	14	7	1.1
a tree	8	4	0.3
a triangle	5	3	0.2
a very	5	4	0.2
a while	8	3	0.3
a whole	7	6	0.5
able to	20	7	0.01
about it	7	5	0.02
about that	20	11	0.2
about the	7	5	0.02
about this	7	4	0.02
all day	9	8	0.1
all I	6	6	0.07
all of	17	9	0.3
all over	14	8	0.2
all that	6	6	0.07
all the	59	17	2
all them	6	4	0.05
all this	6	4	0.05
all those	5	4	0.04
allowed to	46	15	0.2
am I	20	13	0.08
an orange	5	3	0.01
and a	26	9	2.2
and ask	7	3	0.2
and black	5	3	0.1
and David	5	3	0.1
and do	8	4	0.3
and every	9	5	0.4
and get	44	15	6.2
and go	6	6	0.4
and have	7	5	0.3
and he	35	13	4.3
and I	95	20	18
and if	10	8	0.8
and it	42	15	6
and look	5	4	0.2
and me	9	5	0.4
and my	7	6	0.4
and now	6	4	0.2
and one	13	7	0.9
and play	6	5	0.3
and put	8	7	0.5
and see	12	10	1.1
and she	21	5	1
and show	9	7	0.6
and so	6	3	0.2
and take	6	5	0.3
and tell	6	6	0.4
and that	16	18	9.5
and the	36	15	5.1
and then	46	14	6.1
and there	17	11	1.8
and they	29	14	3.8
and this	10	6	0.6
and two	6	4	0.2
and up	5	4	0.2
and we	29	12	3.3
and went	7	4	0.3
and what	6	6	0.4
and white	6	4	0.2
and you	59	20	11.2
another one	29	12	0.2
any more	15	9	0.06
are going	6	5	0.4
are the	6	6	0.08
are they	21	13	0.6
are you	87	20	3.7
aren't you	12	9	0.02
around and	5	4	0.01
around the	6	5	0.01
as well	6	5	0.01
at all	8	6	0.09
at home	14	6	0.2
at it	11	6	0.1
at me	5	5	0.3
at my	11	8	0.2
at our	6	3	0.03
at school	13	8	0.2
at that	9	4	0.07
at the	39	13	1.3
at this	13	8	0.2
away and	7	5	0.01
away from	13	7	0.03
back here	6	4	0.03
back in	30	11	0.4
back to	18	11	0.3
be a	21	8	0.4
be able	19	7	0.3
be back	8	5	0.08
be here	5	4	0.04

Sequence	Freq.	No. of Speakers	Index
be in	6	6	0.08
be on	11	8	0.2
be quiet	20	8	0.3
be up	10	6	0.1
because I	58	22	2.1
because it	18	14	0.4
because she	10	5	0.08
because the	6	3	0.03
because there	6	5	0.05
because they	19	12	0.4
because we	8	7	0.09
because you	19	9	0.3
better get	7	5	0.02
better not	8	8	0.04
big lunch	10	5	0.04
big one	11	7	0.06
bit of	18	10	0.06
but he	8	6	0.08
but I	41	18	1.2
but it	17	12	0.3
but not	11	6	0.1
but she	6	4	0.04
but the	6	6	0.06
but they	8	6	0.08
but we	8	6	0.08
but what	5	4	0.03
but when	10	6	0.1
but you	21	12	0.4
came back	5	4	0.01
came down	6	5	0.01
came from	5	5	0.01
came out	10	7	0.02
came to	6	3	0.01
can be	7	5	0.2
can do	24	11	1.3
can get	24	11	1.3
can go	16	9	0.7
can have	16	8	0.6
can hear	42	10	2
can I	150	19	13.7
can just	6	4	0.1
can make	9	6	0.3
can only	9	7	0.3
can play	11	6	0.3
can put	8	6	0.2
can see	10	6	0.3
can take	6	4	0.1
can they	5	3	0.07
can use	13	5	0.3
can we	21	9	0.9
can you	51	14	3.4
can't do	9	6	0.08
can't even	7	5	0.05
can't find	9	5	0.06
can't get	26	10	0.4
can't hear	15	8	0.2
can't see	15	7	0.2
can't you	6	6	0.05
come and	16	8	0.3
come back	8	5	0.1
come down	12	4	0.1
come here	36	12	1.3
come in	16	9	0.4
come on	183	18	9.5
come out	19	10	0.6
come over	10	6	0.2
come to	6	5	0.09
come up	19	9	0.5
comes out	6	4	0.01
coming down	12	5	0.03
coming out	8	7	0.02
could be	6	4	0.01
could do	5	3	0.01
could have	10	6	0.03
could you	10	5	0.03
daddy and	5	5	0.02
did he	11	10	0.2
did I	9	7	0.1
did it	12	10	0.2
did not	10	6	0.1
did she	5	4	0.04
did so	5	4	0.04
did that	5	3	0.03
did the	7	4	0.05
did you	101	18	3.3
didn't get	7	5	0.03
didn't have	9	5	0.04
didn't I	6	5	0.03
didn't know	7	4	0.02
didn't want	5	5	0.02
didn't you	8	5	0.02
do a	24	10	1.2
do anything	5	3	0.07
do I	24	13	1.6
do it	84	17	7.1
do my	7	3	0.1
do now	8	5	0.2
do some	11	8	0.4
do that	43	17	3.6
do the	17	7	0.6
do them	7	6	0.2
do this	15	8	0.6
do we	9	5	0.2
do you	180	21	18.8
do your	6	5	0.2
does he	6	4	0.01
does it	13	4	0.02
does not	5	4	0.01
does that	6	3	0.01
doesn't matter	17	12	0.08
doing a	6	4	0.01
doing it	7	5	0.02
doing that	8	5	0.02
done a	7	7	0.02
done it	10	6	0.02
done my	5	4	0.01
don't care	7	5	0.2
don't do	16	10	0.7
don't get	10	8	0.4
don't go	9	7	0.3
don't have	27	12	1.4
don't I	9	6	0.2
don't know	108	20	9.5
don't let	7	6	0.2
don't like	20	11	1

TWO-WORD SEQUENCES FREQUENTLY USED BY AUSTRALIAN CHILDREN, AGE 6½—ALPHABETICAL LISTING (cont.)

Sequence	Freq.	No. of Speakers	Index	Sequence	Freq.	No. of Speakers	Index	Sequence	Freq.	No. of Speakers	Index
don't put	9	8	0.3	four six	4	3	0.01	go into	6	6	0.2
don't run	5	4	0.09	from here	5	4	0.01	go like	9	5	0.2
don't say	6	4	0.1	from me	5	4	0.01	go off	6	4	0.1
don't tell	6	3	0.08	from the	14	10	0.1	go on	43	14	2.7
don't think	10	10	0.4	get a	31	13	2	go out	11	8	0.4
don't touch	11	7	0.3	get all	8	5	0.2	go outside	5	4	0.09
don't want	56	17	4.2	get another	6	4	0.1	go over	8	8	0.3
don't you	42	18	3.3	get away	7	5	0.2	go right	5	5	0.1
down and	14	8	0.3	get back	12	8	0.5	go round	9	5	0.2
down here	21	11	0.6	get down	10	9	0.4	go through	5	3	0.07
down in	8	7	0.1	get in	29	11	1.5	go to	65	17	5
down on	11	5	0.3	get it	53	16	4	go up	25	11	1.2
down the	22	11	0.6	get me	15	4	0.3	go upstairs	7	4	0.1
down there	46	18	2	get my	17	10	0.8	goes in	6	4	0.01
down to	26	12	0.8	get off	11	8	0.4	goes there	5	4	0.08
draw a	14	6	0.01	get on	16	10	0.8	goes up	7	7	0.02
eight nine	14	4	0.01	get one	12	8	0.5	going down	11	5	0.2
every time	13	6	0.01	get out	67	16	5.1	going home	8	6	0.2
excuse me	21	7	0.01	get set	9	4	0.2	going in	5	5	0.1
find it	15	9	0.04	get some	6	5	0.1	going on	6	4	0.09
find the	5	5	0.01	get something	6	4	0.1	going to	360	22	30.7
first one	7	5	0.01	get that	18	9	0.8	going up	15	6	0.4
five cents	9	6	0.05	get the	21	11	1.1	going around	5	3	0.06
five six	26	7	0.2	get them	8	7	0.3	good for	5	3	0.02
for a	30	16	1.2	get this	10	6	0.3	good girl	7	4	0.04
for it	7	4	0.07	get to	6	4	0.8	good morning	12	7	0.1
for me	41	12	1.2	get up	21	10	1	good on (congratulations)	6	5	0.04
for mummy (mommy)	5	3	0.04	get you	12	9	0.5	good one	14	7	0.1
for my	6	6	0.09	get your	16	9	0.7	got a	115	19	12.6
for tea	8	4	0.08	give it	12	6	0.05	got all	10	6	0.4
for that	9	5	0.1	give me	35	15	0.3	got another	9	6	0.3
for the	11	7	0.2	give them	9	5	0.03	got any	11	8	0.5
for them	7	6	0.1	give us	15	7	0.07	got four	6	4	0.1
for today	5	3	0.04	give you	10	6	0.04	got in	5	5	0.1
for you	14	9	0.3	go and	62	17	4.8	got it	62	17	6.1
for your	5	5	0.06	go away	7	4	0.1	got me	6	5	0.2
forgot to	6	6	0.01	go back	14	10	0.6	got my	12	7	0.5
found it	12	7	0.01	go down	27	12	1.5	got no	9	6	0.3
four and	5	3	0.02	go downstairs	6	5	0.1	got one	36	14	2.9
four equals	10	3	0.03	go first	7	3	0.1	got some	13	9	0.7
four five	45	12	0.6	go home	12	6	0.3	got that	10	8	0.5
				go in	24	10	1.1				

Sequence	Freq.	No. of Speakers	Index	Sequence	Freq.	No. of Speakers	Index	Sequence	Freq.	No. of Speakers	Index
got the	44	15	3.8	he goes	7	4	0.09	home with	6	5	0.02
got these	5	4	0.1	he got	11	6	0.2	house and	6	3	0.01
got this	10	6	0.4	he had	8	6	0.2	how can	12	7	0.1
got three	7	7	0.3	he is	10	8	0.3	how come	8	5	0.07
got to	103	17	10.1	he just	7	4	0.09	how did	10	5	0.08
got too	5	4	0.1	he might	5	4	0.06	how do	37	14	0.9
got two	13	9	0.7	he put	5	4	0.06	how I	10	5	0.08
guess what	22	6	0.01	he said	11	7	0.2	how many	33	11	0.6
had a	19	10	1.6	he wants	6	5	0.09	how much	10	7	0.1
had it	6	4	0.02	he was	14	9	0.4	how they	8	5	0.07
had the	7	5	0.03	he went	7	3	0.07	how to	29	11	0.5
had to	20	11	0.2	hear it	15	7	0.08	how you	5	4	0.03
hand and	6	5	0.01	hear me	37	9	0.3	hundred and	19	4	0.01
hard to	8	5	0.01	hear us	11	3	0.03	hurry up	14	8	0.01
has got	6	4	0.01	hear you	7	3	0.02	I always	6	5	0.9
has to	10	8	0.02	help me	6	6	0.01	I am	27	13	11
have a	82	19	7	here and	11	7	0.3	I beat	8	5	1.3
have any	7	5	0.2	here comes	7	5	0.1	I bet	10	5	1.6
have got	6	5	0.1	here for	9	7	0.2	I better	5	5	0.8
have I	8	7	0.3	here I	10	6	0.2	I brought	11	7	2.4
have it	20	9	0.8	here it	13	5	0.3	I can	116	20	73
have my	6	5	0.1	here you	12	8	0.4	I can't	72	16	36.2
have one	19	9	0.8	here's (is)	48	20	3.7	I come	14	7	3.1
have some	17	10	0.8	hey Brad	8	4	0.1	I could	16	9	4.6
have that	10	8	0.4	hey can	5	4	0.06	I couldn't	9	4	1.2
have the	14	4	0.3	hey come	5	3	0.05	I cut	7	3	0.7
have this	11	7	0.3	hey dad	6	3	0.06	I did	45	16	22.7
have to	178	19	15.1	hey daddy	8	3	0.08	I didn't	53	15	25
have you	41	16	2.9	hey let	7	4	0.09	I do	40	14	17.6
have your	6	5	0.1	hey look	19	12	0.7	I done	16	6	3
haven't done	10	6	0.04	hey mum (mom)	11	4	0.1	I don't	215	22	148.9
haven't even	12	6	0.05	hey I	18	7	0.4	I eat	5	4	0.6
haven't got	26	9	0.2	hey that	5	4	0.06	I forgot	15	12	5.7
haven't you	7	6	0.03	hey what	8	6	0.2	I found	17	9	4.8
having a	15	4	0.01	hey yes	5	3	0.05	I gave	6	5	0.9
he came	5	4	0.06	hey you	14	8	0.4	I get	38	16	19.2
he can	12	7	0.3	he'll	10	3	0.09	I go	62	18	35.1
he comes	8	6	0.2	he's (is)	56	17	3	I going	10	7	2.2
he did	7	5	0.1	he's (has)	18	10	0.6	I got	175	22	121.2
he didn't	6	6	0.1	his name	6	3	0.01	I had	37	16	18.6
he does	9	3	0.08	hold it	9	5	0.01	I hate	8	5	1.3
he gets	8	4	0.1								

Sequence	Freq.	No. of Speakers	Index
I haven't	48	15	22.7
I heard	10	6	1.9
I hit	7	4	0.9
I hope	7	5	1.1
I just	39	15	18.4
I know	139	20	87.5
I like	62	14	27.3
I live	5	3	0.5
I love	9	6	1.7
I made	7	4	0.9
I mean	24	13	9.8
I meant	5	3	0.5
I might	21	10	6.6
I need	10	7	2.2
I never	22	8	5.5
I only	17	8	4.3
I play	7	4	0.9
I put	38	14	16.7
I read	8	3	0.7
I said	32	15	15.1
I saw	14	10	4.4
I say	25	12	9.5
I see	10	7	2.2
I should	6	4	0.7
I still	5	5	0.8
I take	14	6	2.7
I talk	20	9	5.7
I tell	8	6	1.5
I think	74	21	48.9
I thought	30	13	12.3
I told	17	7	3.8
I use	7	5	1.1
I want	151	20	95
I wanted	5	3	0.5
I was	49	17	26.2
I watch	5	4	0.6
I went	21	13	8.6
I will	21	10	6.6
I wish	7	5	1.1
I won	6	3	0.6
I wonder	12	6	2.3
I won't	31	15	14.6
I would	12	7	2.7
I wouldn't	11	5	1.7
if he	10	8	0.1
if I	27	13	0.6
if it	18	10	0.3
if she	9	4	0.06
if there	5	3	0.02
if they	7	7	0.2
if we	14	10	0.2
if you	84	18	2.4
in a	42	14	3.6
in an	8	7	0.3
in and	12	8	0.6
in case	6	4	0.1
in for	6	3	0.1
in her	7	5	0.2
in here	35	14	3
in it	32	14	2.7
in mine	5	4	0.1
in my	37	16	3.6
in our	14	8	0.7
in that	22	11	1.5
in the	205	21	26.1
in there	94	17	9.7
in this	17	9	0.9
in your	21	16	2
into a	5	4	0.01
into it	14	8	0.05
into the	14	7	0.05
into there	7	4	0.01
is a	25	10	11.4
is going	7	4	0.1
is he	6	4	0.1
is in	5	3	0.07
is it	83	18	6.8
is just	5	4	0.09
is my	13	5	0.3
is not	9	6	0.2
is on	7	6	0.2
is that	56	14	3.6
is the	31	17	2.4
is this	14	8	0.5
is what	6	5	0.1
is your	10	6	0.3
isn't he	5	3	0.01
isn't it	23	12	0.1
it a	5	4	0.4
it again	16	8	2.4
it all	13	7	1.7
it and	18	11	3.7
it at	11	8	1.6
it away	6	5	0.6
it back	25	10	4.6
it because	5	4	0.4
it come	6	5	0.6
it comes	7	5	0.6
it could	5	5	0.5
it does	6	5	0.6
it doesn't	24	15	6.7
it down	17	10	3.1
it for	16	11	3.3
it gets	6	5	0.6
it go	10	6	1.1
it goes	21	11	4.3
it has	9	4	0.7
it in	57	17	17.9
it is	105	17	33
it isn't	19	7	2.5
it just	8	7	1
it like	8	7	1
it looks	10	8	1.5
it might	9	6	1
it must	10	7	1.3
it now	8	6	0.9
it off	36	9	6
it on	75	19	26.3
it out	34	13	8.2
it over	17	10	3.1
it right	15	9	2.5
it says	9	7	1.2
it then	5	4	0.4
it there	15	8	2.2
it to	28	12	6.2
it up	49	16	14.5
it was	53	16	15.7

Sequence	Freq.	No. of Speakers	Index
it wasn't	9	7	1.2
it will	8	5	0.7
it won't	12	8	1.8
it would	5	5	0.5
it yet	5	5	0.5
it'd (would)	10	5	0.9
it'll	21	10	3.9
it's (is)	421	22	167.9
it's (has)	43	15	11.9
I'd (had)	16	8	4
I'd (would)	16	8	4
I'll	400	22	277
I'm	627	21	414.6
I've	185	21	122.3
just a	19	8	0.4
just about	7	7	0.1
just for	5	3	0.04
just give	5	4	0.05
just go	5	5	0.06
just going	7	4	0.07
just got	10	6	0.1
just have	6	4	0.05
just leave	5	5	0.06
just like	6	3	0.04
just pretend	8	3	0.05
just put	8	6	0.1
just the	5	4	0.05
just went	6	5	0.07
keep it	12	8	0.03
keep on	6	6	0.01
keep that	6	5	0.01
keep this	6	4	0.01
know but	8	3	0.09
know how	33	15	1.9
know I	9	9	0.3
know if	7	5	0.1
know it	10	9	0.3
know that	10	8	0.3
know the	9	5	0.2
know them	5	3	0.06
know those	5	5	0.09
know what	71	15	4

Sequence	Freq.	No. of Speakers	Index
know when	10	6	0.2
know where	36	13	1.8
know why	10	6	0.2
know you	10	5	0.2
ladies are	5	4	0.01
last night	11	8	0.02
last one	7	4	0.02
last time	7	5	0.01
leave it	31	11	0.1
let go	5	4	0.02
let it	6	4	0.02
let me	30	11	0.3
let you	11	8	0.09
lets get	10	6	0.05
lets go	22	9	0.2
lets play	5	5	0.02
lets see	25	9	0.2
like a	34	17	1.3
like I	6	5	0.07
like it	21	9	0.4
like that	51	17	1.9
like the	5	4	0.04
like them	5	5	0.06
like this	34	13	1
like to	8	5	0.09
like you	7	6	0.09
little girl	5	3	0.02
little one (s)	12	7	0.08
long time	10	8	0.02
look at	82	21	4.9
look how	5	4	0.06
look I	16	7	2.3
look like	7	6	0.9
look out	7	3	0.5
look up	7	3	0.4
look what	34	13	9.2
look you	7	4	0.6
looking for	8	3	0.09
looks like	16	9	0.03
lots of	17	10	0.02
made it	8	6	0.01
made a	27	12	0.2

Sequence	Freq.	No. of Speakers	Index
make it	14	6	0.06
make sure	5	4	0.01
make the	7	5	0.03
make them	10	5	0.03
make you	6	4	0.02
may I	17	5	0.01
me a	21	12	1.1
me and	6	4	0.1
me back	5	4	0.09
me it	5	4	0.09
me that	6	6	0.2
me the	9	6	0.2
me to	20	11	1
me up	10	6	0.3
might be	18	10	0.08
might have	6	4	0.01
might watch	5	3	0.01
mum and (mom)	6	4	0.02
mum said (mom)	5	3	0.01
mummy can (mommy)	8	4	0.04
mummy I (mommy)	10	5	0.06
mummy look (mommy)	5	5	0.03
must be	17	11	0.03
my birthday	8	3	0.1
my book (s)	6	6	0.2
my car	5	5	0.1
my desk	5	4	0.09
my father	12	4	0.2
my finger	5	4	0.09
my friend (s)	10	8	0.4
my hand	9	7	0.3
my jumper (s)	6	5	0.1
my leg (s)	5	4	0.09
my little	7	5	0.2
my microphone	5	5	0.1
my mother	15	10	0.7

Sequence	Freq.	No. of Speakers	Index	Sequence	Freq.	No. of Speakers	Index	Sequence	Freq.	No. of Speakers	Index
my mummy (mommy)	7	4	0.1	not on	8	6	0.2	oh oh	11	6	0.3
my name	11	4	0.2	not playing	16	7	0.4	oh see	6	3	0.09
my neck	5	3	0.07	not that	13	10	0.4	oh that	14	10	0.7
my other	5	4	0.09	not the	12	8	0.3	oh the	8	3	0.1
my own	8	6	0.2	no there	7	5	0.1	oh there	6	5	0.2
my pencil	6	5	0.1	not to	6	6	0.1	oh we	8	6	0.3
my place	7	5	0.1	not your	7	6	0.1	oh well	11	6	0.3
my port (school bag)	9	8	0.3	now come	11	6	0.2	oh yes	37	17	3.3
my thing	7	6	0.2	now I	29	15	1.2	oh you	28	13	1.9
my turn	10	3	0.1	now it	7	4	0.07	okay I	9	4	0.2
name is	13	5	0.02	now we	12	6	0.2	on a	15	8	0.9
need a	7	6	0.01	now what	9	6	0.1	on all	6	4	0.2
never get	5	3	0.01	now you	21	9	0.5	on and	16	8	0.9
next one	10	3	0.01	of a	19	10	0.7	on here	11	7	0.6
next to	6	6	0.01	of here	5	4	0.07	on it	29	15	3.1
nine ten	10	3	0.01	of it	32	12	1.4	on lets	6	5	0.2
no because	5	4	0.2	of me	9	8	0.3	on me	23	12	2
no don't	13	5	0.5	of my	13	9	0.4	on mike	7	3	0.2
no get	5	5	0.2	of our	8	6	0.2	on mine	5	5	0.2
no he	8	5	0.3	of that	11	7	0.3	on my	26	13	2.4
no I	91	18	12.1	of the	72	16	4.2	on now	7	7	0.4
no it	40	9	2.7	of them	45	16	2.6	on that	22	10	1.6
no miss	18	3	0.4	of these	18	8	0.5	on the	159	22	25.2
no more	8	9	0.2	of this	19	10	0.7	on there	11	8	0.6
no no	8	5	0.3	of those	11	8	0.3	on this	12	7	0.6
no not	19	10	1.4	of water	6	5	0.1	on to	10	6	0.4
no she	10	6	0.4	of you	9	5	0.2	on top	9	7	0.5
no thank	5	3	0.1	of your	14	8	0.4	on we	8	6	0.4
no that	21	10	1.6	off and	5	5	0.04	on with	7	7	0.4
no the	5	5	0.2	off me	6	5	0.04	on you	26	14	2.6
no they	13	8	0.8	off now	10	5	0.07	on your	30	11	2.4
no we	9	8	0.5	off that	6	6	0.05	one and	28	13	2.9
no you	47	18	6.3	off the	11	9	0.01	one day	9	7	0.5
not a	24	11	0.9	oh boy	38	7	1.4	one do	9	5	0.4
not allowed	46	12	1.9	oh dear	5	4	0.1	one hundred	18	3	0.4
not going	29	12	1.2	oh don't	10	6	0.3	one I	7	6	0.3
not in	11	6	0.2	oh get	12	9	0.6	one in	6	5	0.2
not me	5	3	0.05	oh good	8	8	0.3	one is	7	6	0.3
not mine	7	5	0.1	oh I	59	16	4.9	one more	11	6	0.5
not my	8	6	0.2	oh it	14	11	0.8	one of	62	17	8.4
				oh look	16	9	0.8	one out	5	3	0.1
				oh no	39	13	2.6	one that	24	12	2.3

TWO-WORD SEQUENCES FREQUENTLY USED BY AUSTRALIAN CHILDREN, AGE 6½—ALPHABETICAL LISTING (cont.)

Sequence	Freq.	No. of Speakers	Index
one to	6	3	0.2
one too	6	4	0.2
one two	99	13	10.2
one up	6	3	0.2
one wrong	8	4	0.3
one you	8	5	0.3
one's (is)	14	9	1
only a	8	7	0.5
only do	6	4	0.03
only got	8	5	0.05
only one	5	5	0.03
only two	5	3	0.02
only you	6	4	0.03
or a	5	5	0.02
or I	7	5	0.02
or something	13	9	0.07
or you	5	5	0.02
other one	16	10	0.1
other side	7	5	0.02
other way	6	3	0.01
our car	5	3	0.01
our house	10	5	0.03
our place	7	5	0.02
out and	12	8	0.3
out here	10	6	0.2
out in	5	5	0.08
out of	86	18	4.9
out the	22	10	0.7
out there	13	9	0.4
out you	6	5	0.09
over and	8	4	0.05
over here	23	10	0.4
over it	12	5	0.1
over me	5	4	0.03
over the	13	6	0.1
over there	37	14	0.8
over to	6	4	0.04
picture of	11	7	0.01
play this	5	3	0.01
play with	37	10	0.4
plus four	14	3	0.01

Sequence	Freq.	No. of Speakers	Index
put all	7	7	0.1
put it	91	18	4.3
put me	5	5	0.07
put my	14	9	0.3
put on	5	3	0.04
put that	20	11	0.6
put the	30	16	1.3
put them	26	11	0.8
put this	11	6	0.2
put your	20	8	0.4
read that	16	5	0.01
ready to	7	6	0.01
right down	6	4	0.02
right in	6	4	0.02
right now	5	4	0.02
right there	6	3	0.02
right up	5	5	0.03
said I	8	8	0.4
said it	8	6	0.04
said that	9	8	0.06
said you	7	5	0.03
saw a	7	4	0.01
say anything	5	4	0.02
say it	13	7	0.1
say something	14	5	0.08
say that	13	5	0.08
say to	5	3	0.02
say you	5	4	0.02
see a	5	4	0.04
see how	8	4	0.07
see I	7	6	0.09
see if	14	7	0.2
see it	17	8	0.3
see that	25	13	0.7
see the	12	9	0.2
see there	5	4	0.04
see this	18	10	0.4
see what	14	8	0.2
see you	19	11	0.5
see your	6	3	0.04
seven and	7	4	0.01

Sequence	Freq.	No. of Speakers	Index
she can	9	6	0.1
she can't	5	4	0.04
she comes	6	4	0.05
she did	5	4	0.04
she does	5	4	0.04
she doesn't	8	6	0.1
she had	6	3	0.04
she has	8	5	0.08
she knows	7	5	0.07
she said	13	8	0.2
she wants	5	4	0.04
she was	6	5	0.06
she won't	7	3	0.05
she'll	5	3	0.03
she's (is)	53	17	1.9
she's (has)	16	9	0.3
should be	14	9	0.03
should have	5	5	0.01
show them	5	4	0.01
show you	28	11	0.1
shut up	16	7	0.02
sit down	17	10	0.05
sit here	8	7	0.02
six seven	14	5	0.03
so I	21	12	0.3
so they	6	4	0.02
so we	5	4	0.02
so you	6	5	0.03
some kid (s)	8	5	0.05
some more	19	8	0.2
some of	19	11	0.3
someone else	8	5	0.01
something else	11	5	0.05
something like	6	3	0.02
sometimes I	9	6	0.01
stay down	5	4	0.01
stay here	8	6	0.02
stay out	5	4	0.01
stay up	7	5	0.01
stop it	16	10	0.04
take a	9	6	0.07

TWO-WORD SEQUENCES FREQUENTLY USED BY AUSTRALIAN CHILDREN, AGE 6½—ALPHABETICAL LISTING (cont.)

Sequence	Freq.	No. of Speakers	Index	Sequence	Freq.	No. of Speakers	Index	Sequence	Freq.	No. of Speakers	Index
take my	6	4	0.03	that thing	24	11	3.2	the front	14	7	1.5
take one	13	5	0.08	that to	6	6	0.4	the gate (s)	6	5	0.4
take that	5	4	0.03	that up	6	5	0.4	the girl (s)	12	8	1.4
take the	18	10	0.2	that was	23	12	3.3	the ground	9	5	0.7
take them	7	6	0.05	that way	18	10	2.2	the head	15	7	1.6
take this	26	12	0.4	that we	5	5	0.3	the house	15	6	1.3
take two	6	4	0.03	that what	6	4	0.3	the kid (s)	5	3	0.2
take you	5	5	0.03	that won't	5	5	0.3	the lady (s)	20	8	2.4
take your	6	5	0.04	that word	20	10	2.4	the last	12	8	1.4
talk in	9	8	0.04	that you	10	9	1.1	the leader	10	3	0.4
talk into	13	6	0.04	that your	8	6	0.6	the little	15	10	2.2
talk through	13	4	0.03	that's (is)	367	22	97.5	the man	13	7	1.4
talk to	8	8	0.03	that's (has)	6	5	0.4	the matter	7	5	0.5
tape recorder	26	8	0.07	the air	6	4	0.4	the microphone	18	7	1.9
tell me	11	9	0.05	the answer (s)	11	4	0.7	the middle	10	9	1.3
tell them	8	4	0.02	the back	19	11	3.4	the mike	7	5	0.5
tell you	20	9	0.09	the ball	6	6	0.5	the morning	7	6	0.6
ten eleven	7	4	0.02	the battery (s)	7	3	0.3	the next	17	6	1.5
thank you	44	14	0.2	the bell	10	3	0.4	the noise	9	3	0.4
that all	6	5	0.4	the best	19	7	2	the one (s)	37	15	8.2
that and	13	9	1.4	the big	13	7	0.3	the only	5	5	0.4
that big	19	9	2.1	the biggest	10	5	0.7	the other (s)	67	19	18.8
that came	6	4	0.3	the bin (s)	5	3	0.2	the people	8	5	0.6
that for	17	11	2.3	the blue	6	4	0.3	the picture (s)	5	3	0.2
that I	17	11	2.3	the boat (s)	8	5	0.6	the rest	6	4	0.3
that in	6	5	0.4	the book (s)	11	8	1.3	the road	12	5	0.9
that is	10	7	0.8	the bottom	10	6	0.9	the room	6	3	0.3
that isn't	5	5	0.3	the boy (s)	6	4	0.3	the rubbish	7	5	0.5
that little	10	7	0.8	the bridge	7	3	0.3	the same	11	7	1.1
that looks	8	5	0.5	the bus (s)	17	6	0.4	the school	7	5	0.5
that means	9	5	0.5	the car	15	8	1.7	the second	9	4	0.5
that mine	6	5	0.4	the cat	8	3	0.3	the shop (s)	6	5	0.4
that much	5	5	0.3	the chair (s)	9	6	0.8	the side	8	6	0.7
that off	7	7	0.6	the coat (s)	7	3	0.3	the swing	12	4	0.7
that on	8	6	0.6	the day (s)	5	5	0.4	the table (s)	13	8	1.6
that one	158	20	38.2	the dirt	7	5	0.5	the tape	25	7	2.6
that out	7	6	0.5	the dog	16	4	1	the teacher (s)	14	7	0.2
that say	5	4	0.2	the door (s)	23	12	4.1	the thing (s)	28	11	4.6
that side	5	3	0.2	the end	16	5	1.2	the three	6	5	0.4
that tape	6	5	0.4	the fire	9	3	0.4	the time	19	7	2
that the	6	3	0.2	the first	15	8	1.8	the toilet	13	7	1.4
that there	5	4	0.2	the floor	6	5	0.4	the top	15	9	2

Sequence	Freq.	No. of Speakers	Index
the tree (s)	10	3	0.4
the truck	8	3	0.3
the two	6	4	0.3
the water	10	6	0.9
the way	24	7	2.5
the whole	12	6	1.1
the window	15	8	1.8
the wire (s)	5	3	0.2
the word (s)	5	4	0.3
the wrong	8	7	0.8
them all	6	4	0.06
them back	6	6	0.09
them down	5	4	0.05
them I	5	3	0.04
them in	17	10	0.4
them on	9	7	0.2
them out	5	4	0.05
them over	5	3	0.04
them up	19	7	0.3
then he	10	5	0.06
then I	15	9	0.3
then it	7	5	0.04
then they	12	9	0.1
then we	8	5	0.05
then you	16	6	0.1
there and	38	15	3.4
there but	5	4	0.2
there for	8	7	0.3
there he	6	4	0.1
there is	5	3	0.09
there it	15	9	0.8
there was	21	6	0.8
there we	5	4	0.1
there you	7	7	0.3
there's	125	19	14.1
these are	8	7	0.04
these things	5	4	0.01
they are	20	8	0.6
they can	30	9	1
they can't	9	8	0.3
they come	5	4	0.08
they do	9	5	0.2

Sequence	Freq.	No. of Speakers	Index
they don't	6	5	0.1
they got	12	6	0.3
they had	6	5	0.1
they hear	7	4	0.1
they just	5	4	0.08
they put	11	7	0.3
they were	16	10	0.6
they won't	5	5	0.09
they'll	14	6	0.3
they're	130	20	9.9
they've	17	8	0.5
thing in	6	4	0.03
thing off	7	4	0.04
thing on	5	4	0.03
thing that	6	5	0.04
thing up	6	3	0.03
things on	9	3	0.04
think I	22	10	0.2
think it	18	13	0.2
think so	5	4	0.02
think that	9	8	0.06
think they	5	5	0.02
think you	7	6	0.04
this afternoon	5	4	0.1
this book	7	3	0.1
this for	8	4	0.2
this is	91	19	9
this morning	10	8	0.4
this off	17	8	0.7
this on	19	9	0.9
this one	66	18	6.2
this page	7	5	0.2
this stuff	7	5	0.2
this thing	19	9	0.9
this time	20	8	0.8
this way	10	7	0.4
this word	10	4	0.2
those things	7	6	0.02
those two	7	4	0.01
thought you	10	6	0.01
three four	68	12	1.4
through that	10	4	0.01

Sequence	Freq.	No. of Speakers	Index
through the	10	7	0.02
through there	8	5	0.01
throw it	23	8	0.03
till I	12	5	0.01
time I	15	12	0.2
to be	52	17	12.1
to bed	31	11	4.7
to bring	7	6	0.6
to catch	9	7	0.9
to come	16	8	1.8
to cut	5	4	0.3
to do	114	21	32.8
to draw	9	7	0.9
to drive	9	5	0.6
to eat	10	8	1.1
to find	9	7	0.9
to get	114	21	32.8
to give	12	8	1.3
to go	132	20	36.2
to have	50	15	10.3
to hear	15	4	0.8
to here	10	6	0.8
to him	6	5	0.4
to keep	11	7	1.1
to know	8	6	0.7
to leave	9	5	0.6
to make	37	13	6.6
to me	32	14	6.2
to my	11	9	1.4
to number	6	3	0.3
to one	6	4	0.3
to our	7	5	0.5
to pay	6	4	0.3
to play	64	16	14
to put	38	16	8.3
to read	8	4	0.4
to rub	5	4	0.3
to run	6	3	0.3
to say	19	13	3.4
to school	30	15	6.2
to see	26	14	5
to show	7	5	0.5

Sequence	Freq.	No. of Speakers	Index	Sequence	Freq.	No. of Speakers	Index	Sequence	Freq.	No. of Speakers	Index
to sit	13	6	1.1	up and	24	12	1.3	was the	8	6	0.09
to sleep	6	6	0.5	up at	8	6	0.2	watch it	11	8	0.03
to stay	19	11	2.9	up here	30	13	1.8	watch out	7	6	0.01
to take	47	15	9.7	up in	25	14	1.6	watch this	8	6	0.01
to talk	16	12	2.6	up like	6	5	0.1	we are	15	7	0.5
to tell	18	8	2	up now	7	5	0.2	we can	25	11	1.3
to that	8	7	0.8	up on	9	6	0.3	we can't	6	5	0.08
to the	69	17	16.1	up that	8	4	0.2	we could	7	5	0.2
to them	8	5	0.6	up the	11	8	0.4	we didn't	6	4	0.1
to there	8	6	0.7	up there	71	18	6	we do	21	11	1.1
to this	9	6	0.7	up to	56	14	3.7	we don't	13	9	0.5
to throw	6	6	0.5	up with	6	6	0.2	we get	10	7	0.3
to try	9	6	0.7	up you	5	5	0.1	we go	21	11	1.1
to turn	9	5	0.6	us it	8	3	0.01	we going	7	6	0.2
to use	8	6	0.7	use it	6	4	0.01	we got	22	11	1.1
to wait	9	5	0.6	use that	7	4	0.01	we had	9	5	0.2
to wear	13	8	1.4	use your	7	4	0.01	we have	28	11	1.4
to work	8	5	0.6	very good	14	9	0.03	we haven't	5	4	0.09
to write	12	5	0.8	wait a	8	4	0.01	we know	5	5	0.1
to you	10	8	1.1	wait for	15	9	0.06	we might	6	3	0.08
to your	9	6	0.7	wait on	19	7	0.06	we need	7	3	0.1
today is	5	3	0.01	wait there	10	5	0.02	we put	7	4	0.1
told me	15	9	0.03	wait till	8	6	0.02	we saw	7	3	0.1
told you	6	5	0.01	wait until	5	3	0.01	we want	9	6	0.3
too hard	5	4	0.02	want a	13	8	0.3	we were	14	7	0.5
too many	9	5	0.04	want it	24	11	0.8	we won't	5	3	0.07
too much	9	5	0.04	want me	9	7	0.2	well I	28	12	0.5
too strong	5	3	0.01	want my	8	8	0.2	well it	9	5	0.07
top of	12	9	0.01	want some	8	5	0.1	well look	5	4	0.03
touch it	13	8	0.01	want that	5	3	0.05	well they	6	3	0.03
try and	15	8	0.02	want this	8	3	0.07	well you	23	10	0.3
try it	8	7	0.01	want to	237	21	15.4	went down	8	7	0.03
turn it	18	7	0.07	want you	6	5	0.09	went to	14	9	0.07
turn that	6	5	0.02	wanted to	11	7	0.01	were going	8	5	0.02
two lady (s)	12	3	0.1	wants to	19	13	0.07	were you	6	3	0.01
two more	13	5	0.2	was a	27	12	0.6	we'd (had)	6	5	0.1
two of	6	4	0.07	was going	12	8	0.2	we'd (would)	9	3	0.1
two three	95	13	3.6	was in	14	12	0.3	we'll	55	14	3.6
under the	12	9	0.02	was it	8	8	0.1	we're	83	15	5.8
under there	7	5	0.04	was just	6	6	0.07	we've	40	13	2.4
until I	5	3	0.01	was only	5	3	0.03	what a	11	6	0.5
up a	8	6	0.8	was that	8	7	0.1	what about	13	5	0.5

TWO-WORD SEQUENCES FREQUENTLY USED BY AUSTRALIAN CHILDREN, AGE 6½—ALPHABETICAL LISTING (cont.)

Sequence	Freq.	No. of Speakers	Index	Sequence	Freq.	No. of Speakers	Index	Sequence	Freq.	No. of Speakers	Index
what are	36	12	3	where's (has)	5	4	0.07	you a	9	7	1.3
what can	5	4	0.1	which is	7	5	0.01	you all	6	3	0.4
what did	32	12	2.7	which one	31	6	0.05	you and	15	8	2.5
what do	28	14	2.8	who wants	22	7	0.1	you are	27	15	8.4
what does	9	4	2.6	who's (is)	21	12	0.2	you aren't	7	4	0.6
what else	5	3	0.1	why can't	7	5	0.2	you be	8	6	1
what for	5	4	0.1	why did	10	7	0.08	you better	12	11	2.7
what happened	14	9	0.9	why do	14	8	0.1	you bring	6	3	0.4
what have	6	6	0.3	why don't	15	9	0.2	you call	6	5	0.6
what he	8	4	0.2	why I	8	7	0.06	you can	131	21	56.9
what I	63	16	7.1	will be	12	10	0.1	you can't	32	11	7.3
what is	30	11	2.3	will I	22	8	0.2	you come	13	10	2.7
what it	15	9	1	will we	7	4	0.02	you could	13	5	1.3
what sort	5	4	0.1	will you	19	11	0.2	you did	11	8	1.8
what the	6	6	0.3	with a	17	7	0.2	you didn't	11	9	2.1
what they	6	5	0.2	with her	6	3	0.03	you do	45	13	12.1
what time	6	6	0.3	with it	21	9	0.3	you doing	16	9	3
what was	7	5	0.3	with me	22	9	0.3	you done	9	4	0.8
what we	11	8	0.6	with my	9	6	0.09	you don't	68	18	25.3
what would	7	5	0.3	with that	8	4	0.05	you get	58	17	20.4
what you	26	11	2	with the	35	14	0.8	you give	9	5	0.9
what's (is)	159	18	20.1	with this	11	8	0.2	you go	48	17	16.9
when daddy	5	3	0.03	with us	9	6	0.09	you going	41	17	14.4
when he	9	6	0.1	with you	7	5	0.06	you got	88	17	30.9
when I	68	18	2.2	with your	5	3	0.02	you had	10	7	1.4
when it	24	8	0.4	won't be	17	9	0.1	you have	60	19	23.6
when the	7	6	0.08	won't let	6	4	0.02	you haven't	23	11	5.2
when we	21	10	0.4	would be	7	6	0.02	you hear	31	8	5.1
when you	43	15	1.2	would you	15	8	0.05	you help	6	6	0.8
where are	11	7	0.3	wouldn't be	5	3	0.01	you just	26	12	6.5
where do	10	5	0.2	wouldn't have	8	3	0.01	you keep	5	5	0.5
where does	5	3	0.05	wouldn't it	5	4	0.01	you know	140	19	55
where I	15	8	0.4	yes a	6	2	0.09	you like	15	8	2.5
where is	33	12	1.3	yes and	12	7	0.6	you lose	5	3	0.3
where it	10	7	0.2	yes but	26	13	2.6	you make	6	4	0.5
where my	5	4	0.07	yes I	55	16	6.8	you mean	14	8	2.3
where that	6	5	0.1	yes it	19	12	1.8	you might	5	4	0.4
where the	16	8	0.4	yes miss	26	4	0.8	you move	5	3	0.3
where they	9	7	0.2	yes that	10	5	0.4	you mummy	5	4	0.4
where you	11	8	0.3	yes there	5	4	0.2	you must	5	4	0.4
where'd (did)	11	6	0.2	yes we	13	6	0.6	you need	11	8	1.8
where's (is)	89	18	5.4	yes you	31	10	2.4	you never	7	4	0.6

Sequence	Freq.	No. of Speakers	Index
you on	5	3	0.3
you only	8	5	0.8
you out	8	6	1
you please	5	3	0.3
you put	33	14	9.6
you read	11	3	0.7
you right	6	4	0.5
you run	5	5	0.5
you said	14	9	2.6
you saw	7	3	0.5
you say	24	11	5.5
you see	35	12	8.7
you should	10	6	1.2
you sit	5	4	0.4
you spell	16	5	1.7
you take	13	8	2.2
you talk	14	6	1.8
you tell	6	4	0.5
you the	6	4	0.5
you think	20	8	3.3
you throw	5	3	0.3
you to	11	8	1.8
you told	6	3	0.4
you turn	7	4	0.6
you two	12	5	1.2
you up	14	8	2.3
you use	5	5	0.5
you wait	5	3	0.3
you want	83	19	32.6
you wanted	5	4	0.4
you watch	8	4	0.7
you were	16	9	3
you when	5	3	0.3
you won't	14	8	2.3
you wouldn't	7	5	0.7
your car (s)	12	4	0.1
your chair	5	3	0.04
your ear (s)	6	5	0.09
your eyes	7	5	0.06
your finger (s)	5	4	0.06
your foot	10	5	0.1
your hand (s)	15	10	0.4
your head	8	3	0.07
your mark (s)	14	4	0.2
your pencil	5	5	0.07
your place	6	4	0.07
your rubber	5	4	0.06
your turn	11	3	0.1
you'd (had)	11	4	0.9
you'd (would)	9	5	0.9
you'll	52	16	17.2
you're	120	21	82.5
you've	44	14	12.8
's the	126	19	30
'd (had) better	28	11	0.05
'd (would) be	8	7	0.02
'd (would) like	13	7	0.03
'll be	53	15	3.7
'll come	7	6	0.2
'll do	35	12	2
'll get	33	12	1.8
'll give	8	6	0.2
'll go	39	14	2.6
'll have	61	18	5.1
'll just	16	10	0.7
'll let	6	4	0.08
'll make	10	6	0.3
'll never	5	3	0.07
'll only	11	4	0.2
'll put	23	10	1.1
'll say	5	4	0.09
'll see	9	7	0.3
'll show	26	11	1.3
'll take	23	9	1
'll talk	5	4	0.09
'll tell	20	10	0.9
'll try	5	4	0.09
'm a	14	8	0.5
'm coming	10	5	0.2
'm doing	19	9	0.8
'm finished	8	5	0.2
'm getting	17	9	0.7
'm going	101	20	18.4
'm having	4	4	0.3
'm in	6	3	0.09
'm just	8	6	0.2
'm not	98	19	9
'm on	6	3	0.09
'm only	10	5	0.2
'm playing	6	6	0.2
' sitting	7	4	0.1
'm telling	14	5	0.3
'm the	27	7	0.9
'm up	20	7	0.7
'm waiting	5	3	0.07
're a	16	9	0.5
're doing	6	5	0.09
're going	71	17	3.8
're having	8	4	0.1
're in	13	10	0.5
're just	5	5	0.08
're not	58	13	2.4
're on	8	5	0.1
're only	7	5	0.1
're still	6	4	0.07
're the	14	7	0.3
're up	15	4	0.2
's a	152	21	40
's all	19	13	3.1
's alright	6	6	0.5
's an	7	4	0.4
's another	15	9	1.7
's coming	12	8	1.2
's Diane	7	4	0.4
's down	7	6	0.5
's easy	9	6	0.7
's for	8	6	0.6
's getting	6	3	0.2
's going	48	15	9
's good	7	4	0.4
's hard	8	5	0.5
's her	8	7	0.7
's his	7	6	0.5
's how	7	4	0.4
's in	29	13	4.7
's it	13	7	1.2

TWO-WORD SEQUENCES FREQUENTLY USED BY AUSTRALIAN CHILDREN, AGE 6½—ALPHABETICAL LISTING (cont.)

Sequence	Freq.	No. of Speakers	Index
's just	14	7	1.2
's like	8	7	0.7
's me	5	3	0.2
's mine	26	10	3.3
's my	50	16	10
's not	83	18	18.7
's off	10	3	0.4
's on	35	11	4.8
's one	20	9	2.3
's only	27	9	3
's our	7	3	0.3
's out	5	5	0.3
's ready	9	3	0.3
's real	5	4	0.3
's really	6	4	0.3
's right	17	9	1.9
's some	13	9	1.5
's something	8	6	0.6
's that	91	18	20.5
's the	126	19	30
's there	7	3	0.3
's this	22	9	2.5
's too	10	8	1
's turned	5	5	0.3
's two	12	8	1.2
's up	9	7	0.8
's what	39	12	5.9
's where	13	9	1.5
's why	13	9	1.5
's wrong	10	5	0.6
's your	26	12	3.9
's (has) got	84	17	1.1
's (has) been	13	9	0.09
've already	5	4	0.04
've been	9	7	0.1
've done	6	4	0.05
've finished	7	5	0.08
've forgotten	5	3	0.03
've got	182	21	8.6
've had	5	4	0.04
've only	7	6	0.09

AGE 2½—ALPHABETICAL LISTING

Sequence	Freq.	No. of Speakers	Index
got one of	6	3	16
have a look	9	4	9.4
he's a (is)	4	3	138.9
he's going (is)	20	3	699.8
he's (has) got	6	6	294.9
I got this	6	5	107.2
I like this	3	3	4.9
I want to	19	9	1985.5
in the box	3	3	11.3
it's a (is)	3	3	25.1
it's off (is)	10	3	83.5
I'm going	7	4	48.9
look at the	7	7	479.6
that's a (is)	14	6	1070.2
there you are	8	7	96.9
want to get	7	3	55.5
'm going to	3	2	0.2
's (has) got a	5	5	3.5
've got one	3	3	0.01

AGE 3½—ALPHABETICAL LISTING

Sequence	Freq.	No. of Speakers	Index
a big boy	3	3	2.9
a little bit	3	3	15.3
and I will	4	3	2.6
climb up here	4	3	0.05
cup of tea	6	3	0.01
do you want	7	4	15.9
do you know	3	3	6.8
don't know what	4	3	4.7
got a big	5	3	24.9
got a little	4	3	19.8
got to go	4	4	10.6
he's a (is)	5	5	43
he's going (is)	18	5	156
he's in (is)	4	3	20.4
he's (has) got	4	4	2.1
I can see	7	5	96
I don't know	18	8	537
I don't want	8	3	89
I got a	11	6	434.1
I got to	6	4	157.6
I haven't got	4	4	4.9
I know what	4	3	8.1
I show you	3	3	1
I want to	11	7	240.6
in the water	5	3	17.1
it's a (is)	12	6	111.1
it's not (is)	8	4	49.1
I'll come	3	3	31.3
I'll have	4	3	41.2
I'm going	30	13	4998.5
I'm not	9	7	806.8
I'm on	3	3	114.2
I've got	5	4	4.7
look at that	5	3	11.5
look at this	6	3	14
no that's (is)	8	6	9.2
one of these	3	3	1
put it in	5	4	2.2
that's a (is)	17	8	793.6
that's my (is)	6	5	174.9
that's the (is)	4	3	69.2
there you are	6	5	2.5
this is a	8	5	24.4
up in the	4	3	0.5
want it off	5	3	1.1
want to get	3	3	3.5
we got to	8	4	14.1
we're going	11	4	29.8
we've got	5	3	0.8
what's that (is)	5	4	1.9
'm going to	16	9	27.4
's (has) got a	4	4	0.2
've got a	3	3	0.1

THREE-WORD SEQUENCES FREQUENTLY USED BY AUSTRALIAN CHILDREN, AGE 4½—ALPHABETICAL LISTING

Sequence	Freq.	No. of Speakers	Index	Sequence	Freq.	No. of Speakers	Index
a big one	7	5	28.4	that's the	9	4	186
be in the	4	4	0.3	that's what (is)	10	6	310.4
can have a	4	4	1.2	the other one	3	3	3.7
can I have	4	3	0.7	there's some (is)	3	3	1.4
do you know	14	7	13.7	this is a	7	5	18.4
do you want	5	3	2.2	want to take	4	4	3.6
going to do	4	3	11	we have to	3	3	0.6
going to have	4	3	11	we saw a	4	3	0.6
he's (has) got	6	4	0.9	what I made	8	4	16.6
he's not (is)	5	3	7.1	what I'm	6	4	12.5
I can see	6	3	29.6	what's that (is)	7	4	10.3
I don't know	12	6	113.5	what's this (is)	5	5	9.1
I got a	6	5	107.1	why can you	6	4	0.02
I got gun	3	3	31.5	you have to	7	5	12.5
I had a	4	3	8.7	you know what	16	9	245.7
I had to	3	3	6.4	'm going to	20	11	84.7
I haven't got	3	3	1.3	's (has) got a	3	3	0.3
I think I	5	4	16.4	've got a	5	5	0.5
I want to	14	8	310.3				
in the morning	3	3	10.6				
is what I	6	3	1.6				
it has got	3	3	2.1				
it's a (is)	8	4	116.2				
it's going (is)	3	3	32				
it's not (is)	3	3	32				
I'll go	5	4	78.5				
I'll take	4	4	62.8				
I'm going	23	13	3707.2				
I'm making	4	4	256.4				
I'm not	5	4	245.5				
I've got	9	7	36.9				
know what I	3	3	6.5				
look after the	4	3	0.4				
look what I	13	5	8.7				
not going to	3	3	0.2				
on the road	3	3	4				
one of these	10	7	51.6				
one of those	4	3	2.1				
put it on	6	5	1.3				
take it off	4	3	0.2				
that's a (is)	17	9	793				
that's all I	3	3	45.6				

Sequence	Freq.	No. of Speakers	Index
a big fat	3	3	0.4
a little bit	14	8	8.4
all the big	3	3	0.1
all the time	9	6	0.8
all the way	5	4	0.3
and a girl (s)	4	4	1.1
and a six	3	3	0.6
and get it	8	4	0.9
and I can	4	4	3.3
and I don't	4	4	3.3
and I got	5	5	5.2
and I have	4	3	2.5
and I said	4	3	2.5
and I was	3	3	1.9
and it went	7	3	1.1
and it's (is)	9	6	2.9
and I'll	15	8	24.8
and I'm	15	9	27.9
and she was	4	4	0.5
and she's (is)	4	4	0.5
and that one	3	3	0.5
and that's (is)	18	8	7.9
and the other	3	3	0.4
and then I	6	4	1.3
and then they	3	3	0.5
and then you	4	4	0.9
and this is	5	4	0.3
and you and	3	3	1.1
and you can	4	3	1.4
and you get	3	3	1.1
and you got	5	3	1.8
and you're	4	4	1.9
are you doing	17	6	2.1
are you going	14	7	2.1
at the bottom	3	3	0.1
at the end	4	4	0.2
at the top	3	3	0.1
because I got	7	3	0.6
because it's (is)	12	4	0.3
because I'm	5	4	0.6
because I've	6	4	0.7
but I can	5	4	0.3
but I can't	7	5	0.6
but I don't	3	3	0.1
but I got	3	3	0.1
but it's (is)	7	5	0.1
but I'm	7	5	0.6
can do it	9	6	0.5
can I go	6	5	0.4
can I have	29	11	4.2
come on let's	16	6	8.3
come on name (person)	21	9	16.4
did you do	5	5	0.5
did you get	8	4	0.7
did you hear	5	3	0.3
did you say	8	5	0.8
did you see	12	5	1.2
do it for	4	3	0.6
do it like	7	5	1.7
do you do	10	5	4.3
do you have	7	4	2.4
do you know	16	8	11
do you like	4	3	1
do you think	13	5	5.6
do you want	32	13	13.8
don't know all	3	3	1.2
don't know how	8	5	5.6
don't know what	18	10	25.3
don't know where	6	5	4.2
don't want any	7	3	0.4
don't want it	6	5	0.5
don't want to	12	7	1.4
down there and	3	3	0.1
four five six	18	9	0.3
get in there	5	4	0.2
get in trouble	4	3	1
get it over	6	4	0.5
get out of	18	7	2.3
get up there	5	3	0.2
give me a	7	5	0.1
give me it	9	4	0.1
go and get	12	6	1.6
go on name (person)	3	3	0.1
go to school	3	3	0.2
got to the	6	5	0.6
go up and	4	4	0.2
going to be	16	8	27.6
going to beat	8	5	8.6
going to catch	3	3	1.9
going to do	12	7	18.1
going to get	29	9	56.3
going to give	9	6	11.7
going to go	6	5	6.5
going to have	20	9	38.8
going to make	16	6	20.7
going to play	5	3	3.2
going to put	9	7	13.6
going to see	5	3	3.2
going to take	12	4	10.4
going to tell	15	6	19.4
got a lot	3	3	5.3
got a new	4	3	7.1
got a sore	3	3	5.3
got one of	3	3	0.4
got one two	3	3	0.4
got to get	9	4	2.5
got to do	15	5	4.9
got to go	8	6	3.1
got to put	7	4	1.8
have a drink	8	5	2.3
have a little	4	4	0.9
have a look	16	5	4.6
have to do	13	8	13.6
have to get	16	9	18.9
have to go	9	5	5.9
have to have	3	3	11.2
have to leave	3	3	1.2
have to make	4	3	1.6
have to put	9	7	8.2
have to sit	5	3	2
have to stay	3	3	1.2
have to take	7	5	4.6

THREE-WORD SEQUENCES FREQUENTLY USED BY AUSTRALIAN CHILDREN, AGE 5½—ALPHABETICAL LISTING (cont.)

Sequence	Freq.	No. of Speakers	Index	Sequence	Freq.	No. of Speakers	Index	Sequence	Freq.	No. of Speakers	Index
have to turn	3	3	1.2	I had it	5	3	2.5	it for you	10	5	1.9
here you are	9	7	0.3	I had to	3	3	1.5	it in my	3	3	0.5
here's a (is)	4	4	0.3	I have to	27	12	54.5	it in the	7	6	2.5
he's a (is)	10	7	2.3	I haven't got	14	9	12.5	it on me	5	3	1.8
he's going (is)	5	5	1	I just got	3	3	0.8	it on the	7	5	4.3
he's got (has)	14	9	1.9	I know a	3	3	7.4	it to me	11	6	5.9
he's in (is)	4	4	0.6	I know because	6	4	19.8	it to you	7	6	3.8
I can do	18	8	106	I know how	5	4	16.5	it up in	4	3	1.6
I can get	5	4	14.7	I know that	8	5	32.9	it was a	8	4	4.3
I can go	5	4	14.7	I know what	10	7	59.6	it's a (is)	64	14	1146.3
I can hear	4	3	8.8	I like it	4	3	1.7	it's all (is)	10	6	76.8
I can read	5	4	14.7	I only got	4	3	0.9	it's already (is)	4	3	115.5
I can run	8	3	17.7	I only had	3	3	0.7	it's broken (is)	4	3	14.4
I can't do	14	8	55.9	I think I	27	11	99.2	it's called (is)	3	3	11.5
I can't find	8	3	12	I think it	5	3	5	it's going (is)	9	5	57.6
I can't get	6	4	12	I think she	3	3	4	it's good (is)	4	3	15.3
I can't make	3	3	4.5	I thought I	3	3	0.5	it's hot (is)	4	3	15.3
I can't use	5	3	7.5	I thought it	4	3	0.6	it's like (is)	3	3	11.5
I did so	3	3	2.1	I thought you	4	4	0.9	it's mine (is)	6	5	38.4
I did that	8	5	9.4	I want a	3	3	4	it's my (is)	4	4	20.5
I didn't get	4	3	3.7	I want some	3	3	4	it's not (is)	36	13	598.8
I didn't have	4	4	4.9	I want to	47	16	332.8	it's on (is)	8	6	61.5
I didn't see	3	3	2.8	I was going	6	4	5.9	it's only (is)	7	4	35.9
I didn't want	5	4	6.2	if I can	11	6	0.6	it's supposed (is)	5	3	19.2
I don't care	7	3	24.7	if I don't	4	3	0.1	it's that (is)	3	3	11.5
I don't have	7	6	49.4	if you can	8	3	0.4	it's the (is)	6	5	38.4
I don't know	108	15	1903.4	if you do	5	4	0.3	it's too (is)	4	4	20.5
I don't like	7	4	32.9	if you don't	8	5	0.6	it's up (is)	9	5	57.6
I don't think	6	4	28.2	if you want	12	6	1.1	it's your (s) (is)	5	4	25.6
I don't want	29	11	374.9	in a minute	7	6	0.9	it's (has) got	13	8	3.7
I go to	5	5	3	in my class	18	5	5.5	I'll be	15	6	154.3
I go up	4	3	1.5	in my hand	3	3	0.6	I'll do	12	7	144.1
I got a	34	13	456.4	in my port (school bag)	9	7	3.9	I'll drink	3	3	15.5
I got another	5	3	15.5	in the air	3	3	1.5	I'll get	31	10	531.3
I got four	4	4	16.5	in the box	6	4	4	I'll give	5	3	25.7
I got it	12	8	99.2	in the car	6	4	4	I'll go	20	9	308.6
I got one	18	11	204.5	in the house	5	5	4.2	I'll have	27	11	509
I got six	3	3	9.3	in the middle	4	3	2	I'll hold	7	5	60
I got this	4	3	12.4	in the morning	4	4	2.7	I'll just	4	3	20.6
I got to	25	8	206.6	in the water	7	4	4.7	I'll keep	3	3	15.5
I got two	4	3	16.5	in there and	3	3	0.5	I'll make	3	3	15.5
I had a	8	6	8.1								

THREE-WORD SEQUENCES FREQUENTLY USED BY AUSTRALIAN CHILDREN, AGE 5½—ALPHABETICAL LISTING (cont.)

Sequence	Freq.	No. of Speakers	Index	Sequence	Freq.	No. of Speakers	Index	Sequence	Freq.	No. of Speakers	Index
I'll put	20	8	274.3	look at all	5	3	0.6	on the roof	12	5	6.3
I'll read	12	3	61.7	look at my	17	7	4.5	one of the	4	3	0.4
I'll see	6	4	41.2	look at that	12	8	3.6	one of them	13	6	2.3
I'll show	14	7	168	look at the	11	6	2.5	one of these	3	3	0.3
I'll take	6	4	41.2	look at this	11	8	3.3	one of those	12	6	2.1
I'll tell	10	9	154.3	look I'll	5	4	0.1	one two three	61	11	49.2
I'll try	6	4	41.2	look what I	7	5	0.2	out of here	7	6	0.9
I'm a	13	7	260.2	look what name (person)	4	4	0.1	out of it	4	3	0.2
I'm doing	16	8	366.3	me and name (person)	4	3	0.1	out of my	5	4	0.4
I'm drawing	4	3	34.3	no I can	5	4	2	out of the	7	5	0.7
I'm five	3	3	25.8	no I can't	5	5	2.5	put it back	4	4	0.4
I'm getting	7	5	100.2	no I didn't	9	6	5.3	put it down	6	4	0.6
I'm going	126	17	6125.8	no I don't	9	6	5.3	put it in	10	7	1.8
I'm having	8	5	114.5	no I want	4	3	1.2	put it on	19	7	3.4
I'm hot	7	3	60.1	no I won't	6	5	3	put them in	9	5	0.2
I'm in	7	6	120.2	no it isn't	8	4	1.1	put this in	8	5	0.4
I'm just	5	4	57.2	no it's (is)	13	7	3.1	put this on	8	6	0.4
I'm making	5	5	71.5	no I'm	21	7	14.5	put your hand (s)	9	3	0.1
I'm not	69	15	2959.9	no you can't	5	3	0.7	she's a (is)	5	4	0.5
I'm putting	5	3	42.9	no you don't	7	5	1.7	she's not (is)	6	4	0.6
I'm sitting	3	3	25.8	no you won't	3	3	0.5	that and that	3	3	0.2
I'm sorry	3	3	25.8	no you're	8	5	2	that one's (is)	8	4	4.4
I'm taking	5	4	57.2	now I have	4	3	0.2	that was a	5	3	0.5
I'm telling	11	4	125.9	now I'll	7	4	0.5	that's a (is)	26	11	152.7
I'm the	11	8	251.8	now I'm	11	7	1.3	that's all (is)	12	9	57.7
I'm too	3	3	25.8	oh I can	4	4	1	that's for (is)	10	7	37.4
I'm trying	4	3	34.3	oh I can't	7	5	2.3	that's how (is)	9	8	38.5
I'm up	4	4	45.7	oh I don't	9	6	3.5	that's it (is)	3	3	4.8
I've been	8	6	29.8	oh I got	3	3	0.6	that's mine (is)	5	4	10.7
I've finished	4	3	7.4	oh I know	3	3	0.6	that's my (is)	20	8	85.5
I've got	61	12	453.5	oh I thought	3	3	0.6	that's name (person) (is)	13	5	34.7
I've never	4	3	7.4	oh I'll	5	3	1	that's not (is)	10	6	32.1
I've only	5	5	15.5	oh I'm	8	6	3.1	that's one (is)	5	4	10.7
I've used	3	3	5.6	oh that's (is)	12	8	1.1	that's only	3	3	4.8
know how many	4	3	0.1	on the back	3	3	0.9	that's right (is)	7	6	22.5
know how to	18	7	1.1	on the floor	4	3	1.2	that's the (is)	18	8	76.9
know what I	3	3	0.3	on the ground	8	6	5	that's what (is)	17	6	54.5
know what it	7	5	1.1	on the port (on the school bag)	3	3	0.9	that's where (is)	4	3	6.4
know where it	4	3	0.1					that's why (is)	6	3	9.6
know where the	5	4	0.2					that's your (is)	3	3	4.8
like that and	3	3	0.1								

THREE-WORD SEQUENCES FREQUENTLY USED BY AUSTRALIAN CHILDREN, AGE 5½—ALPHABETICAL LISTING (cont.)

Sequence	Freq.	No. of Speakers	Index
the back way	4	3	0.4
the other one	8	4	1.7
the other side	5	3	0.8
there's a (is)	27	11	26.9
there's no	8	5	3.6
there's one (is)	4	4	1.4
there's the (is)	5	3	1.4
there's two (is)	5	3	1.4
there's your	4	4	1.4
they're for	3	3	0.5
they're going	25	7	10.5
they're having	5	3	0.9
they're mine	3	3	0.5
they're not	9	9	4.9
they're the	6	5	1.8
think I'll	6	5	0.1
this is a	8	7	3.4
this is my	8	5	2.4
this is the	8	7	3.4
this is what	4	4	1
this one's (is)	9	6	3.1
three four five	28	10	2.3
to be a	5	5	2.2
to be in	3	3	0.8
to do it	9	6	5.2
to do that	11	7	7.4
to do the	5	4	1.9
to get a	3	3	1.4
to get in	4	3	1.9
to get it	8	6	7.6
to get the	6	3	2.8
to get up	4	3	1.9
to go and	6	5	3.6
to go down	3	3	1.1
to go in	5	3	1.8
to go on	4	3	1.4
to go to	15	10	18.1
to have a	8	5	3.4
to have one	3	3	0.8
to have some	4	3	1
to make a	10	6	1.9
to play with	10	7	4.1

Sequence	Freq.	No. of Speakers	Index
to put it	6	4	1.6
to put this	7	5	2.4
to see if	4	3	0.5
to see what	3	3	0.4
to take my	4	4	0.6
to the toilet	8	7	4.4
two three four	42	12	9.4
up and down	5	5	0.2
up the hill	4	3	0.1
up the top	4	3	0.1
want to do	7	4	1.2
want to get	6	5	1.2
want to go	7	7	3.3
want to have	10	4	1.7
want to know	4	4	0.7
want to look	3	3	0.4
want to play	17	7	4.9
want to see	8	7	2.3
want to tell	11	5	2.4
we have to	17	8	1.2
went to the	5	5	0.2
we'll have	6	4	0.3
we'll make	5	3	0.2
we're going	20	8	7.4
we're not	12	5	2.8
we've got	17	7	1.9
what are we	9	5	1.1
what are you	27	10	6.7
what I did	3	3	0.3
what I found	4	3	0.4
what I got	3	3	0.3
what I'm	8	3	0.7
what I've	4	3	0.4
what's that (is)	28	12	28.4
what's the (is)	13	8	8.8
what's this (is)	14	6	7.1
what's wrong (is)	3	3	0.8
where's my (is)	9	7	1
where's name (person) (is)	12	8	3.2
where's the (is)	15	10	2.5

Sequence	Freq.	No. of Speakers	Index
yes and I	5	4	0.5
yes and there	4	3	0.3
yes and you	3	3	0.2
yes and (name)	3	3	0.2
yes I am	6	5	2.4
yes I can	5	3	1.2
yes I got	4	3	0.9
yes I knew	3	3	0.7
yes I will	3	3	0.7
yes it has	3	3	0.3
yes it is	6	5	0.9
yes it's (is)	13	7	2.7
yes I'll	6	4	1.9
yes I'm	3	3	0.7
you are not	4	4	1.4
you can do	6	4	4.7
you can have	11	7	14.9
you can use	5	3	5.8
you can't do	3	3	0.8
you can't get	3	3	0.8
you can't see	3	3	0.8
you don't have	4	4	2.8
you don't know	9	6	4.8
you get a	4	4	1.2
you get it	5	3	1.1
you get up	3	3	0.7
you go and	4	4	1
you got a	6	5	2.9
you got to	18	9	15.6
you have a	4	4	2.2
you have to	38	12	60.3
you know I	3	3	2.3
you know that	7	4	7.2
you know the	3	3	2.3
you know what	18	6	57.5
you know where	3	3	2.3
you know why	4	4	4.1
you put it	4	4	0.5

THREE-WORD SEQUENCES FREQUENTLY USED BY AUSTRALIAN CHILDREN

AGE 5½—ALPHABETICAL LISTING (cont.)

Sequence	Freq.	No. of Speakers	Index	Sequence	Freq.	No. of Speakers	Index
you want to	21	6	7.9	's not allowed	3	3	1.2
you'll get	3	3	0.4	's not for	3	3	1.2
you'll have	6	4	0.9	's on the	8	5	0.6
you're a	14	7	59.4	's that word	7	3	1.6
you're doing	4	4	9.7	's the man	3	3	1.2
you're getting	3	3	5.5	's the matter	4	4	2.2
you're going	7	6	25.5	's the one	5	3	2
you're just	5	4	12.1	's the other	4	3	0.6
you're making	3	3	5.5	've got a	21	8	4.7
you're not	50	15	454.4	've got one	6	6	1
you're the	4	3	7.3	've got some	5	4	0.6
you've got	21	11	12.9	've got to	23	9	5.8
'll be the	4	4	0.2				
'll get a	3	3	0.2				
'll get it	4	3	0.2				
'll go and	7	4	0.3				
'll have a	10	5	0.9				
'll have to	15	9	2.3				
'll put them	3	3	0.1				
'm going to	69	18	27.2				
'm not allowed	16	4	1.6				
'm not going	9	7	1.6				
'm not playing	7	3	0.5				
're going to	44	10	9.3				
're not allowed	26	8	8.2				
're not going	8	6	1.9				
're not sup-posed	3	3	0.4				
's a big	9	7	18.4				
's a bit	5	4	5.8				
's a different	4	3	3.5				
's a good	9	4	10.5				
's a little	4	4	4.7				
's a microphone	7	4	8.2				
's all the	4	3	0.4				
's going for	3	3	0.7				
's going to	27	13	27.3				
's got a (has)	16	8	1.3				
's got the (has)	7	4	0.5				
's in grade	10	3	1.6				
's in the	4	4	0.9				
's not a	6	6	5				

THREE-WORD SEQUENCES FREQUENTLY USED BY AUSTRALIAN CHILDREN, AGE 6½—ALPHABETICAL LISTING

Sequence	Freq.	No. of Speakers	Index
a big one	6	4	0.8
a bit of	13	8	2.7
a drink of	5	3	0.1
a good girl	3	3	0.3
a good one	10	6	2.5
a hole in	5	4	0.1
a little bit	3	3	0.4
a little one	4	3	0.6
a long time	6	7	0.5
a look at	5	4	0.2
a lot of	3	5	0.3
a picture of	5	5	0.3
a tape recorder	5	6	0.3
all the time	13	6	1
and every time	8	4	0.1
and get him	3	3	0.3
and get it	7	5	1.3
and get my	7	4	1.1
and get one	3	3	0.3
and he said	4	4	0.4
and he's (is)	3	3	0.2
and I got	3	3	0.9
and I had	3	3	0.9
and I put	6	5	3.2
and I was	5	5	2.7
and I want	4	3	1.3
and it was	4	4	0.6
and it's (is)	12	7	3.1
and I'll	13	7	9.9
and I'm	11	8	9.5
and I've	6	6	3.9
and put it	6	6	0.5
and see if	4	4	0.1
and that one	14	5	4
and that's (is)	21	8	9.6
and the little	3	3	0.3
and the man	4	3	0.4
and the other	3	3	0.3
and then it	5	5	0.9
and then they	9	5	1.6
and then you	8	4	1.2
and there's (is)	11	8	0.9
and they're	6	5	0.7
and this is	5	5	0.1
and we'll	4	3	0.2
and we're	5	4	0.4
and you can	7	5	2.3
and you go	3	3	0.6
and you know	7	5	2.3
and you see	3	3	0.6
and you're	4	4	1.1
are going to	5	5	0.1
are you doing	15	9	3
are you getting	3	3	0.2
are you going	22	11	5.4
are you up	5	3	0.3
at the back	4	4	0.1
back in a	8	3	0.1
back in the	9	7	0.2
be able to	19	7	0.2
because I can't	6	3	0.1
because I don't	9	6	0.7
because I haven't	3	3	0.1
because it's (is)	7	7	0.1
because I'm	7	4	0.4
because they're	8	7	0.1
but I had	3	3	0.1
but I know	3	3	0.1
but I won't	4	3	0.1
but it's (is)	6	5	0.1
but I'm	14	11	1.1
can do it	9	5	0.3
can get in	3	3	0.1
can get it	3	3	0.1
can get up	3	3	0.1
can have it	6	4	0.1
can hear it	6	3	0.2
can hear me	14	3	0.5
can I do	5	5	2.1
can I get	5	4	1.6
can I go	14	7	8.1
can I have	46	15	56.8
can I put	5	4	1.6
can I see	5	3	1.2
can I take	6	3	1.5
can I use	5	3	1.2
can I watch	4	3	1
can we do	4	4	0.1
can we have	6	3	0.1
can you get	3	3	0.2
come on lets	6	5	1.7
come on we	5	3	0.9
come on you	6	4	1.3
come up here	7	4	0.1
did you do	6	6	0.7
did you get	13	8	2.1
did you have	5	3	0.3
did you hear	22	5	2.2
did you put	4	3	0.2
did you say	6	3	0.4
did you see	4	3	0.2
did you take	4	3	0.2
do I have	10	5	0.5
do it again	8	5	1.7
do it for	4	3	0.5
do it in	5	4	0.9
do it like	3	3	0.4
do it to	3	3	0.4
do that one	7	5	0.8
do you do	9	4	4.1
do you get	4	3	1.3
do you have	11	5	6.2
do you know	38	13	55.8
do you like	7	6	4.7
do you mean	3	3	0.9
do you need	4	3	1.3
do you spell	16	5	9
do you think	14	7	11.1
do you want	34	15	57.7
don't do it	7	4	0.1
don't do that	6	4	0.1
don't have to	22	10	1.9
don't know			
how	11	7	4.3

THREE-WORD SEQUENCES FREQUENTLY USED BY AUSTRALIAN CHILDREN, AGE 6½—ALPHABETICAL LISTING (cont.)

Sequence	Freq.	No. of Speakers	Index	Sequence	Freq.	No. of Speakers	Index	Sequence	Freq.	No. of Speakers	Index
don't know what	10	7	4	go to bed	23	8	5.6	got to take	6	4	1.4
don't know where	5	3	0.9	go to school	11	7	2.3	have a drink	6	5	1.3
don't like this	3	3	0.1	go to sleep	3	3	0.3	have a go	8	5	1.7
don't put it	5	5	0.1	go to the	11	7	2.3	have a look	16	7	4.7
don't touch it	6	4	0.1	go up and	3	3	0.1	have one of	7	4	0.1
don't want any	3	3	0.2	go up there	7	3	0.2	have to do	17	8	12.4
don't want it	5	4	0.5	going to be	24	13	57.8	have to draw	3	3	0.8
don't want to	35	13	11.4	going to bring	4	3	2.2	have to get	10	8	7.3
don't you do	3	3	0.2	going to do	30	12	66.7	have to give	4	3	1.1
don't you get	3	3	0.2	going to draw	3	3	1.5	have to go	27	10	24.5
don't you want	5	5	0.5	going to get	27	14	69.9	have to have	4	4	1.5
down there and	4	4	0.2	going to give	3	3	1.5	have to pay	5	3	1.4
down to the	7	5	0.2	going to go	24	7	31	have to put	4	3	1.1
five six seven	13	5	0.1	going to have	29	11	59	have to rub	3	3	0.8
for a long	3	3	0.1	going to make	9	6	9.8	have to say	3	3	0.8
for a minute	4	3	0.1	going to play	10	7	12.9	have to take	5	3	1.4
for a while	5	3	0.1	going to put	13	9	21.5	have to wear	8	5	3.6
four five six	26	7	0.6	going to say	3	3	1.5	have you been	3	3	0.1
get a new	3	3	0.1	going to school	3	3	1.5	have you done	3	3	0.1
get back in	4	4	0.1	going to see	10	9	16.6	have you got	23	12	4.9
get in the	13	7	0.8	going to stay	14	8	20.6	here it is	12	5	0.1
get in there	4	4	0.2	going to take	20	11	40.6	here's a (is)	10	7	1.5
get it on	3	3	0.2	going to talk	4	4	3.1	here's my (is)	10	6	1.3
get it out	7	4	0.7	going to tell	9	5	8.3	here's one (is)	3	3	0.2
get it right	3	3	0.2	going to the	3	3	1.5	here's some (is)	3	3	0.2
get out of	14	9	3.9	going to try	8	5	7.4	here's the (is)	6	6	0.8
get up there	3	3	0.1	got a big	4	3	0.9	he's a (is)	9	6	0.9
give me a	8	5	0.1	got a good	5	4	1.5	he's always (is)	3	3	0.1
give me the	7	5	0.1	got a little	3	3	0.6	he's going (is)	12	7	1.5
go and ask	3	3	0.2	got a micro-phone	7	3	1.6	he's not (is)	8	7	1
go and get	28	11	8.8	got a tail	3	3	0.6	he's (has) got	13	9	0.4
go and tell	3	3	0.2	got it on	3	3	0.3	how do you	34	14	2.4
go back in	4	4	0.1	got one two	3	3	0.1	how to do	8	5	0.1
go down and	6	6	0.3	got to be	9	5	2.7	I am not	3	3	0.6
go down the	3	3	0.1	got to do	8	7	3.4	I beat you	7	4	0.2
go down to	4	3	0.1	got to get	14	8	6.8	I brought it	4	3	0.2
go in the	4	4	0.1	got to give	4	3	0.7	I can carry	3	3	3.7
go on the	13	7	1.5	got to go	19	10	11.1	I can do	13	7	40.2
				got to make	6	4	1.4	I can get	9	6	23.4
				got to put	5	4	1.2	I can hear	8	5	17.5
				got to say	3	3	0.5	I can just	3	3	3.7
								I can make	7	5	15.3

Sequence	Freq.	No. of Speakers	Index
I can only	3	3	3.7
I can see	8	5	17.5
I can't do	4	4	3.6
I can't even	3	3	1.8
I can't find	6	4	5.1
I can't get	6	3	3.6
I can't hear	5	4	4.3
I can't see	9	6	11.6
I did it	5	5	3.4
I did not	6	6	5
I did that	4	3	1.6
I didn't say	4	4	2.5
I didn't want	3	3	1.3
I do now	3	3	0.9
I do some	3	3	0.9
I don't care	6	4	20.8
I don't have	10	6	53.6
I don't know	93	18	1499.3
I don't like	18	10	160.8
I don't need	3	3	7.4
I don't think	8	8	58.1
I don't want	46	16	659.6
I found it	6	4	0.7
I get home	3	3	1
I get it	5	4	2.3
I get up	4	3	1.3
I go and	8	7	11.9
I go down	4	3	2.5
I go like	3	3	1.8
I go to	21	8	35.5
I going to	8	6	0.6
I got a	30	11	241.1
I got four	3	3	6.1
I got it	27	15	295.7
I got one	9	6	38.8
I got that	5	4	14.5
I got the	13	6	56.9
I got this	3	3	6.1
I got to	17	9	111.5
I had a	6	4	2.6
I had to	10	7	7.8
I have a	19	11	104.7

Sequence	Freq.	No. of Speakers	Index
I have one	6	4	11.6
I have some	6	5	15
I have to	47	12	281.7
I haven't done	6	3	2.3
I haven't even	3	3	1.1
I haven't got	17	6	13.8
I haven't had	3	3	1.1
I know how	10	6	31.5
I know I	4	4	8.7
I know it	5	5	13.1
I know the	3	3	4.4
I know them	5	3	7.9
I know what	18	10	94.5
I know where	11	7	40.2
I know you	9	5	23.6
I like it	11	5	9
I like the	4	3	1.9
I like them	3	3	1.4
I might do	3	3	0.3
I put it	6	5	3
I put my	7	4	2.8
I put this	6	3	1.7
I said that	3	3	0.8
I saw you	4	3	0.3
I take this	5	4	0.3
I talk into	5	4	0.7
I tell you	4	3	0.1
I think I	15	8	35.2
I think it	12	9	31.8
I think that	5	4	5.9
I think they	4	4	4.9
I think you	3	3	2.4
I thought it	4	3	0.9
I thought that	3	3	0.6
I thought you	7	5	2.6
I told you	3	3	0.2
I want a	6	4	13.3
I want it	7	5	20
I want my	7	7	27.6
I want some	4	3	6.7
I want the	3	3	4.8
I want to	88	18	905.6

Sequence	Freq.	No. of Speakers	Index
I was going	4	4	2.6
I was in	5	5	3.9
I was just	4	4	2.6
I went down	4	3	0.6
I won't be	6	4	2
I won't let	3	3	0.7
I would like	4	3	0.2
if it's (is)	7	4	0.1
if you can	6	3	0.2
if you do	3	3	0.1
if you don't	5	5	0.4
if you go	4	3	0.2
if you want	16	8	1.8
in a minute	18	8	3.1
in my port (school bag)	6	5	0.6
in that one	5	3	0.1
in the after-noon	3	3	1.3
in the air	6	4	3.7
in the car	4	4	2.6
in the head	5	3	2.3
in the kitchen	3	3	1.3
in the middle	5	5	3.9
in the morning	5	4	3.1
in the other	5	4	3.1
in the pocket	3	3	1.3
in the rubbish	5	3	2.3
in there and	9	8	4.2
in this one	4	3	0.1
is it a	4	4	0.5
is that all	3	3	0.2
is that right	3	3	0.2
is that what	5	3	0.3
is that your	6	4	0.5
it back in	3	3	0.2
it back to	4	3	0.3
it doesn't mat-ter	7	7	2.9
it down there	3	3	0.2
it for you	4	4	0.3
it goes through	2	2	0.2

Sequence	Freq.	No. of Speakers	Index
it in my	6	4	2.5
it in the	12	8	10.4
it in there	9	5	4.8
it is a	4	4	3.3
it is not	6	4	4.6
it is on	5	3	3
it like that	3	3	0.1
it looks like	5	3	0.1
it might be	6	4	0.1
it must be	6	6	0.3
it on a	4	3	1.8
it on and	4	3	1.8
it on my	5	5	3.9
it on the	13	8	16.5
it over here	3	3	0.2
it over the	6	4	0.4
it to me	9	6	2
it up here	3	3	0.7
it was a	8	6	4.5
it was in	3	3	0.7
it'll be	5	4	0.5
it'll go	5	4	0.5
it's a (is)	46	16	743.9
it's all (is)	3	3	8.4
it's getting (is)	4	3	11.8
it's going (is)	20	8	80.6
it's hard (is)	6	5	30.2
it's in (is)	6	5	30.2
it's just (is)	8	4	31.9
it's like (is)	7	6	42.2
it's my (is)	5	5	25.2
it's not (is)	44	13	577.7
it's off (is)	8	3	23.5
it's on (is)	29	11	322.4
it's only (is)	16	7	112.5
it's really (is)	5	4	20.2
it's the (is)	5	4	20.2
it's too (is)	7	7	48.7
it's turned (is)	5	5	25.2
I'd (has) got	31	12	26.7
better	13	7	4
I'd (would)	12	6	1.7
like	27	11	495.8
I'll be	7	3	36
I'll bring	4	3	19.4
I'll come	32	11	587.2
I'll do	23	10	382.2
I'll get	8	6	80.3
I'll give	23	10	382.2
I'll go	36	15	900.2
I'll have	4	3	19.4
I'll hit	3	3	13.8
I'll just	11	7	127.4
I'll let	4	3	19.4
I'll make	6	4	38.8
I'll only	7	3	36
I'll pick	3	3	13.8
I'll put	18	9	268.7
I'll say	4	3	19.4
I'll see	5	4	33.2
I'll show	25	10	415.5
I'll sit	3	3	13.8
I'll take	22	9	329.6
I'll talk	4	3	19.4
I'll tell	20	10	332.4
I'm a	14	8	277.8
I'm allowed	4	4	41.5
I'm coming	10	5	124.4
I'm doing	20	9	447.7
I'm finished	8	5	99.5
I'm getting	17	9	381.4
I'm going	191	20	9531
I'm having	14	4	141
I'm hot	4	3	29
I'm in	6	3	45.6
I'm just	8	6	120.2
I'm looking	3	3	20.7
I'm nearly	3	3	20.7
I'm not	88	19	4170.6
I'm on	6	3	45.6
I'm only	10	5	124.4
I'm playing	6	6	91.2
I'm sitting	7	4	70.5
I'm sorry	4	3	29
I'm staying	3	3	20.7
I'm telling	14	5	174.1
I'm the	27	7	472.6
I'm trying	3	3	20.7
I'm up	20	7	348.2
I'm waiting	5	3	37.3
I've a	4	3	8.6
I've already	5	4	14.7
I've been	5	5	18.3
I've done	4	3	8.6
I've finished	6	5	22
I've forgotten	5	3	11
I've got	108	21	1669
I've had	3	3	6.1
I've made	3	3	6.1
I've only	4	3	8.6
I've seen	4	4	12.2
know how to	19	10	2.1
know what I	15	9	3.3
know what it	6	3	0.4
know what to	5	4	0.5
know what we	4	3	0.1
know where I	6	5	0.3
know where it	5	3	0.2
know where the	5	3	0.2
know where you	4	3	0.1
like a big	3	3	0.1
like that one	3	3	0.1
look at all	6	5	0.9
look at him	3	3	0.2
look at it	6	4	0.7
look at mine	3	3	0.2
look at my	8	5	1.2
look at that	6	4	0.7
look at the	11	9	2.9
look at this	12	7	2.5
look I'll	5	4	0.3
look what happened	5	3	0.8

THREE-WORD SEQUENCES FREQUENTLY USED BY AUSTRALIAN CHILDREN, AGE 6½—ALPHABETICAL LISTING (cont.)

Sequence	Freq.	No. of Speakers	Index
look what I	13	9	6.5
no I can	4	3	0.8
no I can't	5	4	1.5
no I didn't	6	4	1.7
no I don't	11	10	8
no I haven't	6	5	2.2
no I want	4	4	1.2
no I won't	6	5	2.2
no I'm	19	12	16.6
no I've	3	3	0.6
no it isn't	10	6	1
no it's (is)	21	6	2
no that's (is)	12	6	0.7
no they're	5	4	0.1
no we're	4	4	0.1
no you can't	5	4	0.8
no you don't	10	8	3
no you're	9	7	2.5
not allowed to	28	8	2.5
not going to	17	8	1
now I can	5	4	0.1
now I'll	7	6	0.3
now I'm	5	4	0.1
of the girl	3	3	0.2
of the thing	3	3	0.2
of the way	11	3	0.8
of them are	4	3	0.2
oh get out	6	3	0.1
oh I don't	3	3	0.2
oh I know	3	3	0.2
oh I want	3	3	0.2
oh I'm	3	3	0.2
oh it's (is)	6	6	0.2
oh look at	6	5	0.1
oh no I	6	4	0.4
oh that's (is)	7	7	0.2
oh you've	6	6	0.4
on and I	3	3	0.1
on my desk	4	3	0.2
on that side	5	3	0.1
on the back	3	3	1.3
on the bottom	4	3	1.8

Sequence	Freq.	No. of Speakers	Index
on the bus	12	6	10.8
on the chair	5	3	2.3
on the end	5	3	2.3
on the head	8	4	4.8
on the other	3	3	1.3
on the side	5	4	3
on the table	5	4	3
on the tape	4	4	2.3
on the thing	4	3	1.8
on the top	5	3	2.3
on top of	6	4	0.1
on your mark (s)	13	3	0.5
one and that	10	6	1
one do you	9	5	0.1
one of our	3	3	0.4
one of the	10	7	3.5
one of them	17	7	7.7
one of these	13	7	4.6
one of those	9	6	2.7
one two three	84	12	62.1
one's and (is)	4	4	0.1
out of here	4	4	0.5
out of it	7	6	1.2
out of my	5	3	0.4
out of that	3	3	0.2
out of the	25	9	6.6
out of there	4	3	0.3
out of this	11	5	1.6
out the window	5	4	0.1
play with it	6	4	0.1
play with me	8	4	0.1
put it back	15	7	2.7
put it in	18	11	5.1
put it on	29	14	10.3
put it there	6	3	0.5
put them in	10	6	0.3
put them on	5	4	0.1
she's a (is)	5	4	0.2
she's not (is)	6	4	0.3

Sequence	Freq.	No. of Speakers	Index
she's (has) got	11	5	0.1
some of them	7	6	0.1
take this off	6	5	0.1
that and I	3	3	0.1
that one and	11	5	12.6
that one that	9	4	8.4
that one wrong	3	3	1.9
that one's (is)	7	5	8
that's a (is)	43	15	378.2
that's all (is)	15	12	105.3
that's alright (is)	4	4	9.8
that's easy	7	5	20.5
that's good (is)	3	3	4.9
that's her (is)	3	3	4.9
that's his (is)	5	4	11.7
that's how (is)	7	4	16.6
that's it (is)	6	3	10.7
that's mine (is)	8	5	23.4
that's my (is)	18	10	105.3
that's not (is)	17	7	70.2
that's one (is)	3	3	4.9
that's only (is)	4	3	6.8
that's our (is)	5	4	11.7
that's right (is)	15	8	70.2
that's the (is)	42	13	320.6
that's what (is)	32	12	224.2
that's where (is)	12	8	56.5
that's why (is)	13	9	68.2
that's your (s)	12	8	56.5
that's (has) got	5	4	0.05
the end of	8	4	0.2
the first one	4	3	0.1
the last one	5	3	0.1
the next one	10	3	0.3
the one I	3	3	0.4
the one that	11	8	4.3
the other day	3	3	0.9
the other one	13	9	13.2
the other		5	4

Sequence	Freq.	No. of Speakers	Index	Sequence	Freq.	No. of Speakers	Index	Sequence	Freq.	No. of Speakers	Index
the other way	6	3	2.1	to come up	3	3	0.1	to put my	4	4	0.8
the rubbish bin	4	4	0.1	to do a	12	7	16.7	to put the	6	5	1.5
the tape recorder	3	3	0.1	to do it	11	4	8.5	to see it	3	3	0.3
the thing on	4	3	0.3	to do one	4	3	2.3	to stay here	5	4	0.3
the window and	3	3	0.1	to do some	5	4	3.9	to take it	9	5	2.6
then I'll	7	6	0.1	to do that	14	9	24.9	to take this	9	6	3.1
there and I	7	5	0.7	to do the	10	4	7.9	to talk into	3	3	0.1
there and they	3	3	0.2	to draw a	7	5	0.1	to the toilet	8	5	3.9
there and you	3	3	0.2	to get a	10	6	11.8	to try and	6	5	0.1
there it is	14	8	0.5	to get all	3	3	1.6	two three four	59	11	14.2
there was a	8	4	0.1	to get down	3	3	1.6	up in a	4	3	0.1
there's a (is)	25	13	27.6	to get in	6	4	4.6	up in the	13	8	1
there's another (is)	7	6	3.5	to get it	10	7	13.8	up in there	3	3	0.1
there's my (is)	8	3	2	to get my	4	4	3.3	up there and	6	4	0.7
there's one (is)	10	6	5.1	to get on	5	3	3	up there with	4	4	0.5
there's some (is)	8	5	3.4	to get one	4	4	3.3	up to here	5	5	0.6
there's something (is)	4	3	1	to get out	6	4	4.6	up to my	3	3	0.2
there's the (is)	13	8	8.9	to get something	5	4	4.7	up to the	8	3	0.5
there's two (is)	8	6	4.1	to get that	4	3	2.3	up to there	3	3	0.2
there's your (is)	3	3	0.7	to get the	10	7	13.8	want it to	7	6	0.1
they can hear	23	6	0.8	to get you	3	3	1.6	want to be	4	4	1.5
they're going	22	8	10.8	to get your	3	3	1.6	want to come	7	6	3.8
they're in	4	3	0.7	to give me	3	3	0.1	want to do	14	12	15.4
they're not	12	7	5.4	to go and	13	9	25.3	want to eat	3	3	0.8
they're on	3	3	0.5	to go away	3	3	1.8	want to get	18	10	16.6
they're still	5	3	0.9	to go back	4	3	2.5	want to go	28	9	23.1
they've got	10	5	0.2	to go down	8	4	6.9	want to have	11	6	6
this is a	13	6	4.5	to go in	5	4	4.3	want to make	8	4	2.9
this is going	3	3	0.5	to go on	9	4	8	want to play	33	12	36.6
this is how	4	4	0.9	to go out	3	3	2	want to read	4	4	1.5
this is my	10	4	2.2	to go to	16	11	39.8	want to see	6	4	2.2
this is the	15	8	6.5	to go up	9	6	11.6	want to take	9	6	4.9
three four five	44	11	4.1	to have a	14	10	8.6	want to tell	3	3	0.8
to be in	3	3	0.6	to have it	4	3	0.7	was going to	9	7	0.1
to be on	5	4	1.5	to have some	4	4	1	was in the	6	6	0.1
to be up	4	3	0.8	to have that	4	3	0.7	we can do	3	3	0.1
				to keep this	4	3	1	we don't want	4	4	0.1
				to make a	11	6	2.6	we go home	3	3	0.1
				to make it	7	4	1.1	we got a	5	4	0.1
				to play with	18	7	10.7	we got the	4	3	0.1
				to put a	3	3	0.4	we got to	4	4	0.1
								we have a	6	3	0.1

Sequence	Freq.	No. of Speakers	Index
we have to	13	7	0.8
we'll be	5	4	0.4
we'll go	6	6	0.8
we'll have	6	5	0.6
we'll just	4	4	0.4
we're going	30	11	11.7
we're not	5	3	0.5
we're the	3	3	0.3
we've got	32	13	6.1
what are they	8	4	0.6
what are you	29	11	5.8
what did he	5	4	0.3
what did you	18	9	2.6
what do you	23	14	5.2
what does that	3	3	0.1
what happened to	4	4	0.1
what I did	4	3	0.5
what I got	4	4	0.7
what is it	24	6	2
what it is	9	7	0.4
what I'm	18	7	5.4
what I've	5	5	1.1
what's a	7	4	3.4
what's her	3	3	1
what's in	11	8	10.7
what's that	65	17	133.7
what's the	23	9	25.1
what's this	16	9	17.5
when I get	11	8	1.2
when I put	4	4	0.2
when I want	3	3	0.1
when I was	6	6	0.5
when it's	13	6	0.2
when I'm	4	4	0.2
when you come	3	3	0.1
when you going	5	3	0.1
when you're	6	6	0.3
where do you	8	5	0.1
where is it	22	8	1.5
where is she	3	3	0.1
where is the	4	3	0.1
where it is	7	5	0.1
where's my	7	4	0.9
where's that	9	4	1.2
where's the	29	14	13
why don't you	13	9	0.1
yes I did	4	3	0.5
yes I do	5	3	0.6
yes I know	11	5	2.3
yes I'm	6	5	1.2
yes it is	6	5	0.3
yes it's (is)	16	10	1.7
yes you can	10	6	0.9
you be quiet	5	3	0.1
you can do	4	4	5.7
you can get	9	4	12.5
you can go	6	6	12.6
you can have	14	8	38.1
you can play	5	4	6.8
you can put	7	6	14.2
you can start	4	3	4
you can stay	3	3	2.8
you can take	5	4	6.8
you can use	11	4	14.8
you can't get	5	3	0.7
you can't hear	4	4	0.7
you come and	3	3	0.1
you come down	4	3	0.2
you do it	11	6	4.8
you don't have	13	9	17.7
you don't know	9	6	8.1
you don't need	4	4	2.5
you don't want	4	4	2.5
you get that	3	3	1
you get the	3	3	1
you get them	4	4	1
you get this	4	3	1
you get your	6		3.7
you give me	4	4	0.1
you go and	9	8	7.3
you go down	5	4	2
you going to	30	13	33.8
you got a	14	9	23.5
you got it	3	3	1.5
you got to	36	10	67.1
you have to	33	14	65.5
you haven't even	7	3	0.7
you haven't got	5	4	0.6
you know how	9	7	20.9
you know that	6	5	9.9
you know those	5	5	8.3
you know what	40	11	145.8
you know when	9	5	14.9
you know where	12	9	35.8
you know why	9	5	14.9
you put it	10	8	4.6
you said it	3	3	0.1
you said you	3	3	0.1
you take the	4	4	0.2
you up to	6	4	0.3
you want it	7	3	4.2
you want to	54	19	201.2
you were going	4	3	0.2
you won't be	4	4	0.2
you'd (had) better	10	4	0.2
you'll be	6	5	3.1
you'll break	3	3	0.9
you'll go	3	3	0.9
you'll have	17	10	17.2
you're a	16	9	71.8
you're doing	4	3	5.8
you're going	19	10	94

Sequence	Freq.	No. of Speakers	Index	Sequence	Freq.	No. of Speakers	Index	Sequence	Freq.	No. of Speakers	Index
you're just	5	5	12.4	's a good	13	6	20	've got a	30	12	18.6
you're not	39	13	255.7	's a little	6	4	5.6	've got another	6	4	1.2
you're only	5	4	9.9	's a micro-phone	8	4	7.6	've got it	15	6	4.6
you're the	10	4	19.8	's a one	3	3	2	've got my	3	3	0.4
you're up	12	3	18.1	's all I	5	5	0.5	've got one	7	4	1.5
you've got	32	12	29.3	's another one	7	6	0.4	've got some	4	3	0.6
you've only	3	3	0.6	's going to	32	14	24.4	've got the	11	6	3.4
'll be a	5	4	0.4	's her name	4	4	0.1	've got three	3	3	0.4
'll be able	4	3	0.3	's in the	4	3	0.3	've got to	40	11	22.3
'll be back	8	3	0.5	's in there	11	7	2.2	've got two	6	4	1.2
'll be up	3	3	0.2	's like a	4	4	0.1				
'll do it	16	8	1.5	's my friend	3	3	0.5				
'll get a	3	3	0.1	's not a	10	6	6.7				
'll get it	4	3	0.1	's not going	4	3	1.3				
'll get you	3	3	0.1	's not in	5	4	2.2				
'll give you	8	6	0.1	's not mine	4	3	1.3				
'll go and	14	7	1.5	's not the	3	3	0.9				
'll have a	7	5	1.1	's not your	6	5	3.4				
'll have one	3	3	0.3	's some more	3	3	0.1				
'll have some	4	3	0.4	's that for	11	7	9.4				
'll have to	34	13	13.6	's that one	7	6	5.1				
'll put it	7	4	0.2	's that word	14	6	10.5				
'll put the	4	3	0.1	's the first	4	4	3				
'll show you	23	10	1.8	's the last	3	3	1.5				
'll take it	6	4	0.1	's the matter	7	5	6.3				
'll tell you	9	7	0.4	's the one	7	4	5.7				
'm doing a	5	3	0.1	's the other	8	7	10.2				
'm going to	167	20	370.2	's the thing	8	5	7.2				
'm going up	7	4	3.1	's the wrong	3	3	1.5				
'm not allowed	7	4	1.5	's this one	5	3	0.2				
'm not going	18	9	8.7	's this word	7	3	0.3				
'm not playing	11	6	3.6	's what I	13	7	3.2				
'm up to	11	3	0.1	's what you	7	5	1.2				
're going home	3	3	0.2	's where I	3	3	0.1				
're going to	50	16	18.1	's where the	4	4	0.1				
're in the	6	3	0.1	's why I	6	3	0.2				
're not allowed	22	8	2.5	's (has) got a	17	9	1				
're not going	6	3	0.3	's (has) got no	3	3	0.1				
're not playing	4	3	0.2	's (has) got one	4	4	0.1				
's a big	5	5	6	's (has) got the	4	4	0.1				
's a bit	3	3	2	's (has) got to	13	6	0.5				
's a girl	3	3	2								

CHAPTER SEVEN

FREQUENCY LISTS

It should be noted that although most of the listings contain 100 items each, at the younger age levels (2½ through 4½) the number of three-word sequences found in the children's language did not reach 100.

The lists in this chapter include only those units used with the very highest frequency at each age level, and thus they provide some insights into the respective core languages. Items are arranged in the order of frequency from highest to lowest, in separate age-level groupings as follows.

THE 100 SINGLE WORDS MOST FREQUENTLY USED BY AUSTRALIAN CHILDREN, AGE 2½—FREQUENCY-ORDER LISTING

Sequence	Freq.	No. of Speakers	Index
there	389	13	389
look	363	13	363
is ('s)	357	13	357
that	369	12	341
I	314	12	290
he	312	12	288
a	272	13	272
here	245	13	245
no	232	13	232
yes	229	13	229
in	204	13	204
it	211	12	195
you	172	13	172
me	183	12	169
got	161	13	161
mummy (mommy)	169	11	143
the	152	12	140
on	138	13	138
one(s)	138	13	138
to	148	12	137
want	128	13	128
go(s)	131	12	121
up	119	13	119
see	115	12	106
my	123	11	104
him	126	10	97
have ('ve)	103	12	95
this	96	11	82
what	82	13	82
put	113	9	77
come	87	11	74
get	114	8	70
out	109	8	67
are ('re)	73	12	67
going	97	8	60
don't	66	11	56
lady(s)	14	5	54
can	66	9	46
too	50	12	46
at	48	12	44
down	45	13	43

Sequence	Freq.	No. of Speakers	Index
oh	46	12	43
take	61	9	43
and	57	9	39
big	71	7	38
they	43	11	36
make	65	7	35
mine	50	9	35
has ('s)	44	10	34
now	39	11	33
two	51	8	31
where	43	9	30
not	43	9	30
dog(s)	35	11	30
back	39	9	27
car(s)	44	7	24
house(s)	44	7	24
do	43	7	23
like	29	10	22
of	32	9	22
bird(s)	48	6	22
can't	26	10	20
little	28	9	19
be	28	9	19
daddy	35	7	19
these	28	8	17
thing(s)	32	7	17
all	37	6	17
man(s)	31	7	17
hello	23	9	16
off	34	6	16
gone	24	8	15
we	27	7	14
boy(s)	24	7	13
talk(s)	27	6	12
watch	21	7	11
more	29	5	11
am ('m)	21	7	11
will ('ll)	20	7	11
way	21	7	11
water	21	7	11
bite(s)	23	6	11
frog(s)	26	5	10

Sequence	Freq.	No. of Speakers	Index
for	19	7	10
bed(s)	26	5	10
box	20	6	10
nice	42	3	10
another	19	9	9
baby(s)	20	6	9
horse(s)	20	6	9
did	16	7	9
walk	19	6	9
them	22	5	8
right	21	5	8
over	16	7	8
let(s)	14	7	8
your	23	4	7
bridge	23	4	7
tea	13	7	7
door(s)	17	5	7

Sequence	Freq.	No. of Speakers	Index	Sequence	Freq.	No. of Speakers	Index	Sequence	Freq.	No. of Speakers	Index
I	450	18	450	down	48	16	43	another	19	9	9.5
is ('s)	338	17	319	all	52	13	38	again	15	10	9.4
a	314	17	296	like	47	14	37	head(s)	21	8	9.3
you	257	18	257	now	52	12	34.4	home	20	8	8.8
it	266	17	252	out	51	12	34	more	20	8	8.8
that	238	17	225	at	50	12	33	was	17	9	8.6
do	190	18	190	they	52	11	32	why	15	10	8.3
the	222	14	172	thing(s)	37	15	31	haven't	15	10	8.3
in	153	18	153	oh	50	11	31	has ('s)	15	10	8.3
got	153	17	144	little	43	13	31	around	17	8	7.6
on	150	17	142	him	52	11	31	but	15	8	7.1
he	226	11	138	your	42	12	28	just	17	7	7
we	125	18	125	big	41	12	27.1	bit(s)	12	10	6.9
and	150	15	125	know	45	11	27	good	12	10	6.7
no	125	18	125	two	39	12	25	think	23	5	6.7
look	125	18	125	of	39	11	24	truck	19	6	6.3
there	117	18	117	his	37	10	21				
here	117	18	117	can't	28	13	20				
one(s)	123	17	116	back	33	11	20				
to	120	17	113	where	30	12	20				
yes	126	16	112	too	30	11	19				
up	125	16	111	when	25	13	18				
are	113	17	107	them	26	12	17				
this	123	15	102	hey	28	13	17				
can	95	18	95	let(s)	27	11	16				
go(s)	92	16	82	boy(s)	28	10	15.3				
come	88	16	78	with	24	11	15				
me	88	15	73	car(s)	30	9	15				
going	80	16	71	over	28	9	14				
don't	83	15	69	off	23	11	14				
have ('ve)	79	15	66	make	24	11	14				
what	75	15	66	cat	41	6	13.7				
will ('ll)	68	17	64	be	27	9	13.3				
not	68	17	64	these	29	8	13				
my	67	17	63	mine	18	13	13				
want	71	16	63	because	28	8	13				
get	74	14	58	goes	22	10	12				
put	71	14	55	take	25	9	12				
am ('m)	62	15	52	only	19	10	11				
for	61	14	48	well	20	9	10				
some	54	16	48	paint(s)	37	5	10				
see	65	12	44	might	27	7	10				

THE 100 SINGLE WORDS MOST FREQUENTLY USED BY AUSTRALIAN CHILDREN, AGE 4½—FREQUENCY-ORDER LISTING

Sequence	Freq.	No. of Speakers	Index
I	489	20	445
a	275	22	275
that	253	22	253
is	272	21	247
the	253	20	230
it	236	21	225
you	320	20	219
to	155	20	141
and	198	20	180
one(s)	161	18	132
in	126	22	126
this	127	19	110
what	133	18	109
have ('ve)	120	19	104
look	97	22	97
got	111	19	96
on	101	20	92
yes	102	19	88
we	94	20	86
can	89	21	85
no	97	19	84
do	89	18	73
there	84	17	70
go	87	17	67
he	86	17	66
know	80	18	65
am ('m)	74	19	64
me	73	19	63
going	75	18	61
are	67	19	58
my	73	16	53
here	58	19	50
up	65	16	47
of	57	17	44
will ('ll)	63	15	43
don't	56	17	43
all	55	17	43
with	46	18	38
see	48	17	37
now	50	16	36
get	49	16	36
not	43	18	35
want	57	14	35
oh	58	13	34
hey	44	17	34
they	55	13	33
come	45	15	31
put	44	15	30
take	38	17	29
make	41	14	26
like	41	14	26
them	36	15	25
for	39	14	25
thing(s)	30	17	23
these	40	12	22
little	38	13	22
where	30	15	21
those	24	19	21
out	31	14	20
but	37	12	20
off	30	14	19
big	35	11	18
mine	29	13	17
at	28	14	17
too	29	12	16
has ('s)	29	12	16
can't	26	12	16
might	26	13	15
down	29	11	15
be	26	13	15
some	22	14	14
just	21	15	14
because	26	12	14
could	25	12	14
she	27	11	14
when	25	13	13
then	33	9	13
so	24	12	13
way	24	11	12
two	26	10	12
did	22	11	11
right	22	10	10
would ('d)	21	10	10
man(s)	22	10	10
had ('d)	22	10	10
boy(s)	26	8	10
house(s)	21	7	9
was	22	9	9
talk(s)	20	10	9
if	23	9	9
home	9	6	9
think	17	10	8
over	23	9	8
leave	19	9	8
saw	17	9	8
play	15	10	7
miss	19	8	7
how	15	10	7
house	21	7	7
after	15	10	7

Sequence	Freq.	No. of Speakers	Index	Sequence	Freq.	No. of Speakers	Index	Sequence	Freq.	No. of Speakers	Index
I	3392	18	449.2	can	410	18	60.3	if	168	16	22
it	2107	18	310.1	here	408	18	60.1	well	185	14	21.2
you	1990	18	292.9	go (s)	403	18	59.3	three	157	16	20.5
is ('s)	1651	18	243	not	393	18	57.8	how	156	16	20.4
(is)	(383)	(11)	(34.5)	he	412	17	57.3	over	156	16	20.4
('s)	(1268)	(18)	(186.6)	they	356	18	52.4	her	143	17	19.9
the	1459	18	214.7	look	345	18	50.8	said	151	16	19.8
to	1287	18	189.4	she	324	18	47.7	has ('s)	142	17	19.7
a	1248	18	183.7	come	320	18	47.1	(has)	(43)	(16)	(5.6)
that	1223	18	180	out	333	17	46.3	('s)	(99)	(17)	(13.8)
and	1158	18	170.4	put	296	18	43.6	when	139	17	19.3
yes	953	18	140.3	because	275	18	40.5	who	132	17	18.4
no	835	18	122.9	now	271	18	39.9	only	125	18	18.4
one (s)	793	17	110.2	of	266	18	39.1	good	138	16	18.1
on	689	18	101.4	two	274	17	38.1	big	130	17	18
what	666	18	98	down	250	18	36.8	little	136	16	17.8
oh	655	18	96.4	for	263	17	36.6	off	121	17	16.8
in	642	18	94.5	did	256	17	35.6	so	121	17	16.8
have ('ve)	640	18	94.2	see	227	18	33.4	then	113	17	15.7
(have)	(459)	(18)	(67.6)	hey	235	17	32.7	him	111	17	15.4
('ve)	(181)	(18)	(26.6)	was	235	17	32.7	thing(s)	125	15	15.3
got	634	18	93.3	with	221	18	32.5	mum (mom)	139	13	14.8
this	608	18	89.5	where	243	17	32.5	play	112	16	14.7
my	585	18	86.1	at	217	18	31.9	make	111	16	14.5
there	563	18	82.9	them	214	18	31.5	let	126	14	14.4
are ('re)	563	18	82.9	(them)	(166)	(18)	(24.4)	tell	103	17	14.3
(are)	(224)	(17)	(31.2)	('em)	(48)	(12)	(4.7)	back	108	16	14.1
('re)	(339)	(18)	(49.9)	want	237	16	31	take	90	18	13.2
me	552	18	81.2	can't	204	18	30	give	105	15	12.9
don't	529	18	77.9	just	200	18	29.4	girl(s)	103	15	12.6
do	520	18	76.5	like	194	18	28.6	four(s)	107	14	12.3
am ('m)	501	18	73.7	your	206	17	28.6	think	114	13	12.2
(am)	(91)	(15)	(11.2)	but	204	17	28.4				
('m)	(413)	(11)	(37.2)	all	199	17	27.7				
will ('ll)	473	18	69.6	didn't	170	18	25				
(will)	(75)	(16)	(9.8)	be	164	18	24.1				
('ll)	(398)	(18)	(58.6)	some	165	17	22.9				
going	469	18	69	too	155	18	22.8				
know	438	18	64.5	had ('d)	172	16	22.5				
up	437	18	64.3	(had)	(162)	(16)	(21.2)				
get	451	17	62.7	('d)	(10)	(7)	(0.6)				
we	421	18	62	right	171	16	22.4				

Sequence	Freq.	No. of Speakers	Index
I	3950	22	523
you	2595	22	343.6
it	2317	22	306.8
is ('s)	2141	22	283.5
(is)	(568)	(22)	(75.2)
('s)	(1573)	(22)	(208.3)
the	1858	22	246
to	1719	22	227.6
that	1515	22	200.6
a	1357	22	179.7
and	1186	22	157
one(s)	997	22	132
yes	973	22	128.8
no	928	22	122.9
on	905	22	119.8
what	882	22	116.8
have ('ve)	857	22	113.5
(have)	(562)	(22)	(74.4)
('ve)	(295)	(21)	(37.3)
in	761	22	100.8
there	744	22	98.5
got	725	22	96
will ('ll)	708	22	93.7
(will)	(123)	(19)	(14.1)
('ll)	(585)	(22)	(77.5)
am ('m)	682	22	90.3
(am)	(48)	(17)	(4.9)
('m)	(634)	(21)	(80.1)
are ('re)	680	22	90
(are)	(269)	(22)	(35.6)
('re)	(411)	(21)	(51.9)
this	655	22	86.7
oh	647	22	85.7
do	624	22	82.6
can	603	22	79.8
get	594	22	78.7
we	588	22	77.9
up	586	22	77.6
go	568	22	75.2
me	565	22	74.8
my	553	22	73.2
don't	549	22	72.7

Sequence	Freq.	No. of Speakers	Index
going	487	22	64.5
here	502	21	63.4
know	476	22	63
they	476	22	63
of	461	22	61
not	428	22	56.7
where	425	22	56.3
hey	430	21	54.3
out	437	20	52.6
he	391	22	51.8
want	388	22	51.3
two	369	22	48.9
your	364	22	48.2
come	381	21	48.2
look	359	22	47.5
now	349	21	44.1
put	329	22	43.6
them	321	22	42.5
for	307	22	40.6
down	304	22	40.3
just	295	22	39.1
like	279	22	37
see	282	21	35.6
be	281	21	35.5
she	304	19	34.8
all	252	22	33.4
did	244	22	32.3
when	229	22	30.3
was	236	21	29.8
at	225	22	29.8
three (s)	226	21	28.6
because	209	22	27.7
with	209	22	27.7
how	226	20	27.2
but	202	22	26.7
over	200	22	26.5
if	199	22	26.4
off	215	19	24.6
well	185	22	24.5
can't	190	21	24
thing	184	21	23.3
some	167	22	22.1

Sequence	Freq.	No. of Speakers	Index
has ('s)	165	22	21.9
(has)	(54)	(16)	(5.2)
('s)	(111)	(19)	(12.7)
back	162	22	21.5
take	177	20	21.3
good	173	20	20.8
only	159	21	20.1
Mummy	222	15	20
(Mommy)			
then	156	21	19.7
say	155	21	19.6
had ('d)	144	22	19.1
(had)	(110)	(21)	(13.9)
('d)	(34)	(13)	(2.7)
why	157	20	18.9
right	156	19	17.8
four	172	17	17.6
o.k., okay	154	19	17.6
little	133	21	16.8
so	139	20	16.7
play	127	21	16.1
too	126	20	15.2
said	124	20	14.9
time (s)	118	21	14.9
five (s)	153	16	14.7
think	117	21	14.8
would ('d)	128	19	14.6
(would)	(73)	(17)	(7.8)
('d)	(55)	(15)	(5.0)
didn't	115	22	14.5
let ('s)	146	16	14.1
something	116	20	14
big	114	20	13.7

THE 100 TWO-WORD SEQUENCES MOST FREQUENTLY USED BY AUSTRALIAN CHILDREN, AGE 2½—FREQUENCY-ORDER LISTING

Sequence	Freq.	No. of Speakers	Index
that's (is)	47	10	142.9
he's (is)	85	6	131
I want	56	9	130.2
look at	34	10	110
in there	35	12	76.3
there's (is)	26	6	54.1
's a	28	7	46.9
I got	26	6	40.3
I'm	19	8	39.2
that one	16	8	38.9
it's	21	9	31.4
want to	29	9	29.8
in here	28	5	25.5
he's (has)	14	7	25.1
got a	25	7	25.1
look that	12	6	23.2
there you	8	7	19.5
in the	11	7	14.1
no I	13	5	13.5
what's (is)	20	9	13.2
going to	22	10	11.8
's going	16	3	11.6
that a	6	6	10.9
I don't	7	6	10.7
I can't	7	6	10.7
here is	8	6	10.5
he is	85	6	10.4
got one	10	7	10
a look	10	4	9.2
I have	7	5	9
that mine	7	4	8.5
look see	8	3	7.6
you are	8	6	7.4
's not	10	3	7.2
I'll	9	3	7
to get	14	4	6.9
a big	7	4	6.8
me got	15	3	6.8
on the	9	6	6.6
there he	6	3	6.2
I like	6	4	6.1
this one	11	7	5.6
no that	9	3	5.6
's that	6	4	5.6
he can't	7	3	5.5
that way	6	3	5.5
put it	12	6	4.9
get him	20	4	4.9
it up	7	4	4.9
in bed	9	3	4.9
no he	8	3	4.9
on here	10	4	4.8
's my	5	4	4.6
want a	8	5	4.6
it on	6	4	4.1
I take	5	3	3.8
I did	5	3	3.8
I can	5	3	3.8
that on	6	3	3.8
he going	5	3	3.7
make a	30	4	3.7
a mouth	5	3	3.5
go on	8	4	3.5
got this	5	5	3.5
up here	8	4	3.5
one(s) in	7	4	3.5
take it	22	4	3.4
got to	7	3	3.1
got my	7	3	3.1
it out	6	3	3.1
it is	6	3	3.1
to put	7	6	3
yes look	5	3	3
have a	12	6	2.9
want it	6	4	2.8
where's (is)	15	7	2.8
get out	11	4	2.7
it down	5	3	2.5
is the	8	5	2.4
on a	6	3	2.2
one of	6	3	2.2
up there	5	4	2.1
him up	6	5	2.1
the box	4	4	2
want this	6	3	2
see look	7	3	2
don't want	8	5	2
get me	11	3	2
down there	10	5	1.9
on me	7	4	1.8
the door	5	3	1.8
to you	5	3	1.8
that my	7	4	1.7
want that	5	3	1.7
see him	6	3	1.7
's (has) got	14	7	1.6
put this	8	3	1.6
come on	8	3	1.6
up the	5	3	1.5
is it	5	5	1.5

THE 100 TWO-WORD SEQUENCES MOST FREQUENTLY USED BY AUSTRALIAN CHILDREN, AGE 3½—FREQUENCY-ORDER LISTING

Sequence	Freq.	No. of Speakers	Index	Sequence	Freq.	No. of Speakers	Index	Sequence	Freq.	No. of Speakers	Index
I'm	64	16	243	I put	7	5	8.1	it goes	6	3	2.5
I got	44	12	125.1	don't know	26	8	7.6	he's (has)	7	5	2.5
that's	67	14	111.4	you can	9	6	7.5	it isn't	6	3	2.5
's a	47	14	78.1	want to	25	9	7.5	get out	11	7	2.4
I don't	33	9	70.7	go to	19	9	7.4	a dog	5	3	2.4
I'll	28	10	66.6	a big	8	5	6.2	and he	7	5	2.3
I want	25	10	59.4	in a	9	6	6.2	on there	6	5	2.3
I can	20	11	52.2	go on	14	10	6.1	the water	6	4	2.2
he's (is)	45	10	32.8	I haven't	5	5	5.9	up to	8	5	2.2
a little	19	11	32.6	is going	14	8	5.9	you like	4	4	2.1
got a	42	10	32	's my	8	6	5.6	one's (is)	8	4	2.1
it's (is)	67	14	29.2	do that	9	6	5.5	put it	12	6	2.1
do know	28	9	25.3	up here	13	7	5.3	can have	8	5	2
going to	52	13	25.3	it on	8	5	5.3	there you	6	5	1.9
in the	27	10	21.9	it off	8	5	5	the table	5	4	1.9
I think	18	5	21.6	can see	14	7	4.9	on this	6	4	1.8
do want	23	8	18.4	up the	11	7	4.6				
I saw	11	6	15.8	this one	12	7	4.5				
look at	28	8	14.8	I've	5	4	4.5				
do you	18	8	14.4	and a	8	8	4.3				
's going	15	8	14.2	you know	6	5	4.1				
in here	18	9	13.2	the car	9	5	4.1				
I know	11	5	13.1	and I	9	7	4.1				
a car	14	6	13	is that	10	7	3.7				
we're	28	7	12.9	'm going	16	9	3.6				
that one	12	9	12.8	no that	9	6	3.6				
got to	21	8	12.8	he got	12	4	3.4				
this is	24	9	11.6	do it	7	5	3.4				
in there	17	8	11	get up	14	4	3.4				
come on	36	7	10.4	do like	7	5	3.4				
on the	17	8	10.2	up there	10	6	3.3				
I can't	7	6	9.9	he might	9	5	3.3				
's the	12	7	9.9	no I	7	7	3.2				
's not	16	5	9.5	a truck	6	3	2.9				
there's (is)	17	9	9.5	you better	5	4	2.8				
it in	10	7	9.3	you do	5	4	2.8				
it is	11	6	8.8	in it	7	5	2.8				
I have	9	4	8.6	you don't	7	5	2.6				
we got	14	9	8.4	you have	6	3	2.6				
's that	10	7	8.3	you are	6	3	2.6				
it up	9	7	8.3	don't want	14	5	2.6				
you can't	10	6	8.2	yes I	7	6	2.5				

THE 100 TWO-WORD SEQUENCES MOST FREQUENTLY USED BY AUSTRALIAN CHILDREN, AGE 4½—FREQUENCY-ORDER LISTING

Sequence	Freq.	No. of Speakers	Index	Sequence	Freq.	No. of Speakers	Index	Sequence	Freq.	No. of Speakers	Index
I'm	71	9	272.8	it on	8	8	6.5	do it	9	7	2.1
that's (is)	62	16	114.1	and he	11	7	6.3	to take	6	5	2.1
I'll	36	12	87.2	is the	20	10	6	is what	11	6	2
it's (is)	49	16	80.1	and you	8	8	5.2	and the	5	5	2
I got	30	13	78.8	it has	10	5	5.2	it was	5	4	2
I want	25	12	61	want to	26	12	5	you are	4	4	2
you know	26	11	37.8	I mean	6	4	4.9	in it	8	4	1.9
I can	20	9	36.5	I might	6	4	4.9	don't know	14	7	1.9
's a	31	13	36.1	and then	12	5	4.9	a man	4	4	1.9
I don't	19	9	34.7	's going	11	5	4.9	that boy	5	3	1.7
in the	33	14	26.5	got on	9	7	4.6	can have	7	6	1.6
going to	46	16	20.4	have to	15	10	4.5	the big	4	4	1.6
I think	13	7	18.3	I go	6	4	4.5	the water	5	3	1.6
a big	16	9	17.9	you can't	7	5	4.4	to come	5	5	1.6
got a	29	13	16.4	to the	8	8	4.1	to see	5	5	1.6
one of	27	10	16.2	and we	7	7	4	we have	7	6	1.6
know what	39	14	16.1	is not	14	9	3.8				
I had	10	8	16	you go	7	4	3.8				
I know	10	8	16	this one	12	6	3.6				
I saw	12	6	14.7	a car	7	4	3.6				
's not	15	10	13.4	there's (is)	13	9	3.5				
I need	13	5	13.4	the little	6	5	3.5				
I've	9	7	12.9	's that	9	4	3.2				
and I	15	10	12.2	do you	16	6	3.2				
this is	23	10	11.6	in here	8	7	3.2				
what I	23	10	11.5	in there	8	7	3.1				
that one	12	8	11.2	I haven't	5	3	3.1				
I made	13	4	10.7	I did	4	4	3.1				
he's (is)	25	14	10.5	I was	4	4	3.1				
on the	20	12	10	a real	6	4	3				
a little	10	8	9.9	it up	7	4	2.9				
the other	11	8	9.2	look what	13	5	2.9				
I can't	9	5	8.9	that way	8	3	2.8				
I found	9	5	8.9	look at	10	6	2.6				
'm going	24	13	8.5	and that	8	4	2.6				
what's (is)	18	9	8.1	and they	6	5	2.5				
you have	10	6	7.9	no I	10	6	2.3				
you got	9	6	7.3	that and	5	4	2.3				
to do	14	8	7.2	yes I	9	6	2.2				
I like	7	5	7.1	in my	8	5	2.2				
have a	21	11	7	a cow	6	3	2.2				
I could	6	5	6.7	to have	7	5	2.1				

THE 100 TWO-WORD SEQUENCES MOST FREQUENTLY USED BY AUSTRALIAN CHILDREN, AGE 5½—FREQUENCY-ORDER LISTING

Sequence	Freq.	No. of Speakers	Index
I'm	476	18	349.8
I'll	302	17	209.6
it's (is)	363	17	156.5
I don't	220	16	143.7
I got	182	17	126.3
I know	154	16	100.6
I can	147	15	90
I've	116	16	75.8
you're	182	17	74
got a	556	17	72.2
that's (is)	261	17	65.3
I can't	88	17	61
I want	78	17	54.1
I think	77	13	40.9
I didn't	66	14	37.7
's a	146	16	35.6
you know	87	15	31.3
I was	57	13	30.2
I have	44	16	28.7
I did	50	14	28.6
going to	275	17	26.4
and I	121	15	25.3
you can	71	14	23.8
I had	42	12	20.6
in the	147	18	20.4
it is	49	16	19.9
to get	83	15	·19.3
don't know	150	18	17.2
I like	32	13	17
's not	65	17	16.9
that one	81	14	16.7
's the	68	16	16.6
it up	50	13	16.5
it was	50	13	16.5
you have	49	14	16.4
I am	36	11	16.2
have to	161	18	16
I said	35	11	15.7
it on	49	12	15
I go	28	13	14.9
to go	56	17	14.7
and you	65	16	14.5

Sequence	Freq.	No. of Speakers	Index
on the	103	15	12.8
I haven't	27	11	12.1
no I	89	13	12.1
you got	41	12	11.8
to do	54	14	11.7
you can't	43	11	11.3
I just	25	11	11.2
there's (is)	96	17	11.1
it to	36	12	10.9
you don't	41	11	10.8
you are	32	14	10.7
to be	43	16	10.7
I do	26	10	10.6
come on	153	18	10.6
do you	112	15	10.5
to have	52	13	10.4
what's (is)	86	15	10.3
yes I	60	14	9.6
to the	41	15	9.5
's that	48	13	9.5
's going	48	13	9.5
I won't	21	11	9.4
's my	47	13	9.3
you get	35	11	9.2
a little	47	13	9.2
I only	22	10	8.9
one two	83	12	8.9
and a	44	14	8.6
it out	30	11	8.4
to put	38	14	8.2
I might	20	10	8.2
I could	25	8	8.2
I need	22	9	8.1
got to	75	14	8.1
oh I	67	15	7.9
you go	30	11	7.9
I love	19	10	7.8
you want	32	10	7.7
in my	61	16	7.5
I put	18	10	7.3
this is	67	15	7.4
they're	107	16	7.3

Sequence	Freq.	No. of Speakers	Index
it in	26	11	7.3
I get	16	11	7.2
to play	42	11	7.2
this one	59	16	6.9
have a	79	16	6.9
you've	26	11	6.8
and that	44	11	6.7
and then	37	13	6.7
I thought	18	9	6.6
the other	34	11	6.6
's in	39	11	6.6
and it	39	12	6.5
in there	58	14	6.3
got it	54	15	6.2
no you	45	13	6.1
a big	35	11	5.8

Sequence	Freq.	No. of Speakers	Index
I'm	627	21	414.6
I'll	400	22	277
it's (is)	421	22	167.9
I don't	215	22	148.9
I've	185	21	122.3
I got	175	22	121.2
that's (is)	367	22	97.5
I want	151	20	95
I know	139	20	87.5
I have	132	20	83.1
you're	190	21	82.5
I can	116	20	73
you can	131	21	56.9
you know	140	19	55
I think	74	21	48.9
's a	152	21	40
that one	158	20	38.2
I can't	72	16	36.2
to go	132	20	36.2
I go	62	18	35.1
it is	105	17	33
to do	114	21	32.8
to get	114	21	32.8
you want	83	19	32.6
you got	88	17	30.9
going to	360	22	30.7
's the	126	19	30
I like	62	14	27.3
it on	75	19	26.3
I was	49	17	26.2
in the	205	21	26.1
you don't	68	18	25.3
on the	159	22	25.2
I didn't	53	15	25
you have	60	19	23.6
I did	45	16	22.7
I haven't	48	15	22.7
's that	91	18	20.5
you get	58	17	20.4
what's	159	18	20.1
I get	38	16	19.2
do you	180	21	18.8
the other(s)	67	19	18.8
's not	83	18	18.7
I had	37	16	18.6
I just	39	15	18.4
'm going	191	20	18.4
and I	95	20	18
it in	57	17	17.9
I do	40	14	17.6
you'll	52	16	17.2
you go	48	17	16.9
I put	38	14	16.7
to the	69	17	16.1
it was	53	16	15.7
want to	237	21	15.4
have to	178	19	15.1
I said	32	15	15.1
I won't	31	15	14.6
it up	49	16	14.5
you going	41	17	14.4
there's	125	19	14.1
to play	64	16	14
can I	150	19	13.7
you've	44	14	12.8
got a	115	19	12.6
I thought	30	13	12.3
no I	91	18	12.1
to be	52	17	12.1
you do	45	13	12.1
it's (has)	43	15	11.9
is a	25	10	11.4
and you	59	20	11.2
I am	27	13	11
to have	50	15	10.3
one two	99	13	10.2
got to	103	17	10.1
's my	50	16	10
they're	130	20	9.9
I mean	24	13	9.8
in there	94	17	9.7
to take	47	15	9.7
you put	33	14	9.6
and that	56	18	9.5
come on	183	18	9.5
don't know	108	20	9.5
I say	25	12	9.5
look what	34	13	9.2
's going	48	15	9
this is	91	19	9
'm not	98	19	9
you see	35	12	8.7
I went	21	13	8.6
've got	182	21	8.6
one of	62	17	8.4
you are	27	15	8.4
a little	45	17	8.3
to put	38	16	8.3
it out	34	13	8.2
the one(s)	37	15	8.2

THREE-WORD SEQUENCES MOST FREQUENTLY USED BY AUSTRALIAN CHILDREN, AGE 2½—FREQUENCY-ORDER LISTING | AGE 3½—FREQUENCY-ORDER LISTING

Age 2½—Frequency-Order Listing

Sequence	Freq.	No. of Speakers	Index
I want to	19	9	1985.5
that's a	14	6	1070.2
he's going	20	3	699.8
look at the	7	7	479.6
he's (has) got	6	6	294.9
he's a	4	3	138.9
I got this	6	5	107.2
there you are	8	7	96.9
it's off	10	3	83.5
want to get	7	3	55.5
I'm going	7	4	48.9
it's a	3	3	25.1
got one of	6	3	16
in the box	3	3	11.3
have a look	9	4	9.4
I like this	3	3	4.9
's (has) got a	5	5	3.5
'm going to	3	2	0.2
've got one	3	3	0.01

Age 3½—Frequency-Order Listing

Sequence	Freq.	No. of Speakers	Index
I'm going	30	13	4998.5
I'm not	9	7	806.8
that's a	17	8	798.6
I don't know	18	8	537
I got a	11	6	434.1
I want to	11	7	240.6
that's my	6	5	174.9
I got to	6	4	157.6
he's going	18	5	156
I'm on	3	3	114.2
it's a	12	6	111.1
I can see	7	5	96
I don't want	8	3	89
that's the	4	3	69.2
it's not	8	4	49.1
he's a	5	5	43
I'll have	4	3	41.2
I'll come	3	3	31.3
we're going	11	4	29.8
'm going to	16	9	27.4
got a big	5	3	24.9
this is a	8	5	24.4
he's in	4	3	20.4
got a little	4	3	19.8
in the water	5	3	17.1
do you want	7	4	15.9
a little bit	3	3	15.3
we got to	8	4	14.1
look at this	6	3	14
look at that	5	3	11.5
got to go	4	4	10.6
no that's (is)	8	6	9.2
I know what	4	3	8.1
do you know	3	3	6.8
I haven't got	4	4	4.9
I've got	5	4	4.7
don't know what	4	3	4.7
want to get	3	3	3.5
a big boy	3	3	2.9
and I will	4	3	2.6
there you are	6	5	2.5
put it in	5	4	2.2
he's (has) got	4	4	2.1
what's that	5	4	1.9
want it off	5	3	1.1
I show you	5	3	1
one of these	3	3	1
we've got	5	3	0.8
up in the	4	3	0.5
's (has) got a	4	4	0.2
've got a	3	3	0.1
climb up here	4	3	0.05
cup of tea	6	3	0.01

Sequence	Freq.	No. of Speakers	Index	Sequence	Freq.	No. of Speakers	Index
I'm going	23	13	3707.2	it has got	3	3	2.1
that's a	17	9	793	one of those	4	3	2.1
that's what	10	6	310.4	is what I	6	3	1.6
I want to	14	8	310.3	there's some	3	3	1.4
I'm making	4	4	256.4	put it on	6	5	1.3
you know what	16	9	245.7	I haven't got	3	3	1.3
I'm not	5	4	245.5	he's (has) got	6	4	0.9
that's the	9	4	186	can I have	4	3	0.7
it's a	8	4	116.2	we have to	3	3	0.6
I don't know	12	6	113.5	we saw a	4	3	0.6
I got a	6	5	107.1	've got a	5	5	0.5
'm going to	20	11	84.7	look after the	4	3	0.4
I'll go	5	4	78.5	be in the	4	4	0.3
I'll take	4	4	62.8	's (has) got a	3	3	0.3
one of these	10	7	51.6	take it off	4	3	0.2
that's all	3	3	45.6	not going to	3	3	0.2
I've got	9	7	36.9	why can you	6	4	0.02
it's not	3	3	32				
it's going	3	3	32				
I got gun	3	3	31.5				
I can see	6	3	29.6				
a big one	7	5	28.4				
this is a	7	5	18.4				
what I made	8	4	16.6				
I think I	5	4	16.4				
do you know	14	7	13.7				
what I'm	6	4	12.5				
you have to	7	5	12.5				
going to do	4	3	11				
going to have	4	3	11				
in the morning	3	3	10.6				
what's that	7	4	10.3				
what's this	5	5	9.1				
look what I	13	5	8.7				
I had a	4	3	8.7				
he's not	5	3	7.1				
I had to	3	3	6.4				
know what I	3	3	6.5				
on the road	3	3	4				
the other one	3	3	3.7				
want to take	4	4	3.6				
do you want	5	3	2.2				

THE 100 THREE-WORD SEQUENCES MOST FREQUENTLY USED BY AUSTRALIAN CHILDREN, AGE 5½—FREQUENCY-ORDER LISTING

Sequence	Freq.	No. of Speakers	Index
I'm going	126	17	6125.8
I'm not	69	15	2959.9
I don't know	108	15	1903.4
I'll get	31	10	531.3
I'll have	27	11	509
I got a	34	13	456.4
you're not	50	15	454.4
I've got	61	12	453.5
I don't want	29	11	374.9
I'm doing	16	8	366.3
I want to	47	16	332.8
I'll go	20	9	308.6
I'll put	20	8	274.3
I'm a	13	7	260.2
I'm the	11	8	251.8
I got to	25	8	206.6
I got one	18	11	204.5
I'll show	14	7	168
I'll tell	10	9	154.3
I'll be	15	6	154.3
that's a	26	11	152.7
it's a	64	14	145.6
I'll do	12	7	144.1
I'm telling	11	4	125.9
I'm in	7	6	120.2
I'm having	8	5	114.5
I can do	18	8	106
I'm getting	7	5	100.2
I think I	27	11	99.2
I got it	12	8	99.2
that's my	20	8	85.5
I'm making	5	5	71.5
I'll read	12	3	61.7
you have to	38	12	60.3
I'm hot	7	3	60.1
I'll hold	7	5	60
I know what	10	7	59.6
you're a	14	7	59.4
that's all	12	9	57.7
you know what	18	6	57.5
I'm taking	5	4	57.2
I'm just	5	4	57.2

Sequence	Freq.	No. of Speakers	Index
going to get	29	9	56.3
I can't do	14	8	55.9
I have to	27	12	54.5
that's what	17	6	54.5
I don't have	7	6	49.4
one two three	61	11	49.2
I'm up	4	4	45.7
I'm putting	5	3	42.9
I'll try	6	4	41.2
I'll take	6	4	41.2
I'll see	6	4	41.2
going to have	20	9	38.8
that's how	9	8	38.5
that's for	10	7	37.4
I'm trying	4	3	34.3
I'm drawing	4	3	34.3
I know that	8	5	32.9
I don't like	7	4	32.9
that's not	10	6	32.1
I've been	8	6	29.8
what's that	28	12	28.4
I don't think	6	4	28.2
and I'm	15	9	27.9
going to be	16	8	27.6
's going to	27	13	27.3
'm going to	69	18	27.2
that's the	18	8	26.9
there's a	27	11	26.9
I'm sitting	3	3	25.8
I'm five	3	3	25.8
I'm too	3	3	25.8
I'm sorry	3	3	25.8
I'll give	5	3	25.7
you're going	7	6	25.5
don't know what	18	10	25.3
and I'll	15	8	24.8
I don't care	7	3	24.7
that's right	7	6	22.5
going to make	16	6	20.7
I'll just	4	3	20.6
I know because	6	4	19.8

Sequence	Freq.	No. of Speakers	Index
going to tell	15	6	19.4
have to get	16	9	18.9
's a big	9	7	18.4
going to do	12	7	18.1
to go to	15	10	18.1
I can run	8	3	17.7
I got two	4	4	16.5
I got four	4	4	16.5
I know how	5	4	16.5
you got to	18	9	15.6
I got another	5	3	15.5
I've only	5	5	15.5
I'll keep	3	3	15.5
I'll drink	3	3	15.5
I'll make	3	3	15.5
you can have	11	7	14.9
I can read	5	4	14.7

THE 100 THREE-WORD SEQUENCES MOST FREQUENTLY USED BY AUSTRALIAN CHILDREN, AGE 6½—FREQUENCY-ORDER LISTING

Sequence	Freq.	No. of Speakers	Index
I'm going	191	20	9531
I'm not	88	19	4170.6
I've got	108	21	1669
I don't know	93	18	1499.3
I want to	88	18	905.6
I'll have	36	15	900.2
it's a	46	16	743.9
I don't want	46	16	659.6
I'll do	32	11	587.2
it's not	44	13	577.7
I'll be	27	11	495.8
I'm the	27	7	472.6
I'm doing	20	9	447.7
I'll show	25	10	415.5
I'll go	23	10	382.2
I'll get	23	10	382.2
I'm getting	17	9	381.4
that's a	43	15	378.2
'm going to	167	20	370.2
I'm up	20	7	348.2
I'll tell	20	10	332.4
I'll take	22	9	329.6
it's on	29	11	322.4
that's the	42	13	320.6
I got it	27	15	295.7
I have to	47	12	281.7
I'm a	14	8	277.8
I'll put	18	9	268.7
you're not	39	13	255.7
I got a	30	11	241.1
that's what	32	12	224.2
you want to	54	19	201.2
I'm telling	14	5	174.1
I don't like	18	10	160.8
you know what	40	11	145.8
I'm having	14	4	141
what's that	65	17	133.7
I'll just	11	7	127.4
I'm only	10	5	124.4
I'm coming	10	5	124.4
I'm just	8	6	120.2
it's only	16	7	112.5
I got to	17	9	111.5
that's all	15	12	105.3
that's my	18	10	105.3
I have a	19	11	104.7
I'm finished	8	5	99.5
I know what	18	10	94.5
you're going	19	10	94
I'm playing	6	6	91.2
it's going	10	8	80.6
I'll give	8	6	80.3
you're a	16	9	71.8
I'm sitting	7	4	70.5
that's not	17	7	70.2
that's right	15	8	70.2
going to get	27	14	69.9
that's why	13	9	68.2
you got to	36	10	67.1
going to do	30	12	66.7
you have to	33	14	65.5
one two three	84	12	62.1
going to have	29	11	59
I don't think	8	8	58.1
going to be	24	13	57.8
do you want	34	15	57.7
I got the	13	6	56.9
can I have	46	15	56.8
that's where	12	8	56.5
that's your	12	8	56.5
do you know	38	13	55.8
I don't have	10	6	53.6
it's too	7	7	48.7
I'm on	6	3	45.6
I'm in	6	3	45.6
you're in	13	7	45.4
it's like	7	6	42.2
I'm allowed	4	4	41.5
going to take	20	11	40.6
I can do	13	7	40.2
I know where	11	7	40.2
to go to	16	11	39.8
I'll make	6	4	38.8
I got one	9	6	38.8
you can have	14	8	38.1
I'm waiting	5	3	37.3
want to play	33	12	36.6
I'll only	7	3	36
I'll bring	7	3	36
you know where	12	9	35.8
I go to	21	8	35.5
I think I	15	8	35.2
you going to	30	13	33.8
I'll see	5	4	33.2
it's just	8	4	31.9
I think it	12	9	31.8
I know how	10	6	31.5
going to go	24	7	31
it's in	6	5	30.2
it's hard	6	5	30.2

EPILOGUE

The Mount Gravatt Language Research Project has looked at the way children use language at various stages of development. Our perspective is selective, since the theories for what we have done and will be doing in the future are drawn from linguists, psychologists, teachers, and others. Our approach is functional, for we believe that language development reflects progressive mastering of the child's functional potential. And our research is empirical in design, for not only do we support our theoretical implications by checking their psychological reality in terms of children's language, but there has been progressive production of practical outcomes. For example, Levels 1 and 2 of the language reading program will be published in early 1977, following work with children up to the age of $6\frac{1}{2}$ years. Levels 3 and 4 will result from the collection of $8\frac{1}{2}$ year old children's language and Levels 5 and 6 from that of $10\frac{1}{2}$ year old children's language.

Not only are we processing samples of language from Australia, Great Britain, North America, and other areas speaking standard English, but we are also proceeding to analyze language of aboriginal children in Australia and black children in urban North America. Arrangements have also been made to process a sample of Spanish from Lima, Peru.

Meanwhile, we are firming very rapidly our theoretical approach, on the basis of our language collections. This will be tested professionally through interaction with other professionals, on a personal basis and through the journals.

One of the first occasions for such interaction occurred at the Sixth World Congress on Reading, sponsored by the International Reading Association and held in Singapore in the summer of 1976. At that congress Dr. Hart presented a paper entitled "Reading is Languaging in Print." This paper summarizes many of the points that are made in Chapters 1 through 5 of this book, and so we reproduce it here by way of recapitulation.

Speaking, listening, reading, and writing are all different manifestations of what I have referred to in the title of this paper as "languaging." Speaking, listening, reading, and writing are different facets of language functioning. The basic assumption behind the Mount Gravatt Developmental Language-Reading Program is that a reading program should be subsumed under a language program which is aimed at the progressive mastery by each child of his functional language potential.

Young children come to school from a very successful language program—very few indeed have failed to develop a remarkably sophisticated and efficient functional oral language system. They are effective language users in the oral form—they have been and are still highly successful language learners. They have learned through speaking and listening.

Research into communicative interaction between young children, their parents, and their peers at preschool ages is beginning to reveal something of the teaching and learning strategies which prove so successful in those early years. One thing is clear, and that is that these young children are not *taught* the rules of oral language—they develop their own rules; they master the oral form of language by progressively improving and modifying rules which "work" for them in the business of communicating in this thing we call language; and they do it, not in special language lessons, but in everyday meaningful and purposeful interaction with their world and encouraged by the sympathetic and functionally oriented support of their family.

We, as teachers, face the task of assisting children through their second major language task—the mastery of the written form of language. To the present, I am afraid we have to admit that our success rate does not compare favorably with that of their teachers of oral language. I want to suggest that one major reason for this comparative lack of success is that we do not capitalize on the product of that earlier success—that secure oral language competence of young children; and that a second major reason is that we abandon the functional perspective and what have proved to be very productive language experiences in oral language acquisition.

In the Mount Gravatt Program, we have tried to explicate the developing oral language behavior of children and to build from that oral language basis across to competence in written language. We have also tried to develop the program around learning strategies which have proved so successful in oral language development. The development of the Mount Gravatt program, therefore, has necessitated both large-scale research into child language and long-term trials of teaching strategies and materials. Research into child language was essential because what linguists have been saying, or at least implying, for a long time about language functioning has been distinctly unhelpful and, in many respects, misleading. . . .

The Unreality of the Word for Young Children

Young children, who have used only oral language, have no clear idea of word boundaries . . . [and] indeed, there are no clear boundaries between words in oral language. The earliest segments of oral language, i.e., the constituents of the early one- and two-word utterances examined by such people as Brown, Bellugi, Braine, Bloom and others, happen to correspond with what will turn out to be words in written language, but the more difficult segments, those with which children learn to link these early "content" language units into connected utterance, are neither perceived as words nor do they often turn out to be words in the written form of language. An obvious example is "going to" or "gonna." In such utterances as "I'm going to hit you" "going to" is clearly *not* two words to a child. It is not two anything—it is one very useful chunk of oral language. To illustrate further, we could take "used to" in "I used to go to kindergarten." "Used" is certainly not the same segment of language as the "used" in "I used the crayon." In fact, I doubt whether most adults associate the "used" in "used to" with the transitive verb "used" except, perhaps, when they write it. (Some college students still write "use to.")

The development of word boundaries is closely associated with the convention of printing. They are not uniformly detectable or even useful for the child in his oral language. The word boundaries of printed language need, therefore, to be learned by experience with printed language, and, in fact, they do not become functionally essential until the child comes to write. Most recent researchers into child language agree that young children perceive oral language in what Oller calls meaningful "chunks." . . . Linguistically it is still true to say that the smallest meaningful element of language is a morpheme—a word or part of a word; but, as I have implied, a word becomes meaningful only when it is used in context. (What do I mean when I say just "used" or "going"?) Out of context, a word is only slightly more meaningful than the phoneme.

There is, then, no one-to-one correspondence between time gaps which occur in oral speech and the spatial gaps which occur between words in print. There is also no reliable one-to-one correspondence between the meaning of a word in print and that in a sequence of oral language unless the word is in similar context in both cases. Indeed, when the time gap configuration differs from spatial gaps between written words (such as happens with "I'm gonna" and "I am going to"), how could the printed word "am" be meaningful when it is in context? In fact, "I am going to" has an emphatic affirmative function rather than the simple future intention of "I'm gonna." We are dealing here with two different chunks of language which carry two different meanings. The important thing to realize is that the language experience which has led to the extensive oral language experience of young children has *not* included scrutiny of individual words except for what we might loosely call "labelling words," and these children have not had *any* practice in withdrawing such words from a communicative context. This procedure has not been necessary or useful in their oral language functioning. By the time children come to school, they are using language in connected utterance, in which they semiautomatically associate sequences of sound with meaning arising from the communication context. They do not contemplate the meaning or form of words out of context. They just use connected, meaningful, and useful language and they use it very efficiently in their communicative functioning.

When teachers come to teach these children the written form of language, they usually insist upon teaching through a word approach to reading—whether this be through a whole word or phonic approach. Teachers also are very much inclined to remove words from a communicative context. Children understand that language is for communicative use. If young children don't understand what a word is, and if they have been giving meaning to words only through experiencing them in a communicative context, it is hardly surprising when many conclude that this written form of language, so patently important to teachers, has very little to do with the oral language they have mastered and that it does not appear to have a communicative function. When this is the case, we are very likely to produce "recoders" or "word callers" who may or may not become competent in reading and writing, whereas if we aim first at producing "decoders" (who read for meaning), recoding strategies such as word-attack skills can then easily be developed. It has been shown, in fact, that children are likely to develop their own word-attack skills by modifying strategies which worked for them in their oral language.

We must produce decoding skills before we worry about recoding skills; that is, our primary aim must be to foster "reading for meaning" rather than "word calling." Children are used to listening for meaning, and they can readily see sense in reading for meaning.

Both listening for meaning and reading for meaning involve predicting forward. Children are used to predicting as they extract meaning from speech; if the language in reading books is fundamentally different from what they have encountered in oral language, however, predicting for meaning is made very difficult. In other words, barriers against reading for meaning exist when the cues children use for predicting in oral language are not present in the written language which confronts them. Reading must then become a meaningless task which, in some way, known only to adults, may *eventually* become a functionally useful activity.

Comparisons Between Language Samples

We at Mount Gravatt have compared the language used in a number of contemporary reading books and found that there is a very considerable difference between the language used in those books and that used by $5\frac{1}{2}$ year old children. Yet we find a great similarity between the oral language of children from $3\frac{1}{2}$ to $6\frac{1}{2}$ years of age and a striking coincidence between the oral language of children at ages $5\frac{1}{2}$ and $6\frac{1}{2}$. We have examined these similarities and differences at *semantic as well as surface form levels* ... [and have found that] there is some fundamental commonality across the language of children of these ages which has not been caught by the controls applied to the language used in children's readers. [*Illustrative tables supplied in Dr. Hart's paper are omitted here because they duplicate material presented in earlier chapters of this book.*]

Incidentally, it appears that this fundamental factor which writers of children's readers have missed has not been missed by writers of adult reading material. Our only investigations into popular adult reading material reveal greater commonality between the language used in that adult reading material and children's oral language than there is between that of the basal readers we have analyzed and the oral language of children for which they were designed!

What is the factor that has been missed? We think it is control of the sequences of language which are used over and over in the wide variety of situations which involve language. The sequences I refer to are so functionally useful that they constitute some 60% to 70% of every naturalistic oral language corpus if that corpus is sufficiently large and varied in situational context. We call these sequences "signalling sequences" because they signal syntactically and semantically what will follow. We refer to them as constituting the "core" of a language corpus because they play such a major role in facilitating prediction for meaning. They appear to be the essential component of what Smith, Goodman and Meredith ... are demanding in their first two criteria for providing materials for children to read: (1) They (the materials) must contain real language as close as possible to the language the child already knows, and (2) they must emphasize the most common patterns and sequences of oral language. That is, the most expected phenomena should occur with greater frequency.

It is now almost ten years since we set out to uncover the features which are characteristic of child language at various age levels. Our task called for a very different analysis of children's language from those currently available. With financial support, initially from the Van Leer Foundation and in later years from the Australian Educational Research and Development Committee, my teams have collected carefully planned language samples ranging from $2\frac{1}{2}$ years to $6\frac{1}{2}$ years. The subjects at each age level were randomly chosen from all children of that age in the city of Brisbane (population approaching one million). All the language spoken by each subject during the normal on-going activity of an entire day was recorded, transcribed, coded, and then ordered by a computer concordance program which brought together similar word and word sequence forms within their immediate verbal context. An index system gave easy access from each occurrence to the larger verbal context including the speech of other participants in the speech episode and also to notations of the situational context. . . .

It is on this data base that we have analyzed the surface semantic and functional features of the "signalling sequences" and other elements characteristic of the naturalistic utterances of children at each age level. Thus our language/reading materials have been based on what we have learned about child language and the strategies employed in the program have been shaped around such assumptions about child language learning as I outlined in the early part of this paper.

One major task in compiling the reading materials arose from the fact that the core "signalling sequences" appropriate to each age level had to be combined with "contentives" to make complete sentences or meaningful portions of sentences. The "contentives" were taken from two sources: (1) the way children of that age characteristically added "contentives" to "signalling sequences," and (2) concepts which children would normally be developing at that age.

Thus signalling sequences such as "I'm going to," "that's," "it's," "I've got," "I want," "I know" call for "content sequences" in order to complete the sentences. If the theme of the book is the life cycle of the frog, then suitable "content sequences" might be "a tadpole," "a frog's egg," "a frog," "four legs," "my home," "the creek." The reading book is written as one set of sentences which children might use if they were studying the life cycle of a frog from a real-life situation.

The success of the books themselves depends on the language lessons which lead up to their presentation. Each reading book needs to have language lessons which might take up to two weeks time prior to the presentation of the reading book. In these language lessons, which we call Pragmatic Language Lessons, the children talk about real-life situations and use the required "signalling sequences," completing these from the meaning they take from the real-life situation. Samples of sentences elicited from children in this way might be "That's a frog's egg," "It's going to be a tadpole," or "That's a tadpole," "It's got four legs." The children find there are many ways of combining the "signalling sequences" with "content sequences" to make meaningful sentences. The sentences become psychologically real to the children. The "signalling sequences" have been used so frequently by these children in their language that they have no problem applying them orally to the real-life situation set up by the teacher. There is no trouble either in transferring meaning to the written form when it is presented using the same real-life situations as was used for the oral form. This is usually done through cards with sequences presented on them, e.g.,

| that's | a tadpole |

Children are asked first to use oral language, then use the suitable printed form, and finally to "read" from the printed form.

Children thus seek visual cues in order to link visual with oral. There need not be a rule-governed phonic analysis at this stage. The rules could not be expressed by the children in any case. However, through practice at recognizing the written form in association with the oral, children will learn to use three different kinds of cues. These are the cue systems within words, the cue systems in the flow of language, and the cue systems coming from the reader's own experiences. Later, word-attack skills are welcomed by the children once they have worked out how to decode written material and are seeking extra help in identifying new words, particularly new content words.

In summary:

1. Every "signalling sequence" used as a basis for the reading book must be elicited in the first place from the children as part of a sentence which has meaning for them.

2. Hence a real-life situation must be set up as preparation for *each* reading book.

3. All the practice of both oral and read language takes place prior to the presentation of the reading book.

4. The presentation of this book is of very short duration. Thus it remains interesting and motivating, especially if the children have a reasonable chance of taking meaning from what they see.

5. The sentences in this book are likely to be novel combinations of "signalling sequences" and "content sequences" and yet, because of their practice at using various combinations, children are likely to cope with this successfully.

6. The reading book not only becomes a test of the child's ability to read for meaning but also a source of motivation for further reading, since his interest and success are in most cases assured.

7. Each book retains its interest and usefulness, since none need be used long enough to be learned by heart.

8. Word-attack skills are taught once the children have learned to decode for themselves. Thus these skills become cues for prediction of meaning rather than the mere recoding of words into sounds.

For over thirty years the practice of using vocabulary controlled reading books has served us well. However, we can improve on this as a result of our language analysis. . . . The materials offered in the Mount Gravatt Developmental Language Reading Program illustrate the type of innovative material available as a result of the Language Research Project: . . .

1. Thirty reading books with themes relating to:
   a) Me and Other People
   b) Me and the Animate World
   c) Me and the Physical World
   d) Me and Working Things Out
   e) Me and Make Believe
   f) Me and Expressing Myself

2. Signalling sequences selected from core language of children as a basis for language content. These are set out in the Teacher's Manual for each language lesson.

3. Master stencils for duplicating language sequences for children's usage in oral and read language.

4. Thirty outlines of Pragmatic Language Lesson material—one for each reading book.

5. Over thirty Musical Games for language reinforcement—at least one per title.

6. Thirty lists of "listening stories" on the same theme as each of the reading books, for the teacher to read to the children.

7. A complete phonetic analysis of every word used in the thirty books and relevant lists in the appendix so that teachers have ready access to relevant phonic material which is meaningful to the children as they have used the words in their language lesson and reading.

8. The choice of two conventional approaches to word-attack skills or an integrated perceptual training, motor skills practice, and word-attack skills program implemented through drama and puppetry.

A similar plan operates for the twenty books of Level 2. Our research data up to [the age of] $6\frac{1}{2}$ years has allowed us to write books to this stage. During the first half of 1976 we have been collecting language from $8\frac{1}{2}$ year old children. This will be completed shortly after August, and by September we should have the data to enable us to write Levels 3 and 4. We will be collecting both oral and written language from the $8\frac{1}{2}$ year old children.

During 1977, our project extends to the language of $10\frac{1}{2}$ year old children and this material will provide the basis for language to be used in our Levels 5 and 6.

Paralleling these practical outcomes has been the development of a language theory which we hope will aid teachers in their work with children throughout the school years, both primary and secondary. . . .

APPENDIX A

THE CALCULATION OF THE COMMUNICATION INDICES

Calculation of Single-Word Indices

Indices were calculated by weighting the frequency of occurrence of a particular word according to the number of children using it, e.g.,

Word	= sometimes
Actual frequency	= 28
No. of speakers	= 10
Total no. of available speakers	= 22
Weighted frequency	$= \dfrac{28}{1} \times \dfrac{10}{22} = 12.7$

To make possible the comparison of index values between age levels it was necessary to adjust the index to take into consideration the differing amounts of language that were analyzed at each age level.[1] The amount of language (in words) recorded from $4\frac{1}{2}$ year old children was taken as a base and a constant (K) was calculated by expressing the total number of words at each age level as an inverse fraction of the total number of words contained in the $4\frac{1}{2}$ year old sample, e.g.,

$$\text{Total no. of words at } 6\tfrac{1}{2} = 72\ 829$$

$$\text{Total no. of words at } 4\tfrac{1}{2} = 10\ 386$$

$$K = \frac{1}{\dfrac{72\ 829}{10\ 386}} = \frac{10\ 386}{72\ 829} = 0.14$$

The weighted frequency of 12.7, calculated above, was then multiplied by K to give the final index:

Word	= sometimes
Weighted frequency	= 12.7
K for $6\frac{1}{2}$ year olds	= 0.14
Frequency index for word	= 1.78

---

1. A word which occurred 10 times in a sample of 100 words could reasonably be expected to occur 20 times in a sample of 200 words. To get some idea of the relative frequency of the word in each sample, the second sample would have to be divided by a constant (K) of 2.

Calculation of Indices for Two- and Three-Word Sequences

Indices for the two-word sequences were obtained by multiplying the index for the total occurrence of the first word by the index for occurrences of the second word *following in sequence with the first.*

For example, the single-word index for all occurrences of "I" is 522.98. The index for "'m," calculated on the number of times it follows "I," is 79.24. Thus, the sequence index for "I'm" is

$$522.98 \times 79.24 = 41\ 457.$$

This is arbitrarily divided by 100 and rounded off to one decimal place to make comprehension of index relationships easier, giving an index of 414.6.

Similarly, for the three-word sequence "I'm going," the index for the number of times "going" follows "I'm" is calculated first (index = 22.99). This is then multiplied by the sequence index for "I'm," i.e.,

$$41\ 457 \times 22.99 = 953\ 096.$$

This is also divided by 100 to give a three-word sequence index for "I'm going" of 9531.

EXAMPLE OF CALCULATION OF CORRESPONDENCE CORRELATION

The accompanying graph compares the relative list order of two-word sequences which are common to the 100 most frequently used sequences in the language of $5\frac{1}{2}$ year old children and $6\frac{1}{2}$ year old children. The calculation of the correspondence relation is carried out as follows.

Step 1. Assign a value of 10 to all squares falling along the diagonal from bottom left to top right.

Step 2. Assign a value of 9 to all squares immediately to the left and right of this diagonal, a value of 8 to the squares next adjacent, and so on until the squares in the far corners are reached. These are assigned a value of 1.

Step 3. Calculation using number of sequences:
   a) Count sequences in squares assigned a value of 10 (in our sample graph there are 19).
   b) Continue in like fashion with squares assigned a value of 9 (in our sample, 23) and so on for other squares.

Step 4. Set up a table as follows:

No. of sequences	Weighting given	Product
19	10	190
23	9	207
21	8	168
10	7	70
4	6	24
1	5	5
2	4	8
1	3	3
0	2	0
0	1	0
91		675

Step 5. Find the total product and express the concurrence relation, in fractional or decimal form, as the proportion this product bears to 1000, e.g.,

$$\text{concurrence correlation} = \frac{675}{1000} = 0.68.$$

5½ \\ 6½	1–10	11–20	21–30	31–40	41–50	51–60	61–70	71–80	81–90	91–100
91–100	1				the other (s)		you've / I thought		in there / and that 9	10
81–90	2		you want		I get / it in	I put	to play	they're 9	this is 10	9
71–80	3					you go	9	got to 10	9	to put / it out
61–70	4			's that / you get		to the / I won't 9	10	one two / 's my 9	's going	a little
51–60	5			you don't / what's	do you / I do 9	10	there's / to be 9	to have	come on	you are
41–50	6	I go / to go	you got / to do	on the / I haven't 9	I just 10	9	no I	and you		
31–40	7	that one	's the / it on 9	you have 10	9	it up / it was / have to / I said		I am		
21–30	8	you can 9	I like / it is / to get / going to	10	in the 9	I had / 's not / and I			don't know	
11–20	9	that's / I want / I have 10	you know / I think / 's a / I can't	I was 9	I did / I didn't					
1–10	I'm / it's / I don't / I got / I know 0 I'll / I've	you're / I can 9	8	7	6	5	got a 4	3	2	1

LIST ORDER IN 5½ YEAR OLD CHILDREN'S LANGUAGE (vertical axis)

LIST ORDER IN 6½ YEAR OLD CHILDREN'S LANGUAGE (horizontal axis)

BIBLIOGRAPHY

Austin, M. C., Bush, C. L., and Huebner, M. H., *Reading Evaluation*. New York: Ronald Press, 1961.

Bateman, B., Reading and psycholinguistic processes of partially seeing children. *C.E.C. Research Monograph, No. 5*, 1963.

Bateman, B., and Wetherell, J., Psycholinguistic aspects of mental retardation. *Mental Retardation* **3,** 8–13, 1965.

Carroll, J. B., Davies, P., and Richman, B., *Word Frequency Book*. New York: American Heritage, 1971.

Dolch, E. W., *Teaching Primary Reading*. Champaign, Ill.: The Garrard Press, 1950.

Edwards, R. P. A., and Gibbon, V., *Words Your Children Use*. London: Burke Books, 1964.

Ferrier, E. E., *An Investigation of Psycholinguistic Factors Associated with Functional Defects of Articulation*. Unpublished doctoral dissertation, University of Illinois, 1963.

Foster, S. C., *Language Skills for Children with Persistent Articulatory Disorders*. Unpublished master's thesis, Texas Women's University, 1963.

Gates, A. I., *A Reading Vocabulary for the Primary Grades*. Bureau of Publications, Columbia University, 1935.

Goodman, K. S., and Burke, C., *Study of Children's Behavior While Reading Orally*. Final Report, U.S. Office of Education Project S.425, 1968.

Goodman, K. S., and Burke, C., *Study of Oral Reading Miscues That Result in Grammatical Retransformation*. Final Report, U.S. Office of Education Project, 7-E-219, 1969.

Handscombe, R., *Five to Nine: Aspects of Function and Structure in the Spoken Language of Elementary School Children*. Toronto: York University and Board of Education for the Borough of North York, 1972.

Hart, N. W. M., The differential diagnosis of psycholinguistic abilities of the cerebral palsied child and effective remedial procedure. *Special Schools Bulletin (Queensland)*, 1963.

Hart, N. W. M., *Psycholinguistic Abilities of the Cerebral Palsied Child*. Unpublished M.A. thesis, University of Queensland, 1964.

Hart, N. W. M., Research reported in *Psycholinguistic Research in Queensland Schools, 1961–1966, Bulletin No. 34*. Brisbane: Research and Curriculum Branch, Queensland Department of Education, 1968.

Hart, N. W. M., *A Psycholinguistic Approach to the Diagnosis and Remediation of Deficit States in Children Resulting from Primary Language Deprivation*. Unpublished doctoral thesis, University of Queensland, 1970.

Holden, M. H., and MacGinitie, W. H., Children's conceptions of word boundaries in speech and print. *Journal of Educational Psychology* **63,** 6, 551–557, 1972.

Huttenlocher, J., Children's language: word phrase relationship. In *Child Language, A Book of Readings*, ed. by Aaron Bar-Adon and Werner F. Leopold. Englewood Cliffs, N.J.: Prentice-Hall, 1971.

Kass, C. E., *Some Psychological Correlates of Severe Reading Disability (Dyslexia)*. Unpublished doctoral dissertation, University of Illinois, 1962.

Kass, C. E., Psycholinguistic disabilities of children with reading problems. *Exceptional Children* **32,** 8, 1966.

Kirk, S. A., McCarthy, J. J., and Kirk, W., *Illinois Test of Psycholinguistic Abilities, Revised Edition*. Urbana, Ill.: Institute for Research on Exceptional Children, University of Illinois, 1969.

McCarthy, J. J., and Kirk, S. A., *Illinois Test of Psycholinguistic Abilities, Experimental Edition.* Urbana, Ill.: Institute for Research on Exceptional Children, University of Illinois, 1961.

McLeod, J., Dyslexia in Young Children, A Factorial Study, with Special Reference to the Illinois Test of Psycholinguistic Abilities. *I.R.E.C. Papers,* Vol. 2., No. 1, 1967.

Ministry of Education, *Standards of Reading.* London: H.M.S.O., 1957.

Mount Gravatt Language Research Project, Theoretical background, procedures used and a partial analysis of 5½ year old children's language. *Mount Gravatt College of Advanced Education, Language Research Project, Research Report No. 1, 1973.*

Mount Gravatt Language Research Project, Further analysis of data from 2½, 3½, 4½ and 5½ year old children. *Mount Gravatt College of Advanced Education, Language Research Project, Research Report No. 2, 1973.*

Mount Gravatt Language Research Project, Single word and word sequence lists taken from the language of 6½ year old children. *Mount Gravatt College of Advanced Education, Language Research Project, Research Report No. 3, 1974.*

Mount Gravatt Language Research Project, An examination of further theoretical and practical aspects for the construction of language development and reading programs based on children's language. *Mount Gravatt College of Advanced Education, Language Research Project, Research Report No. 4, 1974.*

Mount Gravatt Language Research Project, An alphabetical listing of the most frequently used single words and word sequences in the language of 2½, 3½, 4½, 5½ and 6½ year old children. *Mount Gravatt College of Advanced Education, Language Research Project, Research Report No. 5, 1975.*

Mount Gravatt Language Research Project, Developmental trial of the Mount Gravatt Developmental Language Reading Program. *Mount Gravatt College of Advanced Education, Language Research Project, Research Report No. 6, 1976.*

Oller, J. W., On syntax, semantics and pragmatics. *Linguistics* **83**, 43–55, 1972.

Piaget, Jean, Development and learning. In *Piaget Rediscovered,* ed. by Richard E. Ripple and Verne N. Rockcastle. A Report of the Conference on Cognitive Studies and Curriculum Development (March, 1964). Ithaca, N.Y.: School of Education, Cornell University, 1964.

Rinsland, H. D., *A Basic Vocabulary of Elementary School Children.* New York: Macmillan, 1945.

Smith, F., *Understanding Reading.* New York: Holt, Rinehart and Winston, 1971.

Smith E., Goodman, S., and Meredith, R., The reading process: a psycholinguistic view. In *Resources in Reading—Language Instruction,* ed. by Ruddell, Ahern, Hartson, and Taylor, Englewood Cliffs, N.J.: Prentice-Hall, 1974.

Thorndike, E. L., and Lorge, I., *The Teacher's Word Book of 30,000 Words.* Bureau of Publications, Columbia University, 1944.

Van Leer Program, Research report on some aspects of the language development of pre-school children. Department of Education, Queensland, Bernard Van Leer Project, North Quay, Brisbane, 1970.

Victorian Education Department, *The Education Department of Victoria, Report of Remedial Education Committee,* August, 1965.

Werner, H., and Kaplan, E., Development of word meaning through verbal context, an experimental study. *Journal of Psychology* **29**, 251–57, 1950.